Love Whispers

Reflections of a Seasoned Pastor

Michael D. Dent

Copyright 2019

Love Whispers
Reflections of a Seasoned Pastor

ISBN-13: 9781699386279
Scripture Quotations, unless otherwise indicated, are from New Revised Standard Version Bible, Copyright 1989
National Council of the Churches of Christ in the United States of America.
Used by permission. All rights reserved.

Preface

On June 28, 2017, my life changed in an unexpected and unwelcomed way. I was diagnosed with Mild Cognitive Impairment. MCI is a neurological condition which affects one's short term memory. For some time I had been experiencing some forgetfulness, repeating the same question in five minutes or less time, and misplacing my keys, pen, wallet or cell phone. Naturally, I denied and dismissed the notion anything was wrong with me beyond normal aging deficits. After 65 years of never spending a night in the hospital as a patient, I was depressed and anxious with the diagnosis.

The young neurology expert at the University of Colorado Anschutz Medical Campus was professional, straightforward, and yet hopeful. Nonetheless, my life had taken a new turn toward an uncertain outcome. The best would be no further progression of the mild impairment. The worst case scenario is a rapid deterioration into full-blown Alzheimer's disease and eventually death. The reality of my diagnosis hit home hard when Sharon, my wife of 43 years, and I picked up the prescription at the pharmacy later that day. The label on the pill bottle had my name on it with this command, *"Take one tablet by mouth for mild to moderate Alzheimer type dementia."*

Sharon and I took a month of vacation and discernment leave in July to pray, discuss, discern, and decide what was next in our love affairs with life, ministry and one another. In August I delicately disclosed my diagnosis in a confidential meeting with the church's personnel committee members. By the grace of God, the chair of the committee just happened to be a retired neurologist. Michele was a divine gift to the committee and our family.

With the committee's endorsement, I shared with the congregation at the close of each morning service this statement on a September Sunday morning. With Sharon joining me at the center pulpit, I spoke from the heart with tears in my eyes on that special day:

Every year every one of us has a birthday. Birthdays are good! The more you have, the longer you live! Today is my birthday – number 65!

I have chosen this day to share with you that after 43 years of pastoral ministry – including the past eleven years serving as pastor of Trinity United Methodist Church, I will be retiring from active ministry on June 30, 2018 – the end of the Methodist Annual Conference year.

There are three things I ask of you in the next ten months:

#1: That you join me and all our pastors and staff members to make this twelfth and final year in partnership in ministry the very best it can possibly be to the glory of God.

#2: That you pray for our Staff-Parish Relations Committee, our District Superintendent, Cabinet, and Bishop as they work together in the months ahead in discernment to lead to the appointment next spring of the 28th senior pastor of Denver's first church.

#3: That you pray for Sharon and me as we face a recently diagnosed health challenge with an uncertain outcome. Just three days before leaving on vacation in July, we learned that I have a neurological condition called – MCI – mild cognitive impairment. Where this diagnosis and further neurological testing will lead, we do not know at this time.

What we do know is that your compassion, encouragement, and prayers will bless us daily as we move forward with you in the strength of God's grace and mercy in our final 10 months of ministry together. Thank you all for your support, encouragement, prayers and partnership in the ministry of Jesus Christ through Trinity Church "from the first day until now."

We shared more than a few tears that day after the service, you can bet. More than that, Sharon and I were the recipients of abundant kind words, hugs and promises of prayer. Cards, notes, letters, and emails lifted our spirits with gracious words, scriptures and prayers. We were most grateful for the outpouring of affection and support. This pastoral love affair between shepherd and sheep undergirded us with hope, encouragement, and peace.

Over the next eight months I participated in several research testing and exams at the Anschutz Medical Campus. These voluntary procedures included a lumbar puncture, MRI, memory tests and ophthalmology exams and exercises. In the MRI procedure, lying still for seventy minutes in a tube without moving or scratching my nose brought me very close to Jesus! These procedures may not help me, but the research results may well benefit others who are diagnosed with cognitive impairments.

As it turned out, we had to retire in April 2018 due to my health condition. The good gift of retirement enabled me to begin this memoir sooner than expected. Because of the nature of my health challenge and our lifelong commitment to tithing, Sharon and I have I decided to donate a tithe (10%) of the proceeds of this book to the Alzheimer's Association. One in three seniors dies with Alzheimer's or other dementia. Your family is likely to be touched by dementia, if it has not already. Thank you for your investment in the effort to reduce Alzheimer's disease, which accounts for up to eighty percent of all dementia. A cure for the disease remains elusive.

I am grateful for the opportunity to share with you these many diverse personal and pastoral stories of love whispering and grace abounding in many spaces and faces. Perhaps they will bring you some deep joy and laughter, holy reflection and introspection, and memories and musings. May they move you to remember and be thankful for the parents, progeny, pastors, partners , teachers and other people who have been vital love whisperers across the years of your life's journey.

Michael D. Dent
Pastor, 1973-2018
Texas and Colorado

In grateful memory of my Beloved Father and Mother, Brother and Sister

"The memory of the righteous is ever blessed."
Proverbs 10:7

Contents

Introduction

Growing up in the church meant singing the songs of the faith. Over the years one falls in love with *Amazing Grace, A Mighty Fortress Is Our God, Holy, Holy, Holy* and many others. Growing up in a mainline American congregation in the middle of the twentieth century, I cut my teeth on these and other familiar hymns in weekly morning and evening worship services. One popular song which still stands out is *Blessed Assurance*. Written in 1873 by prolific, blind Methodist composer Fanny Crosby, the perennial Top Ten Hymn has a line which has always touched and remained in my ears and my heart.

The whole hymn is about heaven. The second stanza concludes with this magnificent double auditory image by the sightless songwriter, "Echoes of mercy, whispers of love." Those six words have remained in my brain ever since. No mild cognitive impairment, dementia or Alzheimer's will ever take away, I pray, the echoes of God's mercy and the whispers of divine love from my head nor my heart.

Love Whispers is the title and theme of this offering, reminding us of the divine grace which abounds in the places, spaces and faces we encounter and experience daily. The1969 youth musical hit *Pass It On* proclaimed we want to "shout God's love from the mountaintop." However, we might also do well to let love whisper through our lives in our relationships, service, citizenship, stewardship and discipleship.

I am grateful to be the recipient of abundant whispers of love over the past two-thirds of a century, including serving as a Methodist pastor for 44.5 years. As a shepherd, I have been privileged to speak gently again and again Jesus' words of grace at the graves of God's children of all ages, "Do not let your hearts be troubled. Believe in God, believe also in me... My sheep hear my voice. I know them, and they follow me. I give them eternal life, and they will never perish."

As a freshman college student, I attended a convocation on ministry for persons pondering the prospect of becoming pastors. The event was held in the fall in the piney woods of East Texas at Lakeview Methodist Assembly. The attendees were mostly young men. The speaker was from Minnesota. Though it has been almost fifty years ago, I remember well - MCI does not affect long term memory, thank you, Jesus! - Bishop Richard Raines said that serving as a pastor is "the highest, hardest, holiest and happiest calling a person can have." Though that assertion is debatable, it has been true for me since being licensed to preach one year out of high school.

Thank you for sharing this journey as a sibling in love whispering and whispering love. Writing it is therapeutic for my brain. I am deeply humbled by the multitude of diverse ministries, missions, community service and broad spectrum of amazing children of God whom I have encountered thus far in this world. God does love diversity! You will meet some unique folks in the pages ahead.

Though removed in time and space, these saints are still speaking. You will meet family members, U.S. Presidents, Olympic gold medalists, heroes and sheroes, saints and sinners, teachers and preachers. You will connect and likely see yourself as a Love Whisperer and a recipient of love whispers. You will visit faraway places and sacred spaces. You will share history and mystery. You will laugh and cry. You will experience the privileges and heartbreaks of being a pastor. You will taste serving a community and not just a church. You will be challenged to "Enlarge the site of your tent and let the curtains of your habitations be stretched out; do not hold back; lengthen your cords and strengthen your stakes." (Isaiah 54:2) In other words, buckle your seatbelts!

With a fair number of other lucky folks, Sharon and I have had the good fortune to live in two of the most beautiful and unique states in the nation. The Lone Star State is the only state which was an independent nation before joining the Union. We enjoyed Texas and had no intentions to ever leave. As with other natives, I have often said, "I was Texas-born and Texas-bred, and when I die, I will be Texas-dead!" Almost all our living relatives reside in the Lone Star State.

However, we both experienced the beauty of the Centennial State in our formative years. Sharon and her family camped in their trailer across Colorado and many other Western states across a decade. In 1968 I spent a week camping and hiking with my Beaumont, Texas Boy Scout Troop in Durango and Mesa Verde National Park.

A decade later Sharon and I went to Winter Park on a youth ski trip which was a memorable for mostly the wrong reasons. The bus could not make it over Berthoud Pass on the icy US Highway 40 road. Everyone had to abandon the vehicle with two exceptions. One was a youth with a heart condition. The other was my wife who was four-months pregnant. The temperature dipped to 25 degrees below during the trip but did not diminish our desire to return to the state with the highest average elevation in the union, 6,800 feet. Talk about a true Rocky Mountain High!

Fifteen years later we took our young children to the YMCA Snow Mountain Ranch near Granby and to visit the State Capitol and U.S. Mint in Denver. Never in our minds did we ever think we might ever live in Colorado, much less pastor there. Who would have believed two Texas empty nesters would discern a love whisper to leave the Lone Star State and locate in the Centennial State and live in the city of Centennial with a population of over 100,000 souls and which was not even incorporated six years before?

Grace truly abounds. I am humbled and grateful to have this opportunity to share a community pastor's life. The first proposed title of this work was *All My Pastoral Love Affairs.* After all, I truly loved preaching, leading worship, teaching, visiting, serving the sacraments, inviting folks to be generous and praying. These were all truly loves for me. I yielded to a Higher Power and decided to remain married.

Are you ready to experience the whispers of love through the spaces, places and faces of a community pastor? I thought so. Let's do it!

Acknowledgments

One day a squirrel was running along a branch high in an oak tree when he came upon a frog. He was startled by the sight of the amphibian high in the sky. The squirrel had to know how this could be. So, he asked his new green friend, "Mr. Frog, please tell me, how did you get so high in the tree?" The frog confessed, "I am not sure exactly how I got here, but there is one thing I do know for sure. I did not get here by myself!"

No one accomplishes anything approaching significance without the encouragement and assistance of saints seen and unseen across the years. I was abundantly blessed with loving families of origin, orientation, procreation, spiritual direction and education. You will meet some of these amazing family members, teachers, professors, pastors, friends and love whisperers.

I am especially grateful for the congregations Sharon and I were privileged to serve over 44 years. These churches were small and large, old and new, conservative and progressive, loving and serving. All witnessed to and whispered love in fruitful and lasting ways. The joy of journeying with the people of Jesus in tough and tender times, seasons of grief and joy, trials and triumphant times, will forever witness to the power of whispering love.

Tons of thanks to special friends Marilyn Hardy and Juli Van Hooser for proof-reading and editing the manuscript, to Dr. Justin Tull and Aaron Stout for their professional assistance and, most of all, to my best friend, best critic, soulmate, mother of my two children, bride for 45 years, patient and kind caregiver and Love Whisperer *par excellence*, Sharon. She is the best.

Family Whispers of Love

Where do you come from? Who are your people? We all have roots and families. The Bible has several genealogical lists of our spiritual ancestors. We do not get to choose our families. They are gifts. Most us can trace back several generations of "our people." We may or may not like what we discover. You may find a preacher and you may find an outlaw. It might the same person! Whoever you may discover, you are going to find some sweet souls who whispered love throughout their time on the planet. Their words and ways conveyed whispers of love in the spaces of their time and place on the planet. I am humbled to share some whisperers of love from the Dent family tree.

GREAT-GRANDFATHER: *PRO-JESUS, PRO-SLAVERY*

Born in 1818 in Wilkes County, Georgia, Richard Hezekiah Dent married Elizabeth Walker on December 30, 1841. Seventy years later that would have meant a nice tax year-end deduction. They did their best to populate the South, producing nine children between 1844 and 1866. Can you imagine having a baby and a twenty-two-year-old? This was BBC – Before Birth Control. One of the nine children was John Turner Dent. At age 16, my great-grandfather enlisted in the army of the Confederate States of America in 1863 in a vain effort to preserve the institution of human slavery. I am grateful he was on the losing side.

A half-dozen years after the Civil War ended, he moved to Sabine County in East Texas. There John Turner Dent met and married Armadilla - a unique name, to say the least - Pace in 1875. Their union produced three children before her early death. John remarried and had three more Dent offspring.

The impact of deep faith and the loving legacy of his life, like many of his generation, was described in glowing terms. His pastor wrote this personal obituary to my great-grandfather who died three months after my father's birth:

It becomes our sad duty to chronicle the sudden and unexpected death of our beloved friend and brother, John T. Dent, at his home in Milam, Texas October 27, 1916. He was born in Wilkes County, Georgia September 24, 1847. As a mere boy he served with distinction in the Confederate Army, came to Sabine County, Texas, in 1870, lived in Sabine County the remainder of his life

Uncle John, as he was affectionately called, joined the Methodist

Episcopal Church South when young and ever lived a consistent Christian life to the end. He was a man of strong character and conviction and, like Abraham, commanded his children and household after him. They are all Christians and members of the M.E. Church, South.

He has been an officer in the Church for a number of years. I do not think I ever knew a more consecrated Christian or loyal member of the church than Uncle John. His pastor always knew that in him he had a friend in whom he could confide anything about the church. He knew the doctrine and polity of his Church. He loved the Church and the preacher. It was an inspiration for the pastor to associate with him. The pastor, who, tired, discouraged, and almost ready to give up, spent a night with Uncle John would go away the next morning ready to fight the battles again.

He was true to his country, to his preacher, to his family, to his Church, and to his God. After listing the names and places of residence of surviving family members, the obituary concluded with a most reassuring promise: *Bereaved wife, children, loved ones and friends, we all know where to find Uncle John. Let us meet him in that house not made with hands, eternal in the heavens, whose builder and maker is God.*

Though the teenager was sadly a product of his day in going to war in a vain effort to preserve an evil institution, John Taylor Dent went on to serve the Lord, his church, his pastor and his family well. I am inspired by his obituary. I can only imagine and hope that some of his spiritual DNA trickled down to the third and fourth generations. Love whispers that grace will lead us home, saints and sinners alike.

GREAT UNCLE: *CIRCUIT PREACHER AND POET*

My Dent ancestry is truly filled with strong Methodists. One was John Turner's son named Isaac "Ike" Orsen, my father's namesake. My Great-Uncle Ike was old when I was born, but I remember him at family reunions each summer in East Texas when four generations gathered to celebrate the Dent clan. Tossing horseshoes, playing dominoes and consuming a vast array delightful dishes and desserts, all homemade, was the agenda. This was BCC – Before Calorie Counting. Uncle Ike was always the one chosen to pray at the Dent family reunions, a role bequeathed to me in the generations to come.

As I became, so was Uncle Ike a Methodist preacher. He never served a city church. He pastored small churches and circuits of smaller congregations across East Texas all his ministry. As was his father, he was a role model answering a call serve the Lord with one's all. On his ninetieth birthday in 1965, Uncle Ike wrote his memoirs. He refused to call them that because he was still living. The final stanza of poetic quatrain as he entered his tenth decade read:

> *For forty-one years I have gone to and fro on the earth*
> *Trying to persuade folks to seek the new birth.*
> *One more item, and with this I close my story –*
> *Someday I hope to enter Christ's home for His Saints in Glory.*

His son, John Wesley Dent (nice Methodist name, of course) wrote in the 1970 Texas Annual Methodist Conference Journal that just before his father died August 2, 1969, he completed his memoirs with these lines:

> *One more word I do want to say*
> *Thank you to all who helped me along my way.*

What a wonderful and winsome example of gratitude, faith, and faithfulness was Uncle Ike! I was sixteen when he graduated to glory. I regret not getting to know him better in his sunset years and look forward to reconnecting somehow, someway, some day. His words still whisper love of God and neighbor.

GRANDPARENTS: *ROLE MODELS PAR EXCELLENCE*

Ike's brother, my grandfather, arrived in 1885. Robert Harrison Dent was a schoolteacher who studied law at home. Without a day of law school, he became a practicing attorney and served as Sabine County Judge and County Attorney in Hemphill, Texas for several terms each. His office was in the County Courthouse where there were always two or three tables of domino games being played outside under the leafy oak trees on the courthouse square. Erected in 1906, the three-story building contained the county offices, sheriff's department, jail and adjacent gallows for administering East Texas justice on the spot. The three-story courthouse is still in service 113 years later.

My brother, sister, and I called our paternal grandparents Mama Dent and Granddaddy. Granddaddy was always "old" to me, as he was 67 when I born in 1952. Now that I am 67, I realize our perspectives change as we age. Do you remember "Don't trust anyone over 30"? "Life begins at 40"? "Seventy is the new 50"? I have often said age is just a number. Some people are old at 20 and some are young at 90.

Our maternal grandparents also lived in Hemphill, population 913, and went to the same First Methodist Church. Our family drove two hours there from our hometown of Beaumont in Southeast Texas at least once a month to visit them. Both grand families had large gardens, fields of crops and fruit trees. Between them they fed us in abundance with fresh corn, watermelon, peaches, butterbeans, squash, tomatoes, pears and tomatoes. Granddaddy subscribed to and planted by the Annual *Farmer's Almanac.*

Next to the Bible and the *Upper Room* daily devotional guide, the almanac was his most treasured reading. He had a collection of the bimonthly *Upper Room* publications dating back to the early 1930s. That left a lasting impression on me of the importance of a daily time of Bible reading, devotional reflection, prayer and a "Thought for the Day." To this day reading the daily *Upper Room* is one of my spiritual practices.

We grandkids usually spent a week with our grandparents each summer. That meant the delights of going swimming at the Conservation Corps or "CC" Lake in nearby Milam, eating a five-cent ice cream at the drive-in dairy mart, walking into town and going to the movies at the Sabine County Theatre on Saturday mornings for ten cents. Sundays in Hemphill always included Sunday School, worship and a big meal at home.

I rejoice that two of my beloved grandparents lived long enough to hear me preach. It was only my third sermon and I was still a teenager. Mamaw and Papaw Killion were quite proud as the message was delivered at their church in Hemphill. I believe my Mama Dent and Granddaddy were listening long distance that evening. My siblings, cousins and I were blessed to have wonderful examples in our grandparents of how to live life well, live long and leave a legacy of love, joy, faith, family and hope. Their lives whispered love in their kindness, gentleness and faithfulness.

They lived by example, not lectures. They fed, led and blessed their grandchildren with values of faith and family, encouragement and empathy and care and compassion. I do not recall any arguments, cross words, or despair in our grandparents. They gave us roots, wings and spiritual things. For their whispers of love, I will forever be thankful.

The tiny town of Hemphill made international headlines February 1, 2003 when the Space Shuttle Columbia exploded during reentry into the earth's atmosphere. Parts of the spacecraft and its crew members were scattered and recovered from a debris field across Sabine County. Ironically, a memorial to the to the seven brave astronauts lost in the tragedy sits in the small East Texas town near the Louisiana border where I used to run and play as a child every summer and wish to be an astronaut someday.

FATHER: *PATRIOT, PROTECTOR, PROVIDER*

My dad was named after his preacher uncle, Rev. I.O. Dent. Daddy did not know that the "I" stood for Isaac, the great First Testament prophet. When my father enlisted in the US Army Air Corps in 1941, he was given the name Ingram because an initial was unacceptable to Uncle Sam. Perhaps Ingram was the maiden name of the mother of the serviceman admitting my father into military that day.

Our family is proud of our loved one's service during World War II. My dad volunteered for service on January 25, 1941. He was assigned to the Army Air Corps and trained at Scott Field in Illinois. He served overseas October 1942 to April 1945 in England, Italy and North Africa. He achieved the rank of Staff Sargent. He answered the call, as did so many young men and some women, to oppose the military forces of Germany, Italy and Japan. He was awarded the EAME Campaign Ribbon with eleven Bronze Stars, the Distinguished Unit Badge with two Oak Leaf Clusters, Good Conduct Medal, American Defense Service Ribbon and Victory Medal. He never spoke of his years in the war or the military tattoos on his arms, but his descendants will always be proud of his service as a member of what Tom Brokaw called and wrote of as *The Greatest Generation.*

My dad came home and wasted no time wooing, winning, and wedding nineteen-year-old Mavis Killion. She had graduated from Hemphill High School as Salutatorian of the Class of 1943. Her 1940 yearbook shares she was the Most Popular Girl as a freshman. The wedding was held May 1, 1946, a Wednesday of all days, at the First Methodist Church of Hemphill. The covenant made that day lasted a half-century, broken only by the death of my father in early 1997. Their marriage covenant was a wonderful witness to whispers of love.

The newlyweds soon moved to Southeast Texas where my father spent his working life as a loyal laborer in the storehouse of the Mobil Oil Refinery in south Beaumont for thirty years. The sleepy community founded in 1835 came to fame on January 10, 1901 when the Spindletop oil gusher erupted on the south side of the city. Hundreds, if not thousands of oil wells were dug, and black gold flowed like water over Niagara Falls. The Golden Triangle of the port cities of Beaumont, Port Arthur, and Orange built refineries, shipyards, and railroads to send petroleum and its products to the far corners of the country and globe.

Immense oil companies, including Mobil, Texaco, Gulf, and Sun Oil, had major plants along or near the Neches River, employing tens of thousands of laborers who operated the refineries 24-7-365. When I was in elementary school in the early sixties, we young children practiced civil defense drills – how to duck under your desk and kiss your posterior goodbye when the feared Soviet Union began bombing us on the refinery-rich Gulf Coast. About the same time, my cousin Mike Smith of Louisiana was mobilized and sent with his National Guard Unit to Florida to repel any Russian enemy troops invading the nation from Cuban shores. Thankfully, cooler heads prevailed, and a missile crisis was averted.

After his early retirement at 60, my father spent the rest of his life caring for others. He looked in on his elderly mother-in-law daily, visited the sick and shut-ins of Wesley United Methodist Church, and volunteered at Some Other Place. SOP is an ecumenical, faith-based coalition which provides food, clothing, gently used furniture, job placement and counseling for those in need in the Beaumont community. He walked daily his grand-dog Spanky, who lived just down the street. Daddy also took pleasure placing the garbage cans of all the widows and seniors in the neighborhood back in their proper places.

There is a special place in the hereafter for those whose lives of love and humility impact for good the lives of others. Following his passing, I wrote a tribute to Daddy in the weekly *Messenger* of Marvin United Methodist Church in Tyler, Texas, where I was serving as senior pastor. The column was picked up and published across the state in the *Cross Connection* of the Texas Conference of the United Methodist Church. The piece highlights my family's Methodist roots and my dad's devotion to his children. It was published the Friday before Heritage Sunday in 1997.

> My father died Feb. 18. He was 80 and lived with Alzheimer's ("old timers" he called it) for three years. His death brought grief to my family, but also gratitude for the rich Methodist heritage he shared, lived, and left with us. I.O. Dent was named after his uncle, an East Texas circuit preacher for The Methodist Church in the late 19th and early 20th centuries. His two cousins, Frank and George Dent, also became Methodist preachers.
>
> My parents were married in 1946 and modeled marital fidelity, forgiveness and faith for their three children for 50 years. My dad sold his favorite shotgun one Christmas, so his children could

have presents. We never had a lot of things, but our home was filled with love, laughter, and God's grace. We seldom missed services at North End Methodist Church in Beaumont. My dad introduced me to Lakeview Methodist Assembly at age eight on a Methodist Men Father-Son Retreat. He and my mom passed on wisdom, respect, hard work and service to others. My late brother became a physician, my sister a teacher and I a Methodist preacher.

In a handwritten will in 1962, my dad wrote, "To my loving children, I would leave this thought. You have unlimited opportunities in this great country of ours. Keep up with your education and remember the precepts and examples of your ancestors. Honor your mother and live the kind of life of which you will be unashamed to face our heavenly Father. Remember me in your prayers and please forgive me where I have failed you." On this Heritage Sunday, I am most grateful to my Father above for the heritage of Methodist Christian love and service my father lived and bequeathed to me and to all who knew and loved him. "For he was a good man, full of the Holy Spirit and faith." (Acts 11:24)

MOTHER: *STRONG IN THE BROKEN PLACES*

My parents paid less than ten thousand dollars for the small, wood-frame house on East Lynwood Drive in north Beaumont. It was my home for the first twenty years of my life, containing six rooms: A living-dining room, three small bedrooms, a bathroom, and a tiny kitchen. It had a single-attached garage, an attic for storage and an old-fashioned dryer in the backyard called a clothesline. My young mother was truly a domestic engineer. She had no education beyond the eleventh grade of Hemphill High School, married a man ten years her senior and had three babies in five years. My sister once told me many years later our mother made my father have "the silver scissors surgery" after I was born so there would be no accidents adding other baby Dents!

For many years we had only one car. I remember vividly the 1957 blue Plymouth with huge fins, gas wars that got down to fifteen cents a gallon and going to the local Farmers' Market on Saturday mornings to peruse and purchase fresh produce from nearby farms. To earn extra cash for the family, my mother went to work as a census taker in 1960. She went house to house to gain the names, ages and occupations of each resident in homes in one of the most economically challenged parts of the city. It was dangerous and hard work. She did it fearlessly to provide for her children. I did not realize then the risks she was taking. Today, of course, the census is taken each ten years electronically and by snail mail.

In the mid-sixties my mother went to work as the secretary for the new Jefferson County Sheriff in downtown Beaumont. Dick Culbertson, a Texas State Highway Patrolman, had been appointed as the new sheriff following charges of corruption against the longtime previous sheriff. A grand jury investigation resulted in indictments tied to organized crime centered around bad boy behavior.

A book entitled *Betting, Booze, and Brothels: Vice, Corruption, and Justice in Jefferson County Texas from Spindletop to the James Commission* was written. One of the community leaders who courageously stood for needed ethical reform in the community was a young, dynamic pastor of the historic downtown First Methodist Church. Dr. John Wesley Hardt served that congregation for 18 years. He was later elected to the office of bishop in the United Methodist Church in 1980. Though my family belonged to another Methodist church in the city, I knew of Dr. Hardt. Our lives and ministries would cross and connect multiple times in varied settings over the next half-century-plus.

Sheriff Culbertson, another Methodist public servant, went on to win six full terms of office in the county of nearly 250,000 residents. Every four years he had an opponent and my family campaigned for Dick with road signs, bumper stickers and fish fry dinners. After all, the way to a voter's heart is through the stomach! As my mother served as the sheriff's secretary, she was deputized and authorized to pack heat. Her like-new pistol is still in the family after more than 50 years. After all, secretaries and preachers very infrequently have need for firearm fights, thank God.

My neat, sweet, petite mother was a life-loving, life-giving woman. She was truly strong in the broken places, having buried two young adult children across the years. Life is not fair to many in this temporary world. Despite the losses of a beloved son in 1981 at 33 and a precious daughter at 54, my mother did not let grief define her life. She whispered love through her tears. I do believe the illness and death of her beloved daughter Marilyn in 2004 hastened her own passing the next year. After my sister graduated to glory, I was conscious of making the best effort of selfcare possible. I believe if mother had lost all three of us, she would have gone into a severe downward spiral. Sadly, a year later my mother spent the final five weeks of her life in St. Elizabeth's Hospital in Beaumont where she received excellent care. She remained steadfast in tough times of great grief and was more than kind and gracious to all the caregivers in that final month.

Truth be told, the death certificate could have listed cause of death as "Broken Heart." I will forever be grateful for the dear woman who brought me into this world. I can also never forget the care and support the woman who sat with, gave ice chips to and wiped the fevered brow of her mother-in-law for over a month. My dear wife was an angel in disguise as a Florence Nightingale daughter-in-law. Sharon was also a strong support to me as I entered a new chapter as an orphan and the last living member of my family of origin.

Two days after my mom's blessed release from her suffering at age 79, over 300 souls shared the glorious celebration of her life and faith. Her obituary appropriately began, "Well done, good and faithful servant. Enter into the joy of your Master." It accurately captured her essence with this single sentence, "Faith, family and friends were the greatest blessings of her life." She was a member of the same church for almost sixty years. Across the decades she was an active member of the Wesleyan Service Guild, Methodist Women, Fidelis Class and Women's Society of Christian Service. She volunteered at Some Other Place after retirement. When her children were young, she drove carpools, served in the PTA and worked in the Little League concession stand.

At her Service of Death and Resurrection in the Wesley United Methodist Church sanctuary on August 20, 2005, the congregation began with the mighty hymn of praise, *All Creatures of our God and King.* The pipe organ led us in singing the signal line, "Thou leadest home the child of God, Christ our Lord the way has trod." Pastors Bill Scales, Jim Bass and Peter Miller led the service. The celebration concluded with the contemporary *Hymn of Promise* and its wonderful lines,

> In our end is our beginning; in our time infinity;
> In our doubt there is believing; in our life, eternity.
> In our death, a resurrection; at the last a victory,
> Unrevealed until its season, something God alone can see.

I celebrate a lifelong joy and gratitude for the gift of my beloved parents, Mavis and I.O., whose precious memories, faith, love and generosity continue to whisper love to me daily.

BROTHER: *ACHIEVER, BELIEVER, HEALER*

Brother Gilbert was my role model and confidante, as well as my roommate for the first thirteen years of my life. He was born in Beaumont in September 1947. I was born in Beaumont in September 1952. He played football, basketball, and baseball. So, did I. He was a student council officer and so was I. He was an Eagle Scout and so was I. He earned the God and Country Award. I am a little chagrined that as the future preacher I did not receive the God and Country Award!

My brother was not an angel. Neither was I, nor were you. He had collection of *Playboy* magazine centerfolds hidden in one of his dresser drawers while in high school. I think he must have been preparing for anatomy classes in medical school! Two of the years I was an undergraduate school student pastor in High Island, Texas, Gilbert was studying at the University of Texas Medical School Branch in Galveston, 32 miles away. We would meet for seafood fare on Bolivar Peninsula. He once took me to the remote room of the school where students learned anatomy by dissecting donated human bodies. Gilbert gave his cadaver a name. He called him Ernest. Whenever my brother went to the morgue, he would say, "I am going to work in earnest."

A year after Gilbert graduated from med school and moved to Dallas for his internship and residency at Baylor Medical Center, I graduated from undergraduate school and moved to Dallas to study theology at Southern Methodist University. A signal highlight of our first year in Dallas together was going to the old Ownby Stadium on the SMU campus and seeing the world's greatest soccer star play in an exhibition match. Neither of us knew much about soccer, but it was a fun time in a full house!

I do remember the special feeling of being with my brother in the presence of the world's best-known athlete of the most popular sport in the world. His name was Pele and was from the nation of Brazil. Twenty-one years later I would be a delegate to the World Methodist Conference in Rio de Janeiro, Brazil, and would remember that signal night with Pele in Dallas with Gilbert cheering a hero to millions across the globe. Thank you, God, for special memories which connect us to those now gone. You might call it a mental and, indeed, a most holy communion.

Another sacred experience shared with my beloved brother was his and Kathy's wedding in Dallas in her parents' home in North Dallas. It was my personal and pastoral privilege to officiate and join this much-loved couple in the covenant of Christian marriage. Cheers, tears, and toasts to many happy years were the order at the reception following. It is always fun to be with Baptists who know they are not going to hell because they drink champagne at a wedding reception!

Gilbert and Kathy's marriage in September 1978 was a medical merger. He was completing his residency in internal medicine and she was a nurse in the thoracic surgery ICU at Baylor Hospital when they met in 1977. In a few months they were engaged and planning to spend a long, happy life of service together. Gilbert and Kathy loved each other deeply and were devoted to their profession. What a bright future lay ahead for this new family, so gifted and so in love!

He had joined an internal medicine group in North Dallas after finishing his residency and passing his state medical board exams. Kathy retired from nursing, so they could travel some and begin a family. They got a most special Texas Independence Day gift when Andrew Powell Dent arrived in Presbyterian Hospital in North Dallas on March 2, 1981. It was candy cigars, flowers and balloons galore!

Life does not always go as planned. Detours, interruptions, and sometimes dramatic and traumatic events invade our lives without warning. Such was the case for my parents' first child, best man at my wedding and father of five-month-old Andrew. Dr. David Streitmatter wrote this tender tribute to his young colleague in the August 1981 *Presby-Scope*, the Medical Staff Monthly Newsletter of Presbyterian Medical Center:

> **Gene Gilbert Dent, M.D.**, born in Beaumont less than 34 years ago, was a graduate of U.T.M.B. at Galveston. He completed his internal medicine residency at Baylor in Dallas in 1977. In his four years in practice, he served his patients, colleagues and Presbyterian Hospital with enthusiasm, energy, humor, and dedication. On July 30, Gilbert was on his way home to his wife and 5-month child, but he and his persimmon Mazda were crushed by the crazed flight of a forged-prescription fugitive. Gilbert never regained consciousness. The tragic news filled us with disbelief. It was a bad dream. Overwhelming grief allowed no room for anger that a happy husband, proud father, and a career that promised much service to be wiped out so senselessly. He loved his new office in Woodhill. His empty desk reminds us

how unpredictable and precious life is. When grief is gone, we shall praise God for his joyful life: a rare combination of youthful enthusiasm and maturity.

My brother remained in a coma for a week before our family made the painful, but necessary decision to remove our loved one from life support. He passed peacefully Friday, August 7, five weeks before his thirty-fourth birthday. Three days later it was my personal and pastoral privilege to stand and speak to an overflowing assembly of friends, neighbors, and hundreds from the medical community. In the strength of God and filled with countless whispers of love during the week, I spoke with confidence and conviction these words on behalf of our family:

> We will not be defeated by what has happened. We will not be overcome. We will not give up. We will not despair. For we are part of a tradition that witnesses to the truth that Love endures all things; that it is stronger than hatred, that good can overcome evil, and that resurrection has the power to overcome even death. The reason my family and many others can come through an experience like this is that we are the followers of another thirty-three-year-old physician who also died at the hands of evil forces beyond his control – One who rose triumphantly to give us the victory over sin and death.

The service music, scriptures and messages brought comfort and hope to our family and those gathered, though there was still deep pain and loss to work through. The normal stages of grief - denial, anger, bargaining and depression - would be a lengthy journey toward acceptance for us all. The sudden, senseless, violent death of someone young is a tragedy beyond measure. In a sense, one does not get over such a loss, only through it. I have stood with far too many families in cemeteries across four decades saying goodbye to beloved children and grandchildren.

Tears, time, talk, trust, touch, and thanksgiving are the six alliterative gifts from God to get us through painful losses. Grief is work. It takes time. It cannot be rushed. Jesus honored our tears. He wept at the death of his friend Lazarus. He promised, "Blessed are those who mourn, for they shall be comforted." We have been sustained by many whispers of love across the years. My sister-in-law later remarried. My nephew grew up, graduated from college on the East Coast, met a Georgia girl, fell in love and asked me to

22

officiate at his wedding. What a joy to be included in that holy creation of a new family on a golf course in Sea Island, Georgia.

Andrew and his wife now have two young boys. They included Dent in the name of one of their sons, Charley, whom I had the privilege of baptizing in May 2019. Joined by his parents and son William, Andrew came to Denver for worship and to celebrate my retirement in April 2018. I felt my beloved brother's presence that day. The circle of life – birth and death – we are all born, and we all die. Blessed are those who travel the journey with faith, hope and love. Love whispers in mysterious ways.

Fast forward 37 years from my brother's death. In December 2018 a retired pastor friend in Tyler invited me to join him and two other guests to hear former Special Prosecutor Ken Starr speak at a Rotary Club Luncheon Meeting. The bigger deal for me that day was that one of the other lunch guests was from my hometown of Beaumont. Eugene and I had attended and graduated from junior high and high school together, but we had not seen each other in 47 years. As we talked, we discovered he had been a patient of my brother for several years in Dallas. I was stunned! I had never met any of my brother's patients. Eugene began to share how Gilbert had cared for him and pretty much saved his life one day. I asked him if he would put into writing the critical medical care he received.

A week later Eugene emailed me from Michigan a detailed recollection of what happened between patient and physician. Here is a portion:

> This will be an attempt to give you the basis of what transpired with your brother, Dr. Gilbert Dent. While combing my hair in the full-sized mirror one morning - without a shirt - it came to my attention that all my ribs were visibly pronounced. I grabbed the scales and found that I had shrunk from 180 lbs. to 138 lbs. Picked up the telephone and got a same day appointment. When I entered Dr. Dent's office, he happened to be walking by the receptionist - took one look at me and yelled out to the P.A. to grab some Latin-based medical equipment followed by the American form of the Latin word statim - STAT! A blood sample was in progress as well as a thorough chewing out for thinking I had not finished my meds. In minutes, he discovered my white blood count was triple, and I was less than 24 hours from

hospitalization - or worse. Multiple injections were administered, 14-day erythromycin prescribed with a 3/7/10 day follow up to which 10 pounds came back in 10 days. Within 6 months, I was 100% up and running. Dr. Dent told me I had every sign of being rheumatic. The World turns rather slowly without someone like Dr. Gilbert Dent in your life. Without him, my World would likely not be spinning at all.

Thanks, Eugene, for being a most unlikely love whisperer after two-score years. Due to patient confidentiality, my brother never spoke of the meaningful medical care he rendered. Billions of persons have benefitted physically, spiritually and emotionally from another thirty-three-year-old physician who went about doing good, bringing healing, hope and new life to folks of all times and places. Eugene, you have echoed grace and multiplied mercy. My family is most grateful our paths crossed in a profound connection. You blessed our family deeply with the memory of a long gone, lastingly loved brother. Thanks be to God for the Great Physician and Older Brother of us all who continues to bless the broken, heal the hurting, counsel the conflicted and whisper love to the least, the last and the lost.

SISTER: *WITTY, WONDERFUL, WISE*

Marilyn did not have it all. She was the middle child, the only girl and had the August birthday, making her usually the youngest in her class each year in school. Though only 37 months apart in age, we were four grades apart in school. Despite the seeming disadvantages she brought to public school, she bloomed where she was planted.

My sister embraced the social scene, tolerated the scholastic side and enjoyed the whole experience of education, socialization and maturation. She laughed often, studied occasionally and found fulfillment in the relationships with her teachers, classmates and even her two brothers who enjoyed occasionally ganging up on her with teasing, taunting, and testing her patience. Gilbert and I were probably jealous because she had her own room and closet.

Marilyn was gregarious. She never met a stranger. She joined school clubs, entertained with the Buffalo Belles, the school's drill team. She sang in the youth choir, was active in the Methodist Youth Fellowship and earned pins for her Sunday School perfect attendance at North End Methodist Church. She did have a crazy streak in the best sense of the word. Once when the local popular teenage radio station - "KAYC, 1450 on your radio dial"- had a contest to determine who had "The Most Unkissable Lips," Marilyn submitted an entry with twelve different shades of various lipsticks. Guess who won the contest? No one was surprised.

I was proud to be her little brother. Several of my teachers across the years had Marilyn in their classes. They recalled her fondly from four years before. She paved the way for me. The excellent public school teachers we had inspired my sister to major in education and to devote three decades to teaching children herself. She enjoyed college as a member of the Delta Zeta sorority. In college she met Dennis from Winnie, Texas. They dated, fell in love, and got engaged. On June 23, 1973, it was my joyous personal and pastoral privilege to join this happy couple in the covenant of Christian marriage at St. Matthew's United Methodist Church in High Island, Texas.

This couple followed the biblical mandate to "be fruitful and multiply" by bringing forth son Chad and daughter Amanda in the years to follow. Marilyn balanced well the roles of wife, mother, teacher, and daughter. She was blessed to live just down the street from our parents who helped with baby-sitting grandchildren and grand dogs across the years. Marilyn walked in the way of her two brothers as a sports fan. She was particularly attached to the Houston Astros and was not averse to hanging over the Astrodome home dugout with her friends to get pictures of the players before and after games.

After thirty years of teaching middle school and special education, Marilyn chose to enter a new chapter of life – retirement! She jumped right in with the joyous experiences of her two children getting married, traveling with her husband on his business trips with Mobil Oil, playing bridge and then finally the awesome joy of welcoming and holding her first grandchild on November 22, 2003. Marilyn connected closely with the words and experience of Christian songwriters and singers Bill and Gloria Gaither:

> How sweet to hold a newborn baby,
> And feel the pride and joy he gives.

Four days later, the day before Thanksgiving, Marilyn was diagnosed with a brain tumor. Surgery on December 11 revealed it was malignant and extensive. Chemotherapy began in early January. Headaches, nausea, and disfigurement followed. Despite her condition, Marilyn was upbeat. She had come face-to-face with death seven years before as a victim of a violent home invasion and terrorizing attack which lasted several hours.

In early January 2004 she wrote these words of faith, confidence and promise in her emails to family and friends: 'Being positive and optimistic is coming very easily for me — for faith in God will do that for that, you know! Love to all, Marilyn." A little later she sent, "Again, dear friends and family, thank you for keeping my family in your thoughts and prayer. God has really blessed us with a wonderful support system like you. With much faith and love, Marilyn."

Early Sunday, February 15, my sister's pain finally ended. In death, she was healed. As all families who love, our family wept at her death, but we also rejoiced in her life of love, laughter, and faith across 54 years. Two days later at her celebration of life and faith at Wesley United Methodist Church, our family's home church for over 50 years, we sang these words from the Gaithers about our risen Savior:

> Because He lives, I can face tomorrow
> Because He lives, all fear is gone
> Because I know He holds the future
> And life is worth the living just because he lives.

Then close Dent family friend and pastor Bill Scales stood to preach. At the end of his funeral message, he shared a personal experience from a few days before. Bill and his wife Janet went to the eightieth birthday celebration of a fellow retired pastor named Kelly Williams. Kelly was longtime senior pastor of the prominent Chapelwood United Methodist Church in Houston. Six years before, this retired minister had taken his ten-year-old grandson to their ranch to help him tend the cows. He had given Derrick a four-wheel all-terrain vehicle which he enjoyed riding at the ranch. But on this day, something went terribly wrong. Derrick tried to maneuver the four-wheeler down through a wash-out which had not been there before. The vehicle somehow turned over, crushing Derrick to death.

For six years the grandfather held himself responsible for the accident. The vehicle had been a gift from him. But a few weeks before my sister's death, something happened that changed everything. Sitting in church listening to the sermon, the grandfather suddenly looked up to the huge cross above the altar at Chapelwood Church and there sitting with his legs dangling from one of the cross bars was Derrick. He was smiling from ear to ear, and saying, "Granddaddy, look, I'm okay. Please stop grieving. I like it here. Please don't cry anymore. I'm okay."

Thinking if he told others of what happened they would surely think he was losing his mind, the grandfather remained silent. But the next evening he received a phone call from Derrick's mother and father who now lived in Dallas. The daughter-in-law said, "John has something to tell you." When the son got on the line he engaged in some small talk. Then he said to his dad, "We went to church yesterday. While I was sitting there, I looked up at the cross and there on one of the cross beams I saw Derrick swinging his legs and saying, 'Look, Daddy! I'm okay. Please don't grieve anymore. I like it here. I'm okay.'"

I am not certain what to make of this experience. I did know the grandfather and trust his experience and that of his son. I have read at many memorial services the words of Jesus, "I will not leave you comfortless... because I live, you also will live...I go to prepare a place for a place for you." To all who have said goodbye to a close loved one in death or will someday – and that is all us – we can find comfort in the experience and expectation that somehow, someway, someday in the mystery of divine grace we will be reconnected with those we no longer see.

I daily, dearly and deeply continue to love in spirit my departed sister Marilyn and confess that I look forward to catching up with her and Gilbert and all our brothers and sisters in Christ who have gone ahead to the Father's house. If we are truly quiet and centered, listening deeply and carefully, we might just hear echoes of mercy and whispers of love from the next room. This is my story. This is my song. And I am sticking to it all the day long.

WIFE: *STRONG, SPIRITUAL, SUPPORT*

"A good wife, who can find? She is far more precious than jewels. The heart of her husband trusts in her, and he will have no lack of gain." I can attest to the truth of this wisdom witness from the Hebrew scriptures. Sharon and I first met in three-year-old Sunday school class in our neighborhood Methodist church in north Beaumont. Though I have no memory of the incident, she clearly recalls that I was a bully. She has vividly recounted countless times with delight a Sunday morning confrontation I allegedly had with her over sixty years ago.

Her compelling storytelling includes details which make her account quite credible. She remembers that Mrs. Helpinstill was our teacher. According to Sharon, I was playing in the blocks with another boy named Tommy Matthews. When that got old, I grabbed a tiny toy truck and began pushing it along the bench against the wall where other classmates were comfortably seated. When I came to Sharon, I revved up my vehicle and with a loud command shouted at her with two single syllable words, "Move, girl!" I then ran my truck into her leg. When her mother came to pick her up, Mrs. Helpinstill had to explain the tears in Sharon's eyes and the bruise on her leg. It was a wonder the future preacher was not expelled from Sunday school for bad boy behavior!

My dear wife and I have had many laughs since then when bumping into each other in the tiny kitchens, bathrooms and closets we have shared over the years. I often said with jest on such occasions, "Move girl!" Having resided with my bride in eighteen apartments, dorms, parsonages and homes over 45 years of marriage, I have spoken these words many times: "It's time to 'Move girl'." By the way, I never found that bullying anyone, especially one's spouse or the Bride of Christ, ever got anyone very far.

Sharon was always strong, spiritual and supportive. She overcame a disease in her freshman year of high school, an out-of-state relocation in her senior year of high school due to her father's job transfer and a painful termination of multiyear relationship early in college. Her faith sustained her in the tough times. Her dad was her rock and her hero. A reserved, gentle man, he was a pilot in the Second Great War, came home and went to work for thirty-seven years. A month after retiring from his oil company accounting position, he began blacking out. Tests followed. He was diagnosed with a malignant brain tumor. Dennis was promoted to glory on December 21, 1983, three months after becoming ill. We celebrated his life of sixty years and his eternal life on December 24. Sharon and our family went to Christmas Eve Candlelight Services to celebrate the arrival of the Babe of Bethlehem. As Sharon wept in bidding goodbye to her dear father that day, she went to worship that evening to rejoice in welcoming a beloved Son who brings light, hope and life in a world of darkness, despair and death.

While Sharon and I went to the same junior high and high school and dated some of each other's best friends, it was not until she went away to college in Oklahoma that we began to date. After her freshman year at the University of Tulsa, she returned to Beaumont for the summer of 1972 to care for her declining grandmother. During that time, she assisted me with my first church job as Summer Youth Director at the First United Methodist Church in Orange, Texas, on the Louisiana border. She was terrific helping with the girls in the group. I fell in love with serving in the church and in love with someone who loved serving in the church.

Sharon went back to Tulsa for her sophomore year. We grew in love

500 miles apart as we sent cards and letters religiously at six cents a pop. I still have a shoe box full of our romantic pursuits in which I chased her until she caught me. Our frequent investment in the U.S. mail service was supplemented by weekly Sunday night station-to-station landline telephone calls. Our love whispers were whisked on by the clock. At fifty cents a minute, we had to limit our verbal expressions of affection to ten minutes a week. Sounds crazy now in our day of countless minutes, but our relationship grew deeper over the distance.

Sharon and her family returned to Beaumont at Thanksgiving and Christmas. When I was licensed to preach in November 1972 and assigned to a student pastorate in January 1973, Sharon knew if we were headed to the altar, she was destined to a road of relocations, living in church-owned houses and being scrutinized by some church members for the clothes she wore, the way she reared our children and whether or not she attended every event at the church. By the grace of God, Sharon accepted a proposal and ring from me at Christmas 1973. She took the lead planning and preparing for a wedding 500 miles and eight months away.

We were united in the in the covenant of Christian marriage in July 1974 by close pastor family friend Bill Scales in a midafternoon service in our home church. In addition to *The Prayer of St. Francis,* the soloist sang *Let It Be Me,* not found in any hymnal, but a personal pledge to a lifetime together. After a simple reception of cake, punch and coffee, and receiving many kind gifts of dishes, linens and the usual helpful items for young newlyweds, we sped off in my 1972 gold, two-door Dodge Charger to Lafayette, Louisiana.

Some of our friends had very artistically decorated our car with white shoe polish, drawing the Methodist Cross and Flame logo, as well as writing our names on the car for all to see. About three the next morning, we were awakened in our second-floor room at the Ramada Inn by some unrelated, inebriated guests at three in the morning. They were yelling, "Mike! Sharon! Wake up! Where are you?" We did not reply. We found a car wash Sunday morning and quickly scrubbed our names off the honeymoon vehicle! The next three days we spent eating awesome Cajun food and seeing the sights of New Orleans. There is no place quite like the French Quarter to see the vast variety of God's creatures in creative, colorful clothing or not.

For forty-five years Sharon has been a super supportive spouse. She completed her early childhood education degree in four years while relocating several times, caring for her ill grandmother, planning a wedding and becoming a pastor's wife at age 21. Across our marriage she has taught preschool, migrant students in a rural setting, in an elite private school and in a Dallas public school classroom with no aide and 36 students, six of whom spoke only Spanish or Vietnamese. She often voluntarily worked with the mothers of the children she taught to equip them in becoming more effective parents. There will be a special place in the world to come for saints like Sharon who persevere in the classroom against all odds to teach, care for and nourish the minds, hearts and lives of young children. She whispered love in multiple languages and countless lives.

Her service in the classroom not only blessed the children she taught, but also gave her an identity outside her role as the preacher's spouse in the communities we served. She was respected for her professional skills. When our own children arrived, she took excellent care of them, teaching them valuable lessons in academics and life, as well. When I was away at long meetings, on pastoral visits, at conferences or on mission trips, Sharon managed the home well. She was the best. Look up Proverbs 31:26-29 and you will see her image.

In the congregations we served, Sharon was far more than "PW" or "Preacher's Wife," as one of our daughter's friends affectionately called her. She sang in the chancel choir, taught children's Sunday School, and Vacation Bible School. In our time in Denver Sharon taught Julia Cameron's *The Artist Way* book to adults in the Trinity Music and Arts Ministry for several years. She was honored to teach a watercolor class at Laity Lodge in the Texas Hill Country during our time in the Lone Star State.

Sharon stepped up to lead beyond the local churches we served. She was a member of the Texas Conference Spouses Association for thirty years, serving as District President several times, Vice President and President of the Spouses Association and Chair of the Conference Spouses Retreat. She enjoyed installing United Methodist Women officers and teaching UMW programs in many settings. The United Methodist Women are not to be confused with the United Mine Workers. The women have a most impressive history of social concerns, service and mission around the world. Their former names, the Women's Society of Christian Service and the Wesleyan Service Guild, describe well their call to make a significant impact in the world in the Methodist tradition of serving the local and global communities.

I was often blessed to have Sharon be my roommate when I traveled to attend or speak at church conferences across the country and world. We enjoyed ecclesial events in England, Rome, Israel, Greece, Egypt, Scotland, California, New Orleans, Baltimore, Chicago, Arkansas and across Texas. We also had some adult vacation renewal time together in Alaska, Washington, Cozumel, Canada and Jamaica over the years.

As a young pastor I was required to attend many meetings and conferences without her, as she cared for our children. Later in our marriage Sharon was able to make annual quilting and weaving retreats in Colorado. She ended up hosting quilting and sewing retreats annually at our mountain retirement home for six years. A dozen or more of her church and very secular friends gathered to eat, visit, cook, sew, weave and solve the problems of the world. No men, especially pastors, could attend. What happened on those retreats stayed on those retreats. They may not have solved many of the dilemmas of the land, yet they always had a delightful time trying!

Sharon has always been a superb, strong caregiver. She shone brightly over the years in caring for her grandmother, father, mother and mother-in-law in their last days. She surely supported me as I buried my parents and siblings across the years. Following a skiing accident in 2000 in Colorado and surgery a week later in Texas, I was nurtured by Sharon's TLC over six weeks of PT – pain and torture - to full recovery and skiing again. One of Sharon's favorite Bible verses is "I can do all things through Christ who strengthens me." She has proven that by being my mainstay for 45 years. She has done all things well to strengthen, sustain and support her spiritual partner and mate.

Since my MCI diagnosis, she has stepped up her compassionate care. My challenges pale in comparison to her having two C-sections, being thrown off a camel in Egypt and cracking her tailbone on the third day of a 16-day trip, falling and crushing the radial head in her elbow at our son's law school graduation, having two knee replacement surgeries in three months and undergoing monthly infusions for rheumatoid arthritis for years into the present. I am a kindergartener in the school of pain. She is in grad school. Nonetheless, Sharon calls our life together "an adventure." She is honest with me and I with her. We believe in the Biblical proverb, "It is better to marry than to burn." In fact, I believe it best to marry and to burn! We have learned some important lessons over the years to having a lasting marriage:

1. Forgive one another. We all make mistakes.
2. Pray for one another. We all need help.
3. Whisper love to one another. Love covers a multitude of mistakes.

4. Stay close to the Creator. You will be close to one another

5. Master the magic mantra, "Let's eat out tonight."

MISS LEE: *GETTING A GREAT START*

She was my brother's first-grade teacher. She was my sister's first-grade teacher. She was my first-grade teacher. Over a five-year period in the 1950s, Miss Lee launched the public education of the Dent children at French Elementary School in the working-class neighborhood of north Beaumont. The school was named for John Jay French, a Connecticut-born transplant to Texas in the middle of the nineteenth century.

Miss Lee had a most interesting first name. Her parents named her Voyd. Why, I do not know. What I do know and will ever be grateful for is the fact that she filled a void in our lives. She introduced the Dent children and countless others across the decades to a hunger for education. She taught us letters and numerals, words and basic math. She instilled manners, taking turns, helping your classmates, listening to instructions and following the rules. She was stern, yet kind. She lived the biblical wisdom, "Train children in the right way, and when old, they will not stray."

Miss Lee was spot on in her evaluation of her students' skills or their lack of the same. While she graded me very favorably in academic areas, she deservingly gave me an "N" in handwriting. She suggested I needed to take time and work on my printing. Unfortunately, I retained my often less than legible letters. I am persistently plagued by poor penmanship. The advent of computers has been a boon to legible written communication.

My brother, sister and I were all grateful for the firm foundation of public education established by Miss Lee. Forty years after finishing the first grade, I received a phone call from my mother in Beaumont. She shared the news of Miss Lee's death. Though I was unable to attend the celebration of her life and vocation, I was able to call Dr. Ed Brooks Bowles, the pastor of First Baptist Church and tell him the invaluable impact Miss Lee made on three little kids in their first year of school. Gilbert, Marilyn and I all entered helping professions, prepared by the first year in the classroom under Miss Lee's tutelage.

Some folks who attended the funeral told me that Dr. Bowles spoke of the indelible impression made for God and good by Miss Lee in the lives of three first graders from one family in Beaumont in the middle of the twentieth century. Thanks be to God for Voyd Lee and all the many teachers who got us off to great starts with whispers of loving encouragement, affirmation and guidance. May their tribe increase as they shape the lives of those yet on the scene.

MRS. REDD: *SHARING HISTORY WITH HER CHILDREN*

Mrs. Billie Redd went overboard that day. She somehow arranged for a small black and white television set with "rabbit ears" to be rolled into our elementary classroom. Students from the other second grade classes around us piled in to witness an unprecedented event. We saw history made on our tiny TV set. Astronaut John Glenn became the first American to orbit earth in outer space in the Mercury space capsule. We saw him blast off from Cape Canaveral, circle the globe three times and finally splash down in the North Atlantic Ocean.

Seeing this event live was as good as it gets when you are eight years old. In a race to space with Russia, we were catching up with the competition. There was no collision nor collusion with the Russians that day. There were only smiling faces, squeals of delight and celebration of an amazing accomplishment for America. Mrs. Redd made a memory for her students. She went the second mile to make it possible for her children to experience and share history in a happy hour.

Another memorable international event in this era was the regular civil defense drills carried out in Mrs. Redd's and other classrooms. Some families had underground shelters installed on their property with hope of surviving air attacks from Russian bombers. Every Wednesday a civil defense drill was conducted at 12:00 noon. Wailing sirens pierced the air for several minutes each week to ensure the air raid system was operational. As a part of that drill we students were to kneel under our desks and cover our heads. Some fatalistic students added a third directive, "Then kiss your backside goodbye!" Only they did not say backside. It is hard to hear many whispers of love when contemplating the annihilation of humanity. Yet, Mrs. Redd reassured her students all would be well.

MRS. HOLLOMAN: *CARING FOR HER CHILDREN*

The best teachers do more than teach subjects. Math, spelling and reading are vital, but not on the final report card. People do not care how much we know. They want to know how much we care. The best teachers are caregivers. They go the second mile, perhaps the third when necessary. I saw that happen one day in Mrs. Holloman's third grade class. One day one of my fellow students had a most embarrassing accident in the classroom. This student had academic and social challenges. She struggled regularly to fit in the larger group. On this particular day she peed in her pants. The liquid was running down her leg and on to the floor in a puddle. No one knew whether to laugh or cry in the moment.

Mrs. Holloman quickly and quietly took charge of a situation which could have spun suddenly out-of-control. She gave the students a new task to divert their attention. Somehow, she had paper towels nearby and cared for her student's need. Mrs. Holloman taught us all that day a valuable lifelong lesson in caring. It has stuck with me for over 55 years. Love can be whispered in a card, a gift, a prayer, and even in a paper towel.

COACH HOSEA: *STRONG AND SPIRITUAL*

Coach Jay Hosea was every seventh-grade boy's dream. He was young, not out of college more than a handful of years. His premature hair loss made him appear older, at least 30. He was a paragon of physical fitness. He modeled quickly and easily ascending and descending the pegboard on the James Bowie Junior High gym wall. That task was much harder than it looked. He taught us aspiring athletes to lift weights and get ready for the football team next year.

Coach Hosea was very strong in another important area. He was a man of solid faith. Every Monday in athletics class he asked, "How many of you men went to church yesterday?" After the seeing the usually strong show of hands, Coach would simply say, "Men, this is important." He did not preach or pray, but the priority of faith was evident in his short time with us at Bowie. To be called "men" at age 12 or 13 years was life affirming!

The next year Coach Hosea was honored by being promoted to French Hight School and its football coaching staff. Just a couple of months in his new position, he got sick, went to the doctor and was soon diagnosed with a rapidly growing cancer. How could this be? Sadness and sorrow pervaded the Bowie and French school campuses when he died in February 1967. With many other students I went to the funeral at the First Methodist Church in Liberty, Texas. It was my first funeral to attend and I wept profusely. Nothing made sense at that moment. With many classmates I was grieving, though I did not know nor understand the stages of grief, nor the strength of my foundation of faith at the time. That would come later.

What I do know is that I have stopped several times over the years at the Liberty cemetery on US Highway 90. There I would visit Coach Hosea's grave for a short time. I would see and remember several significant things. Coach was only 26 years-old when he died. He was preceded in death by an infant son who was buried beside him. Of signal importance and inspiration are the words of St. Paul, favorites of Coach Hosea, inscribed on his headstone, "I can do all things through Christ who strengthens me."

The short, yet strong spiritual life of my first coach continues to whisper the love of Christ to me. God only knows how many others have been encouraged through the gentle spiritual witness of divine strength and freedom from the fear of death found in the message on a gravestone in Liberty, Texas. Coach Hosea just got to the finish line before the rest of us.

MRS. BROWN: *ANCIENT AND CONTEMPORARY*

Dorothy Brown must have been at least a hundred years old. At least she looked very chronologically gifted to a class of junior students at French High School in Beaumont. Although the Romantic language was taught there, the school was also named for the city pioneer John Jay French. Mrs. Brown may have been around when Mr. French was still above ground. She wore wire rim glasses and could have been mistaken for your great-grandmother.

We were condemned to a semester of American Literature with Old Lady Brown. Our expectations were not high. The highlight of our class was getting to be in groups of 5-6 students tasked with choosing an American lit classic work and presenting it to the class with a present-day parallel experience. Our team chose Mark Twain's *The Adventures of Huckleberry Finn.* That was a sane and safe selection from the vast field available. What was not so safe and sane was choosing a smash 1968 rock song by the Canadian American edgy music group named Steppenwolf to be our contemporary parallel to Huck Finn. We had enough sense not to choose their hit *The Pusher.* We rolled the dice and chose Steppenwolf's bigger hit, *Born to Be Wild.* As an essential part of the soundtrack to the smash movie *Easy Rider,* it was the perfect song of the of the counter-cultural character of Huck Finn. If anyone was ever born to be wild, he was Huckleberry Finn!

The day of reckoning came. Our team introduced our project on Huck Finn in class, set the stage for the contemporary composition, breathed a "Help me Jesus, I'm in trouble prayer" and let the homemade tape recording commence. Would we live through the day? Would Old Lady Brown boot us from her class with a kick in our, uh, backside for a severe lack of class on our adolescent parts and hearts?

Then the recording kicked off with this new generation declaration of independence:

> Get your motor runnin'
> Head out on the highway
> Lookin' for adventure
> And whatever comes our way
> Yeah Darlin' go make it happen
> Take the world in a love embrace
> Fire all of your guns at once and
> Explode into space

The rest is history. Mrs. Brown loved it! She awarded us an A+ on the project. She went from Old Lady Brown to Queen Dorothy, from the Wicked Witch to the Good Witch in the literature department. We went from the outhouse to the penthouse. She went from ancient to contemporary. We went from juniors to seniors in a few months.

A few years later I ran into Mrs. Brown. She did not look ancient. She was kind and gracious. Our chance meeting was at a church, her First Methodist Church in downtown Beaumont. We were both surprised. As surprises go, it was a wonderful one. I expect to run into this timeless saint again somehow, someday, someway. Her whispers of love are still echoing in the heads and hearts of hundreds, even thousands of students who came to some degree of maturity under her wise tutelage.

MR. HOLLAND: *NO OPUS, BUT A HERO*

Donnie Holland showed up in the fall of 1970 as the new industrial arts teacher at French High School. Just out of college, he was tall, at least six-three. He was an immediate asset to the faculty basketball team when it played the local radio station disc jockeys in the fundraising game for the school.

More than that, Mr. Holland was just cool. He wore ankle boots, dark dress shirts and stylish jackets. He pushed the envelope, sporting hair over his ears and long sideburns. Best of all, he became the part-time youth director at my church. He could shoot baskets, shoot pool and shoot the bull with the best of them. All of us guys looked up to him in every way.

He was also blessed with a beautiful young wife. Betty was petite, at least a foot shorter than her husband, and helped in the youth program. She taught at Hebert High School, an African American school on the other side of town.

They were a great team and asset to our church, school and community for a year or two. I was fortunate to hang out some at their apartment. They were just cool folks!

Then suddenly they were gone. Nobody knew what happened. There were rumors of an affair and a divorce. People move on. Change happens. Relationships die. New relationships grow. I always wondered what happened to Mr. Holland. Gone, but not forgotten.

Two decades later I saw his name in the newspaper, his face on the national television news. I was stunned and saddened to learn of his death. The headline proclaimed" *Lt. Col. Donnie Holland Killed In Second Day of Desert Storm."* The newspaper reported, "U. S. Air Force Lt. Col. Donnie Holland, 42, formerly of Bastrop, LA, and the son of Doug and Christine Holland, died in the second day after the aerial attacks began in Iraq in January 1991, as part of Operation Desert Storm. Holland, a pilot, was flying an F-15 Eagle and was reported missing in action on January 17, 1991, after successfully completing intensive bombing operations on the first day of the war. He was listed as missing in action until the end of the war when his remains were returned to U. S. authorities."

He was buried with full military honors, including a "Missing Man" fly over by fellow airmen from his base in North Carolina in F-15 Eagles, a 21-gun salute, and the playing of Taps the grave-side ceremony at the Promised Land Cemetery. Lt. Col. Holland was buried in a family plot where his grandparents are buried.

The lives and loves of those who cross our paths across the years – teachers, neighbors, family members, church folk – may never conceive an opus – yet they well may bless our lives decades later with deeds of sacrifice, echoes of mercy and whispers of love. Mr. Holland surely did.

Home Church: Space of Grace

COMMUNITY: *ALL IN THE FAMILY*

I was fortunate to have two loving homes growing up. One was my nuclear family – father, mother, brother and sister. The other was our church family consisting of over 800 diverse friends in faith, located two blocks from our home. North End Methodist Church began in 1912 and moved to its second location in 1950 where the Dents joined three years later. The new facility was remembered in these glowing terms, "The new building was a palace with tall ceilings, wide halls, tiled floors, broad staircases, classrooms, offices, restrooms, a kitchen, a Fellowship Hall, and gigantic parking lots." As good as it was, no building is perfect. The church history notes that in the late 1950's, "After being in the church several years, walls were added between the toilet stalls." Being in a family does have its limits.

When the new education wing and youth center were added to the church in 1958, it was the cool space to be for my friends and me for the next dozen years. Furnished with two pool tables, a bumper pool table, shuffleboard court built into the floor, a juke box, built-in booths for weekly snack suppers, and a soft drink machine, this was the place to be! In the early years a six-ounce Coca Cola in glass bottle from a machine costs six cents.

The congregation was a cross-section of the north side with a few professionals, some managers and many refinery workers, teachers, and laborers. There were some retirees and many young families. Family is the best word to describe the varied congregation. There were a fair number of singles. Looking back, I recognize we had gay members in our congregation of God's people. The best way to describe my home church is a gracious space where all were welcomed. I always felt that I belonged. That is wonderful feeling. The church was truly one big happy family. This perception was accurate and remained valid until my becoming a pastor and began attending monthly meetings of the Finance Committee, Board of Trustees and Personnel Committee. Occasionally the church is one big unhappy family. But it is a family.

Seriously and joyously, my home church was a home, a place and space of grace where all were welcome. The North End Methodist Church family had open doors, open minds and warm hearts. Everyone was genuinely welcomed, even a three-year-old bully in the blocks in Sunday School. Having a place to belong is a beautiful thing. A healthy faith family will forever echo mercy, whisper love and offer blessed assurance. There is no more valuable gift than that of a spiritual community. We all have a need to believe, become and belong. Love is warm word of welcome, a gentle whisper that you have a place of grace in this space.

SPIRITUALITY: *MYSTERY AND TRANSFORMATION*

Church is not just a gathering place. Something special, sacred and spiritual often stirs in our inner being when we dwell in the space of grace called church. There is something deep and profound that touches souls in the community called church. God's family provides the context to connect to the Creator at a depth far beyond daily life, politics, sports or the stock market. This space of grace gives us the setting to reflect on and be in touch with our soul, the innermost depths of our spirit.

As we encounter the Holy, we are transformed. Our souls and spirits are searched and shaped, touched and transformed. My local church provided me the space to "dabble in the mysteries of the Almighty" and to discover that the foundation of faith is firm. I was being transformed by the renewal of my mind to discover God will's and way for my life without even knowing it. Loving whispers, merciful echoes and abounding grace were mysteriously growing my life for good.

EDUCATION: *LOVE GOD WITH YOUR MIND*

My home church gave me a Revised Standard Bible in the third grade. My Sunday school teachers taught me to read the Bible, ask questions and study the history of the Judeo-Christian heritage. My Junior Methodist Youth Fellowship taught me to memorize the 66 books of the Bible. That gift has blessed my ministry to this day. My fifth-grade Sunday school teacher, Juanita Landry, influenced me to enter the pastoral ministry. I went to Vacation Bible School for a week every summer. I can still taste the oatmeal cookies and grape punch! Jane Webb spoke of the synoptic gospels and the "Q source." My teachers taught me above all else to love the Lord my God with all my heart, mind, soul and strength and to love my neighbor as myself. They never despised nor disparaged other religions or races.

My Christian education was expanded on Sunday evenings in Junior MYF (Methodist Youth Fellowship). We had a Bible story taught by Mildred Sampson. She made the Old Testament tales and characters come alive. Of course, we enjoyed games and refreshments, too. The boys in the group were occasionally rowdy and a little raunchy. Though I was baptized and joined the church on Palm Sunday 1964 when I was eleven years old, the six years following in the youth group brought serious seasons of learning, growing and maturing in the faith. My friends and I loved it that at our home church we did not have to check our brains at the door when we came to church. Questions were welcomed. Doubts were not doubted. Loving God with our minds is a Biblical mandate. Methodism was born as a movement in a university setting. Methodism requires an educated clergy.

WORSHIP: *LOVE GOD WITH YOUR HEART*

Every Sunday morning…every Sunday night…and the annual week of morning and evening revival services, my growing up in the church was filled with worship. And I embraced it. The only Sunday evening I wanted to miss was the annual showing of *The Wizard of Oz.* After all, "There is no place like home" on the night of the yearly telecast of the best-known and most commercially successful adaptation of L. Frank Baum's 1900 children's book. Our parents graciously allowed us kids to enjoy the annual battle between witches good and evil.

Sunday morning worship with robed choir and clergy brought grandeur and glory, mystery and majesty to the church's Happy Hour. Smiling faces and joyful souls of all ages shared in the worship and praise of the Holy. Indeed, we stood and sang the soaring strains of "Holy, Holy, Holy, Lord God Almighty," every first Sunday of the month. Worship was an exercise in doxology and theology. It softened my heart, grew my heart and prepared my heart to love God and neighbor.

Worship was, is and ever shall be the primary practice of loving God with our heart. Worship, both individual and community, is central to our spiritual development as we praise, pray, confess, offer ourselves and our gifts to God. As we come into God's presence in worship, we are reminded of who we are in a world where often up is down and down is up. God desires, demands and delights in our heartfelt praise. Worship reminds us of who we are in the midst of all that would make us forget.

SERVICE: *LOVE YOUR NEIGHBOR*

Loving God is great, necessary, number one and indispensable. Yet there is more. A connected command from the Christ is to love our neighbors as ourselves. My church taught me to care, to serve, to give, and to help others.

The church provided service projects for us to put our faith into practice. We gave special offerings for missions near and far. We visited senior citizens in a housing project, and invited neighborhood children to attend the annual Vacation Bible School, revivals and summer youth weeks.

North End Methodist Church was a service station. It was not about "serve us," however. The congregation helped launch a community, ecumenical mission which provided food, clothing, job referrals, and counseling. Named Some Other Place and led by a female Methodist pastor, it is still a vital mission among the underserved in the Beaumont community over 50 years later. The church also invested in mission projects of hospitals, schools, colleges and pastor training overseas. Missionaries to African nations, South America and the Far East would send letters and bring reports of how we were serving and loving our neighbors with grace in places near and far. Those letters and reports were whispers of love.

VOCATION: *DISCOVER YOUR CALL*

How does an individual choose what to do with his or her life? One young lad on the farm had a vision. He told his father he had seen three large, distinct letters in the sky. The young man believed the message of "GPC" was for him, a call to "Go preach Christ." His father had a different interpretation of the message. He said, "Son, that doesn't mean go preach Christ. It means 'Go plow corn!'" None of us can be completely certain of our life's work, yet tradition teaches we have a vocation. Vocation and a job are not the same thing. Vocation comes from the Latin word *vocare,* meaning to call. A vocation is a calling, a summons of sorts, a strong inclination of a course of action to take. People in public service, medicine, education, nursing, criminal justice and, of course, ministry often speak of being called to their life's work.

My call to pastoral ministry did not come dramatically in two seconds, minutes, or even two years. The reality is it came over two decades through countless kind people who loved God and who loved God's children, even and especially when they did crazy stuff on the way to some measure of maturity. The experiences, events and everyday people at North End Methodist were used by God to call me and others into ordained ministry. The congregation produced twelve individuals who entered pastoral ministry from the congregation between 1948 and 2006. I am grateful to be one of those.

My first sermon was in an evening service at my home church in December 1971, seven months out of high school. The title was *Jesus: The*

Liberator. One cannot go wrong with Jesus! The pastor asked me to preach again in January and several other times in 1972. As the Summer Youth Director in nearby Orange, Texas I was privileged to preach in that prestigious pulpit at the historic First UMC. The response of that historic congregation was encouraging and gracious. A call to preach which was literally a score of years in the making came to fruition on my twentieth birthday in mid-September. I "surrendered to the call" and committed myself to serve Jesus Christ as a minister of the Good News.

Call is first. As did young Samuel (1 Samuel 3:9), young Michael heard God calling. My call came over many years, but the commitment became concrete on the day I departed my teenage years. After the commitment came cultivation. Methodists are nothing if not methodical in their scrutiny of candidates for ministry. I adjusted my degree plan at Lamar, called Sharon in Tulsa, and began immediately working on the requirements for being approved for a License to Preach in The United Methodist Church. First steps included an application sent to take a Course of Study through the denomination's ministry office in Nashville, and interviews with my pastor, Beaumont District Committee on Ministry, and the congregation's Pastor-Parish Relations Committee.

Not being a stranger to these folks, I was approved at each level after due conversation and deliberation. Once the course of study was completed, the church called a special Charge Conference to consider approving me to receive a License to Preach. The process took several months to complete. My calling first voiced in the fifth grade was officially confirmed with the issuance of the license on November 25, 1972. Life would never be the same. My time of complete cultivation would take another eight years of study and service.

My pastoral ministry of 44 years began in a place and space of grace, a family called "church" where there was mystery and majesty, and where I learned to love my Maker with my head and heart, and my neighbor and myself. I also learned that I was loved eternally and unconditionally by the One who is love. The tender memories and mercies of those formative years will forever whisper the fundamental grace which grounds us all in a space of community called church.

Coming of Age in the Sixties

RACE RELATIONS: *DESEGREGATION, DEATHS, A DREAM*

The extended decade from the late 1950s into the early 1970s was a tumultuous time across the land. Conflict in Southeast Asia and in the Southern United States dominated the headlines many days of the years I was moving from childhood to adolescence. No place was conflict more present than in the arena of race relations. The Weingarten's Grocery Store where my family shopped had prominent signs declaring Colored or White on the water fountains and restroom doors. The practice was not questioned. In my early years though, there were no signs, but certain schools, churches and businesses were open to one race or another. Frankly, the "N" word was used openly to designate particular people and the part of town in which they lived.

Racial segregation seemed to be accepted without question in that time and place. But it was more than separation. I recall black patrons at the movie theatre in my grandparents' hometown having to enter by an exterior stairwell. Once inside the balcony, they had no access to the restrooms and concessions. No one publicly questioned the overt practice of discrimination.

My wife and I clearly remember dressing in black face in our first-grade, year-end school program. Almost sixty years later I had the privilege of meeting The Little Rock Nine. These African American students risked their lives to desegregate schools in Arkansas. They were threatened, taunted and spat on for enrolling in a public school. President Dwight Eisenhower had to intervene to make the integration possible. Times were changing, but it would be another decade before integration became a reality in Beaumont. My classmates and I were taught in fifth-grade music class the words and tune of Dixie, the de facto national anthem of the Confederate States of America. Partial integration came to the public schools of Beaumont in the mid-'60s.

The assassinations of President John Kennedy, Dr. Martin Luther King, Jr., and Senator Robert Kennedy over a five-year period brought disbelief, grief and anxiety to a nation needing a vision forward. The young dreamers were gunned down. Tensions intensified in racial and political arenas. Riots came to Detroit and Watts. A law and order candidate with a southern strategy emerged to lead the land. Racial tension did not abate. The nation was coming of age. So was I.

The moral mandate of Dr. King seemed to be lost. His dream of freedom and equality for all was put on hold. His love became a faint whisper, yet it echoes mercy over a half-century since his death. I painfully confess that as a fifteen-year old junior high student in the South, I did not grasp the inequality, injustice and institutional racism prevalent at the time of his death at age 39. May the 1964 Nobel Peace Prize winner rest in peace and his dream continue to bring life and shalom for all of God's children in century 21.

MUSICAL REVOLUTION: *ROCK AND ROLL IS HERE TO STAY*

Music historians trace rock and roll to as early as the 1940s. It expanded in the 1950s and exploded in the 1960s with the British Invasion. The sounds, songs and sights of the Beatles' arrival in the U.S. in 1964 began the wave of rock bands from across the pond. Other popular rock and roll groups the forefront of the "Invasion." included the Rolling Stones, the Who, the Kinks, the Dave Clark Five, Herman's Hermits, the Zombies, the Hollies, and the Animals. we

Despite their parents' protestations, the three Dent children were home on the four Sunday evenings when the Beatles sang and played live on the Ed Sullivan Show beginning February 1964. The Beatles appeared three more times in person and made filmed performances later. The Dave Clark Five, with a less rebellious reputation than the Beatles, made 13 appearances on the show, more than any other UK music group.

My brother, sister and I purchased and shared 45-RPM record hits of the popular British Bands, as well of the smooth sounds of USA's Beach Boys, Buffalo Springfield, Creedence Clearwater Revival, Monkees, Ike and Tina Turner, the Byrds and the Doors. Over forty years later I would pray for the Beach Boys in a public concert in Downtown Denver. Like prayer, rock and roll is here to stay, like it or not. Believe it or not, rock and roll cruises are now a staple in the boomer cruise industry. Anybody in for a cruise with Paul Revere and the Raiders or a variation thereof?

POVERTY AND POLLUTION: *WAR IS DECLARED*

The War on Poverty is the unofficial name for legislation initially introduced by United States President Lyndon B. Johnson during his State of the Union address in January 1964. In office for less than two months after his predecessor's assassination, Johnson proposed new programs in response to a national poverty rate of around 19 percent. The speech led the United States Congress to pass the Economic Opportunity Act, which established the Office of Economic Opportunity to administer the local application of federal funds targeted against poverty.

As a part of the Great Society, Johnson believed in expanding the federal government's roles in education and health care as poverty reduction strategies. These policies were also viewed as a continuation of President Franklin Roosevelt's New Deal, which ran from 1933 to 1937. The president from Texas had a grand plan: "Our aim is not only to relieve the symptom of poverty, but to cure it and, above all, to prevent it." The legacy of the War on Poverty policy initiative continues such federal programs as Head Start, Volunteers in Service to America and Job Corps.

War was also declared on pollution in the 1960s. Along with technological advances, the Industrial Revolution of the mid-19th century introduced new sources of air and water contamination. By the middle of the twentieth century, the impact of these changes was felt in countries across the globe. In the 1960s, an environmental movement began to stem the tide of pollutants flowing into the planet's ecosystems.

I well remember as a high school student in 1969 when chemical waste was released into the Cuyahoga River in Ohio, causing it to burst into flames. The fiery waterway became a symbol of how industrial pollution was destroying America's natural resources. Out of this movement came the annual Earth Day and legislative victories enacting the Clean Air and the Clean Act Water Acts in 1970 and 1972. The war on pollution on a global level is still being waged. I hope the satirical sticker of the *Mad* magazine edition from the mid-sixties does not ever come to pass. The reverse biblical parallel proclaimed, "In the end man destroyed the heavens and the earth." The verdict is still out. Hope yet whispers, "The earth is mine." (See Psalm 24:1.)

1968: A YEAR FOR THE AGES: *PROTESTS, PROPHETS, PAIN*

In my 67 years of earthy existence, no year stands out as does 1968 on personal, national, international and outer space levels. There was political drama and trauma, great grief and glorious gain, turning points and breaking points, culture clashes and tragic assassinations. I entered high school as one of the first in my class to be able to drive legally – some advantages to having an early September birthday! – and became interested in presidential politics and car dating for the first time, not necessarily in that order.

The year began with the Green Bay Packers defeating the Oakland Raiders on January 14 for the National Football Championship in the final year before the term Super Bowl was introduced. On January 21 the Vietnam War Battle of Khe Sanh began. It was one of the most publicized and controversial battles of the war, lasting to April 8. A U.S. B-52 Stratofortress crashed in Greenland, discharging 4 nuclear bombs. North Korea seized the USS *Pueblo*, claiming the ship violated its territorial waters while spying. A half-century later North Korea is still a pain the U.S. backside. A civil rights protest staged at a white-only bowling alley in Orangeburg, South Carolina was broken up by highway patrol. Three college students were killed.

President Lyndon B. Johnson barely edged out antiwar candidate Eugene McCarthy in the New Hampshire Democratic primary, a vote which highlighted the deep divisions in the country, and the party, over Vietnam. In the My Lai Massacre American troops killed scores of civilians. U.S. Senator Robert F. Kennedy entered the race for the Democratic Party presidential nomination. Students at Howard University in Washington, D.C. signaled a new era of militant student activism on college campuses in the U.S. Students staged rallies, protests and a five-day sit-in, laying siege to the administration building, shutting down the university in protest over its ROTC program and the Vietnam War and demanding a more Afrocentric curriculum. On March 31 President Johnson announced he would not seek re-election.

On April 3 Dr. Martin Luther King Jr. delivered his "I've Been to the Mountaintop" speech in a Memphis, Tennessee church The next day he was assassinated at age 39. Riots erupted in major American cities, lasting for several days. On April 11 President Johnson signed the Civil Rights Act of 1968. The United Methodist Church was created by the union of the former Methodist and Evangelical United Brethren churches. From April 23–30 student protesters at Columbia University in New York City took over administration buildings and shut down the university. On May 13 one million protesting students marched through the streets of Paris.

On May 17 nine protestors entered the Selective Service offices in Catonsville, Maryland, took dozens of selective service draft records, and burned them with napalm as a protest against the Vietnam War. Radical feminist Valerie Solanas shot artist Andy Warhol on June 3 at his New York City studio. U.S. presidential candidate Senator Robert F. Kennedy was shot at the Ambassador Hotel in Los Angeles on June 5. He died from his wounds the next day. He was 42. Two assassinations in two months silenced the voices of young prophetic voices.

Meeting August 5–8, the Republican National Convention in Miami Beach, Florida nominated Richard Nixon for U.S. President and Spiro Agnew for Vice President. The Medal of Honor was posthumously awarded to James

Anderson, Jr. on August 21. He was the first African-American U.S. Marine to be given this award.

In late August police clashed with anti-war protesters in Chicago outside the 1968 Democratic National Convention, which nominated Hubert Humphrey for U.S. President and Edmund Muskie for Vice President. The riots and subsequent trials were a vital part of the activism of the Youth International Party, or Yippies.

On August 28 John Gordon Mein, U.S. Ambassador to Guatemala, was assassinated on the streets of Guatemala City, the first U.S. Ambassador assassinated in the line of duty. On September 7, 150 women arrived in Atlantic City, New Jersey to protest against the Miss America Pageant, as exploitative of women. The Tet Offensive came to an end in South Vietnam on September 23. The next day *60 Minutes* debuted on CBS and is still on the air as of November 2019.

In October the Tlatelolco massacre student demonstration ended in a in bloodbath at La Plaza de las Tres Culturas in Tlatelolco, Mexico City, Mexico, ten days before the opening of the 1968 Summer Olympics. As many as 300 were estimated to have been killed. José Feliciano performed "The Star-Spangled Banner" at Tiger Stadium in Detroit during Game 5 pre-game ceremonies of the 1968 World Series between the Tigers and the St. Louis Cardinals. His personalized, slow, Latin jazz performance proved highly controversial, opening the door for later interpretations of the national anthem. NASA launched *Apollo 7*, the first manned Apollo mission. The United States Department of Defense announced that the U.S. Army planned to send about 24,000 troops back to Vietnam for involuntary second tours.

In Mexico City, African-American athletes Tommie Smith and John Carlos bowed their heads and raise their fists in a black power salute after winning, respectively, the gold and bronze medals in the Olympic men's 200 meters. On October 22 the Gun Control Act of 1968 was enacted. On Halloween, U.S. President Lyndon B. Johnson announced to the nation that he had ordered a complete cessation of "all air, naval, and artillery bombardment of North Vietnam" effective All Saints Day. In the November 5 U.S. presidential election, Republican candidate Richard Nixon defeated the Democratic candidate, Vice President Hubert Humphrey, and American Independent Party candidate George Wallace. The Alabama governor spoke in my hometown during the campaign. His racist rants are still reverberating over a half-century later. Yale University announced on November 14 it was going to admit women.

The next day Operation Commando Hunt was initiated to interdict men and supplies on the Ho Chi Minh trail, through Laos into South Vietnam. By the end of the operation, three million tons of bombs were dropped on Laos, slowing but not seriously disrupting trail operations. On November 24 four men hijacked a Pan Am flight from JFK International Airport, New York to Havana, Cuba.

This painful, strange year came to an encouraging end. On Christmas Eve the USA spacecraft *Apollo 8* entered orbit around the moon. Astronauts Frank Borman, Jim Lovell and William Anders became the first humans to see the far side of the moon and planet earth as a whole, as well as having traveled further away from the planet than any other people in history. Anders photographed *Earthrise*. The crew also read from the Bible.

In what was the most watched television broadcast at the time, the crew of Apollo 8 read in turn from the first chapter of Genesis, the Hebrew-Christian book of beginnings, as they orbited the moon. The astronauts recited verses 1-10 verbatim, using the King James Version text. Anders read verses 1–4, Lovell read verses 5–8, and Borman read verses 9–10, concluding the transmission. The transcript captured a holy moment in history for the human family. Crew Commander Borman concluded, "And from the crew of Apollo 8, we close with good night, good luck, a Merry Christmas – and God bless all of you, all of you on the good Earth."

A prayer from a quarter-million miles away declaring creation is good was good tonic after a tough year. And God saw that the earth was good and is good. For love whispers hope even in a year never to be forgotten and never to be repeated.

Good Gifts from the BSA

Following in my brother's footsteps, I enrolled in Cub Scout Pack 65 in 1960 on my eighth birthday. Three years of den meetings, Blue and Gold Banquets and becoming a Webelos Cub Scout were all prelude to joining the Boy Scouts. Crossing over from Cub Scout Pack 65 to Boy Scout Troop 65, both sponsored by North End Methodist Church, was one of the best decisions I ever made. The values I received in Boy Scouts, coupled with those congruent of the faith community, set me in a healthy direction for the rest of life.

VALUES: *SOMETHING TO GUIDE*

Where do values come from? How is character shaped? What is the source of moral fiber? As with countless other boys entering adolescence, it came through the Scout Oath, the Scout Law and the simple Scout Slogan. Every Monday night our 7:00 meeting began with every scout raising his right arm and reciting in unison the Scout Oath: *On my honor, I will do my best, To do my duty to God and my Country and to obey the Scout Law; To help other people at all times; To keep myself physically strong, mentally awake, and morally straight.* As with reciting the Apostles' Creed or other historic affirmation regularly in worship, the weekly recitation of the Scout Law instilled positive, foundational values to live by. Doing one's best, being loyal to Creator and nation, always serving others and taking care of oneself in all arenas of life are vital values in guiding one's life.

Complementing the Scout Oath is the Scout Law. It would likewise be spoken in unison by all present with right hand raised. The dozen components were quickly memorized and imbedded in every scout's memory bank for the rest of his life: *A Scout is Trustworthy, Loyal, Helpful, Friendly, Courteous, Kind, Obedient, Cheerful, Thrifty, Brave, Clean, and Reverent.* Our 30-35 Troop 65 members recited from memory these dozen positive attributes at the start of each meeting.

The third value-based member of the Boy Scout's Holy Trinity was the Scout Slogan. It states simply, *Do a Good Turn Daily.* This succinct slogan is a first cousin to a central command of Christ to "Love your neighbor as yourself." Every Boy Scout looked forward to receiving the monthly magazine called *Boys' Life.* It contained relevant articles, a page of corny jokes, a minimum of ads and "A True Story of Scouts in Action." The tales of Boy Scouts saving lives by doing good turns were truly inspiring. I cannot imagine a finer, firmer foundation of values than those of the Boy Scouts of America on which to build one's life.

SKILLS: *SOMETHING TO DO*

Children have lots of energy and curiosity. Young adolescent boys often have a double dose of both. They need something to do. Boy Scouts gave me much to do, yet it was not meaningless busywork. Troop 65 taught me lasting skills for which I am forever grateful: how to build a fire, cook a tinfoil dinner, pitch a tent, take down a tent, dig a latrine, tie knots, mark a trail, follow a trail, identify constellations in the night sky, light a lantern, fold, present and salute a flag, march in formation, send and receive Morse Code messages. Though I recall still some of the code letters, Morse Code is the single skill from six years of Boy Scouting that has not been employed beyond my years in the troop. You may even need to Google it to know what Morse Code is!

One of the most significant skills scouting schooled me in was aquatics. When I was nine-years old I nearly drowned after jumping into the deep end of a community swimming pool. My mother was in the deep end and beckoned me to join her, believing she was able to assist me, if needed. As soon as I hit the water, I knew I was in over my head, literally and figuratively, and began thrashing about in a panic. My dear mother was in a similar state of alarm and began screaming, "Help, help!" An alert lifeguard and other strong swimmers in the water quickly came to our rescue.

When I joined the Boy Scouts at age 11, I was still not able to swim. Call me a late bloomer, I finally got the hang of it at my first weeklong Scout Summer Camp at Camp Urland near Woodville, Texas. We non-swimmers were grouped together. Everyone going in the pool had to have a "buddy," no matter what one's swimming ability. When the lifeguard blew his whistle, everyone was to immediately find his buddy and hold hands up to be counted by the lifeguards. When asked why we had a buddy system, one newbie scout answered, "So you don't have drown by yourself." That was not my response, but it could have been.

By the time summer camp ended in 1964 I was able to swim, praise God! By the time I completed my youth scouting experience, I had earned merit badges in swimming, lifesaving, rowing and canoeing, all the aquatic badges available at the time. My proudest water accomplishment was completing the marathon Mile Swim. To swim 5,280 feet is no small feat! It took me just over an hour to swim scores of long laps in a designated section of Lake Tejas near

Colmesneil, Texas. The swim took place on the troop's annual Family Campout in August. No pressure, but you did not want to drop out of the extended, exhausting event in front of the sisters of your fellow Scouts whose heads you were hoping to turn.

CAMARADERIE: *SOMEPLACE TO BELONG*

Every healthy human being has a hunger for community. We desire to belong, connect and share life. In 2000 Harvard Sociology Professor Robert Putnam wrote *Bowling Alone: The Collapse and Revival of American Community.* The intriguing title came from his 1995 essay entitled "Bowling Alone: America's Declining Social Capital." Putnam surveyed the decline of social capital in the United States since 1950. He described the reduction in all the forms of in-person social intercourse upon which Americans used to found, educate and enrich the fabric of their social lives.

As a sociology major and pastor, I was interested in his work. Despite the decline of bowling leagues, PTAs and other traditional organizations, people still need community, camaraderie and connection. In addition to my family of origin and church family, Boy Scout Troop 65 was a place of peers, a fellowship of friends and a fun family. There was a genuine bond built in the activities and antics of troop and patrol meetings, campouts and courts of honor, as well as crazy skits, long hikes and scary ghost stories around the campfire.

Perhaps the strongest and most fun connection was created around the campfire on Friday nights. Most of our monthly camping trips were just one-nighters, so the campfire was the time to go over Saturday's plans, sing silly songs and tell ghost stories. Our musical repertoire included such notables as *Old Hiram's Goat, The Ants Go Marching, On Top of Spaghetti* and *Row, Row, Row Your Boat.* We even had our own troop song with a catchy, camaraderie-building tune:

> We're a hiking, camping Troop 65. 65!
> We're a hiking, camping Troop 65. 65!
> We'll got in any weather, just to be together,
> We're a hiking, camping Troop 65. 65!

Not a lot of originality, I suppose, but certainly a lot of spirit and bonds were built in singing with great gusto! Not every meeting had singing, but it did have a spiritual component. While our troop was sponsored by North End

Methodist Church, it had Baptist, Catholic and other faith expressions along with many Methodists. Each Monday meeting concluded promptly at 8:30 p.m. with the same ritual. While standing in our uniforms in our four respective patrols, we waited momentarily for the lights to be turned off. When that happened, we all raised the middle three fingers of our right hands in the dark toward heaven and prayed in unison this Scout Benediction, *"And now may the Great Scoutmaster of all true scouts be with you until we meet again."* Boy Scouts was a great place to be, to become and to belong for me and millions of other budding adolescents coming of age in the middle of the twentieth century.

TRAVEL: *SOMEWHERE TO GO*

Membership has its privileges. Belonging to Troop 65 meant opportunities to travel. Two months before his seventeenth birthday, my brother Gilbert attended the National Scout Jamboree in Valley Forge, Pennsylvania. The theme was *Strengthening America's History.* He was an Explorer Scout in Post 65 by then and thinking about college. His group also visited Philadelphia and its famed Liberty Bell, as well as Washington, D.C. and the its historic monuments and museums. I know Gilbert had an awesome time. What I did not know and could not know at the time was that his life was half-over.

The travel opportunities for me in scouting expanded my horizons. Four special trips were all most memorable. In addition to our annual weeklong Summer Camp at Camp Urland, our troop had several special summer trips. The 1965 trip was a float trip on two large barge rafts over fifty miles down the Neches River. We were Tom Sawyer and Huckleberry Finn all over again! Snakes, mosquitos and heat were no match for our young adolescent minds and bodies. The *Beaumont Enterprise* newspaper featured an article and pictures of the adventure. God bless the dads who designed and built the barges. These men who led the way on this volunteer adventure were truly whispering love to their sons and all the boys of the troop. Every boy on the float trip received the highly coveted Fifty Mile Patch for his accomplishment.

The next summer brought another travel adventure to the troop's members. We went to the rocky Hill Country of Central Texas and camped for a week. It was the farthest some of us young Beaumont boys had ever been from home, me included. Our itinerary included a day in Austin touring the State Capitol, the University of Texas, and Memorial Stadium, home of the 1963 National Football College Champions. A part of the tour was riding an elevator to the top of the UT Tower. At 28 stories it was tallest building in the city at the time. What an amazing view of the Texas Hill Country from the top of tower! The prominent landmark was bathed in orange lights whenever the Longhorn football team came out on the long end of the stick, which was often in that era.

Less than three months after our visit to the Austin campus, a shocking tragedy took place. A 25-year-old architectural engineering student and a former Boy Scout named Charles Whitman entered the building with a cache of weapons. He commandeered the elevator, rode to the top of the tower and began a shooting spree which lasted 96 minutes. By the time he was finally shot and killed by law enforcement on the observation deck, Whitman had killed 14 individuals and wounded 31 others.

Officials discovered later he had killed his wife and mother earlier that morning, and that he had been under treatment for depression for some time. He was taking medications prescribed by five different physicians. Ironically, Whitman joined the Boy Scouts at age 11. He became an Eagle Scout at 12 years three months, reportedly the youngest of any Eagle Scout up to that time. Tragically, his mental illness contributed to what was the largest mass murder by an individual at the time in the nation's history. If I have learned anything as a pastor over many years, it is this: Life is fragile, unpredictable and, therefore, precious. I am stretched to hear any mild whispers of love at all in a mass loss of human life.

My longest and best Boy Scout trip was in the summer of 1968. Troop 65 took a two-week trip to where God resides. Yes, we joined many others from the Lone Star State to journey by car to cool Colorado, the Colorful State. Many of us had never been to the Centennial State. I was one of those newbies and fell flat on my face in awe of the mountains, streams, animals and forests. We toured the strange and marvelous cave dwellings in Mesa Verde National Park, spent time in Pagosa Springs and Durango and stood in four states at one time at the remote, touristy Four Corners Monument.

However, the highlight of the venture was a three-day wilderness hike into the San Juan National Forest for a select small group of senior scouts. All 15 or 16 years of age, we six carried our gear and hiked into a new space with no adults, tents, cabins or conveniences. We were trusted by our adult leaders to do good, do right and do well. It was not easy, yet we would not trade the trip for anything. I was introduced to an amazing state which would become a favorite vacation destination, as well as our home for a dozen years. Thank you, for the introduction to the High Country, Boy Scout Troop 65!

Along with a couple of other Scouts in my troop, I was chosen to be a part of the Order of the Arrow. The Order is the National Honor Society of the Boy Scouts of America, composed of Scouts who best exemplify the Scout Oath and Law in their daily lives as elected by their peers. There is some mystery, silence, ceremony and Native American influence in the initiation. One must hike in, carry only necessities, make camp, maintain silence, and survive with minimal rations. Not everyone is able or willing to meet the stringent requirements. I was fortunate to do so.

As a new member of the Order of the Arrow, I was invited to attend an OA Conference to be held at a Scout camp near Belton, Texas. I was eager to go because I knew there would be a lot of patch trading going on. Patches are multicolored embroidered creations depicting the past and present "lodges" of the OA. Trading and selling patches were skills I was developing to enhance my patch collection and college savings account.

At the conference I left my patch collection in my tent during a session of the gathering. At the conference of honor campers, I had no anxiety that my treasured collection would grow feet and walk away. Apparently, that is what happened. When I came back to my tent, my unsecured valuable patch collection was nowhere to be found. I was shocked, sad and sorry over the theft, but remembered the folksy wisdom from my childhood, "There's a rotten apple in every barrel." No organization is without some flaws, failures and foibles. I also learned you cannot control everything that happens to you, but you can control how you respond to it. That would be a valuable lesson in in my life dealing with personal losses of much greater magnitude than a pilfered pile of patches.

CONNECTIONS: *SOMEONE TO SHARE*

In the approach to 2020, the Boy Scouts of America made some major modifications in membership to accommodate social changes in the country. After over 100 years as the Boy Scouts of America, the organization changed its name. The new moniker became Scouts BSA. In January 2017, the historic organization announced that transgender boys would be allowed to enroll in boys-only programs. Previously, the sex listed on an applicant's birth certificate determined eligibility for these programs. Going forward, the decision would be determined on the gender listed on the application. The first openly transgender boy to join the Scouts in February 2017 was rejected from the Boy

Scouts for being transgender, but the policy was changed after his story became nationally known.,

Another major transformation occurred in October 2017. The Boy Scouts of America announced that girls would be invited into Cub Scouts beginning in fall of 2018, with an early adopter program beginning in January 2018. The announcement included the statement that girls in Cub Scouting will simply be called "Cub Scouts" but that a name would need to be given to the new Boy Scout equivalent program for girls which would be launching. In February 2019 the name became Scouts BSA. On January 16, 2018, Abigail Lemon of Euless, Texas became the BSA's first female Cub Scout. The times, they are a-changing. They always have been, and always will be. Change or perish, say the prophets of the ages.

My time in scouting came with many changes. Maturing from age 11 to 17, from riding a Schwinn bicycle to driving our family's Ford Mustang, from elementary to high school, from *Mad* magazine to still reading *Mad* and now *Sports Illustrated*, from Tenderfoot Scout to Eagle Scout. Change is necessary part of life for an institution and an individual. We change or we die. One thing which remains is the connection. The scouting experience over almost 110 years bonds boys - and now girls - in beneficial behavior outlined and instilled in the recitation and application of the Scout Oath, Law and Slogan.

In whatever community, town or city in which I served as a pastor over 44 years, being a Boy Scout was always as asset. The road from Tenderfoot to Eagle was not easy. Though I was a quality baseball player, I withdrew from my Little League team at age 12. I wept when I handed over my green and gray uniform to my manager, Mr. Day, at his home on Dallas Street in North Beaumont on a late spring Sunday afternoon of 1965. It was a tremendously difficult decision to make. Yet it was the right one. I believed it was unfair to the team to miss four critical games while gone on Scouting trips. There was short-term pain and long-term pleasure from the decision. Love whispered later, "You did the right thing."

Becoming an Eagle Scout brought instant respect, relationships and future invitations to serve and support the Scouting program. In two new church plants I served, Scout troops were launched. Both are still going strong in the Klein and Atascocita communities just north of Houston. I was privileged to attend and often asked to pray at Eagle Scout Courts of Honor of church members in Texas and Colorado. It was a privilege to invest financially in the work of the BSA across the decades.

The connections I made with the Boy Scout Council in Denver were delightful during my dozen years of ministry there. Soon after arriving in the Mile-High City, I was invited by a community leader and church member named Ned Minor to attend a Boy Scout Sports Breakfast. I enjoyed the quality event at the Pepsi Center, home to the Denver Nuggets National Basketball Association Team and the Colorado Avalanche National Hockey Team. After that first experience, I committed to attending every April and making a financial investment in the Denver Boy Scouts. What could possibly be more fun than showing up at 6:00 a.m. in Downtown Denver to eat breakfast with 1,000 of your friends, Boy Scouts, area college and professional coaches and hear speak a prominent professional sports personality?

Five times over the years until retiring, I was invited and honored to offer the invocation at the Sports Breakfast which raised over $1,000,000 annually for the Denver Area Boy Scouts. What a fun opportunity to meet and pray for Baseball Hall of Fame Member Ozzie Smith (AKA *The Wizard of Oz)*, Denver hometown hero and NBA All-Star Chauncy Billups, twice Super Bowl Champion Coach Mike Shanahan, Super Bowl Coach John Fox, and the 2016 Denver Bronco Super Bowl L (50) Super Bowl Championship Coaching Staff.

I went extra early to a reception for pictures and personal conversation with the Broncos coaches before the breakfast. The morning was memorable in meeting Defensive Coordinator Wade Phillips. His famous father Bum was a popular professional football coach. My mother-in-law tutored Bum Phillips at French High School circa 1940 in Beaumont in the same building where I attended fifth and sixth grades. My Aunt Sue taught Wade's future wife Laurie in elementary school in Nederland in the 1950s. To be so big, Texas can also be so small!

What a special opportunity to meet and chat also with Super Bowl Champion Head Coach Gary Kubiak. Less than three years before he had had collapsed on the sideline during an NFL game. In a scary sequence of events he lay still on the stadium indoor floor of the Houston Texans for an extended time before being transported from the stadium to Methodist Hospital. The Houston native and Texas A & M University graduate eventually recovered and returned to the sidelines, only to be released later from his coaching position in December 2013. Fired in his home state, Gary landed in Denver in January 2015 and - along with QB Peyton Manning - led the Broncos to their third Super Bowl Championship in February 2016. Other than Hank Aaron, never have I met a kinder, more gracious sports star than Coach Gary Kubiak.

58

He is a winner on and off the field. It is nice when nice guys finish first.

I am grateful for the connections made in the orbits of sports and Scouts. Faith and Scouts are also closely yoked. Indeed, "A Scout is reverent…I will do my duty to God…" Connecting Jehovah (The LORD) and jocks came easily. Almost as easy was juxtaposing scouting and patriotism. In mid-November 2015 the Denver Boy Scout Council kicked off a new annual event called the "Duty to God Breakfast." Beginning with coffee at an hour almost before God was awake, the breakfast attracted dozens of tables of Boy Scout supporters and friends. As a pastor and Boy Scout, I was honored to be asked to serve as the event's Emcee.

The official welcome to the inaugural breakfast was delivered by prominent community leader, former U.S. Senate candidate, philanthropist, longtime Denver Boy Scout Executive member Pete Coors. It does not take long to count how many times a Methodist minister from Texas is introduced at the historic Western Stock Show Complex by a Colorado Catholic billionaire whose family made its fortune brewing and selling bunches of barrels of beer!

I thanked Mr. Coors and said, "It is a joyful privilege to be a part of this Inaugural Duty to God Breakfast of the Denver Area Council of the Boy Scouts of America. Over 50 years ago I joined Boy Scout Troop 65 in Beaumont, Texas. It was one of the best things that ever happened to me. My life and ministry have been immeasurably enriched by the lessons learned through the Scout Oath and Scout Law, including duty to God and Country. On behalf of the Denver Area Council, I welcome you warmly this wonderful Wednesday morning as we commemorate and celebrate our responsibility to our Creator."

We began the program with a flag ceremony, reciting of the Scout Oath and Law, Pledge of Allegiance and posting of the colors. I was then honored to introduce a friend, colleague in ministry, and a direct descendant of William D. Boyce, the founder of the Boy Scouts of America. Reverend Loren Boyce was the Lead Pastor of the Heritage United Methodist Church in Littleton. As a new father, Loren offered a powerful, personal and poignant prayer of thanksgiving for this event, his newborn son and first child that he might grow up to become a strong Scout serving God and country. The speaker for the morning was Father John P. Fitzgibbons, S.J., President of Regis University in Denver. Father John is one of the most gracious, genuine good guys on the planet. Thank you, God, for whispering love through my new Catholic brothers. Peter and John sound like good biblical names to me!

ACHIEVEMENT: *SOMETHING TO BE PROUD OF*

The road to becoming an Eagle Scout is no picnic in the park. Fifty years ago, only one in 100 boys enrolling in scouts persevered to receive BSA's highest rank. Today that has risen just slightly to 1.5 percent. It has been long recognized that the top thing taking teenage boys from the scouting movement is fumes: perfumes and gasoline. Goodbye good deeds and hello girlfriends and GTOs!

Patience, perseverance and positive parents are helpful gifts to move a boy through the ranks from Tenderfoot, Second Class, First Class, Star, Life and finally to Eagle Scout. It took me six years to finally achieve the highest rank of the scouting program. A scout must earn a minimum of 21 merit badges. Today they include First Aid, Citizenship in the Community, Citizenship in the Nation, Citizenship in the World, Communication, Cooking, Personal Fitness, Emergency Preparedness or Lifesaving, Environmental Science or Sustainability, Personal Management, Swimming or Hiking or Cycling, Camping, and Family Life. Times change. Fifty years ago, there were no Emergency Preparedness, Environmental Sustainability or Family Life merit badges. The world changes. Boy Scouts change.

Never did I think at the time that this award would bring such pride, connections, service and honor in the next fifty years. In two new church plants we launched new Boy Scout troops. As a pastor I was invited to attend many Eagle Scout Courts of Honor of church members across four decades. The new Eagles and their families were always thrilled and thankful to have their family pastor show up and stand up with all other Eagles present for the presentation of the supreme scouting award.

The Denver Area Boy Scout Council was most gracious to invite me to serve on its Board of Directors, attend its camps, tour its Scout Headquarters complete with indoor rock-climbing wall, and pray at its annual Eagle Scout Dinner honoring the new 400 Eagle Scouts and their families at a large Denver Area Hotel. It was at one of those occasions in 2015 I was humbled and honored to be presented with the Outstanding National Eagle Scout Award from the Denver Area Council and the National Eagle Scout Association. I accepted the award on behalf of my beloved late brother who was an Eagle Scout and inspired me to walk in his way. Gilbert also earned the God and Country Award. I am still somewhat embarrassed that I did not follow in his footsteps and earn the religious achievement award!

Like many before and after me, my life was changed for good by being a

Boy Scout. I would never trade the experience for anything. The most memorable, humbling and meaningful experience I had in scouting was not any court of honor, campfire, trip or award honor bestowed. It was not accidentally bumping into U.S. President Gerald Ford in the hallway at a Boy Scout event in Houston in 1980, though that was quite cool.

No, it was a campout with a special needs Scout Troop whose members needed assistance to dress, go to the bathroom, move about, eat a meal and brush their teeth. Another fourteen-year-old Troop 65 member and I had the responsibility and privilege of being helpers on their weekend special needs campout at Lake Tejas. The experience exhausted my body yet exhilarated my soul. Thank you, Scouting USA, for whispering love in so many young lives in the past 110 years. I am proud to be connected to the Scouting movement and its willingness and ability to change with the times. You have achieved much and blessed many.

Money Matters

FIRST JOBS: *EARN ALL YOU CAN*

"The lack of money is the root of all evil." Mark Twain is credited with that insight. The biblical wisdom is quite different and discerning, "The *love* of money is the root of all evil..." Money is the root of much good. Money builds hospitals, educates children, sends missionaries, supports widows, and aids single parents, seniors and the poor. Money does much good for God. Money is not God but can be become a god when sought at all costs. Money matters. We need it. It makes the world go around in a sense. Methodism movement founder John Wesley had three simple rules regarding money. Wesley (1703-1791) was an Anglican priest, a practical theologian, and a methodical organizer. His advice on money is timeless, timely and trustworthy.

Wesley preached a sermon entitled *The Use of Money.* His message laid out three rules for money. The first was "Earn all you can." Most everyone is Wesleyan in this respect. Many folks, if not most all, work hard and invest to earn, grow, gather and gain money. Some go beyond earning. They beg, borrow, steal or swindle to gain the maximum they possibly can. I once visited in a minimum-security federal facility one of my church members who went beyond earning in trying to gain all he could. His gain was in vain and caused him much pain.

Mr. Wesley would exclude any gain by Christians which carries the cost of harming us in body, mind or spirit. Likewise, he nixed anything that harms our neighbor in any aspect, by damaging her body, by failing to exercise due diligence in his protection, or by exploiting weaknesses of mind or failings of character. It is interesting to think about what modern occupations would pass Wesley's tests and what would not.

Even unaware of the Methodist movement mandate to make money to the max, I did my best to contribute to earning money. As a child I gathered, washed and returned soda drink bottles and to our neighborhood convenience store. The return was only a penny or two a bottle. However, a candy bar cost only a nickel at the time, so hustling bottles was a worthwhile business endeavor. I babysat a for few neighbors for fifty cents an hour. When I approached adolescence, my father supported me by providing the mower, gas and transportation when necessary. I had a prosperous lawn mowing business in my neighborhood. I worked hard to gain as much as possible for my future education. At three to five bucks per yard, I was sacking away several hundred dollars over the years for college expenses.

While in junior high, my friend Charlie Snell talked me into being his substitute on his morning newspaper route. I liked Charlie. His dad was a detective for the police department. That was cool. What fun to get up at 3:00 a.m. to fold, pack and deliver several hundred newspapers on a bicycle on a wet cold morning. Not! I do not recall the remuneration, but the gain was not worth the pain. Sorry, Charlie.

Several years later I had a short-term job in high school working for the same newspaper. This time I was not delivering newspapers, but rather manually stuffing the Sunday *Beaumont Enterprise* paper with the comics, *Parade* magazine and commercial inserts from local businesses. About two dozen high school upperclassmen from different schools worked every Saturday from 11:00 p.m. until 5:00 a.m. Sunday. Between the presses running and our inserting the advertisements, we were permitted to go outside and play touch football on the nearly empty downtown newspaper parking lot. What a hoot! A police patrol car would occasionally pass by as we were passing the football. Beaumont's best came to know boys just want to have fun when they can while raking in $1.60 an hour. I was grateful for the $9.60 check I received each Saturday night.

I do not recall any specifics to the Saturday Night Ambush, but I was called into the night boss's office and terminated on the spot. Shocked, saddened and sorry, I asked why and was told I had come in a little late a couple of times. Though I could not recall any significant tardiness, I accepted my fate without argument. The hours and pay were truly not that great and made it hard to get to Sunday School on time and alert. Before leaving the building for the last time, I took a copy of the early run Sunday edition and gave it to my then former boss. There was my picture in newspaper and an article about my receiving the Eagle Scout award. Oh well, learn the lesson. Close the door. Move on. The best is yet to be. More money will be earned in the seasons to come.

Six months later another opportunity to gain green came on the scene. Along with 12-14 other high school juniors and seniors from Beaumont area schools, I was chosen to work for Jefferson County cleaning roads, hauling trash and painting. It was hot, dirty manual labor for which we semi-privileged guys were grateful. We labored 44 hours a week. After all, at $1.75/hour we were paid $154.00 every two weeks. I liked it enough to do it another year before starting college.

As good as the summer job was, it whispered in love to me, "You don't want to do this forever." That was confirmed one hot day when clearing brush along a county road. An angry swarm of bumblebees attacked as I unknowingly invaded their home nest on the ground at the bottom of a fence post. It was a brief, but brave battle as the bees stung me 19 times. That is the number of stings the Emergency Room staff at St. Elizabeth Hospital confirmed.

Later in the ministry I would be stung several times by some of God's precious children who were upset because I unintentionally or not stepped into their space, face or lack of grace. On another level of sharing the pain of others hurts many times in over four decades, I went to cemeteries with hundreds of good friends who had been stung. It was my pastoral privilege to whisper the biblical Q & A of hope and love. St. Paul asked rhetorically, "Where, O death, is your victory? Where, O death is your sting?" He answers with supreme confidence, "The sting of death is sin, and the power of sin is the law." Then not with a whisper but a shout, the acclaimed apostle announces the gracious good news, "Thanks be to God who gives us the victory through our Lord Jesus Christ."

My last pre-ministry job was working part-time in the Tandy Leather Company store in Beaumont during my freshman year of college. It was a small store with only two fulltime employees. The position was perfect with a friendly Baptist boss, flexible hours and a little above minimum wage salary. My responsibilities were packing mail orders, putting out merchandise, waiting on customers and sweeping the store. Everyone ought to work in retail at some time or other to get a sense of serving the public. We had wonderful regular customers who would inspect the leather hides closely and purchase just the right ones for their custom hats, belts, saddles and other leather projects.

I am grateful for that learning experience with handling money and building relationships with the public, as well as gaining an appreciation for leather. Its durability, flexibility and natural beauty contribute to its popular use in making footwear, automobile seats, clothing, bags, book bindings, fashion accessories, and furniture. The earliest record of leather artifacts dates to 2200 B.C.E. Tandy Leather Company was founded in Fort Worth, Texas in 1919. It is still in business after a century. I am thankful to have been a part of one percent of its history. I gained far more than a little spending money in my last year as a teenager.

FIRST BANK ACCOUNT: *SAVE ALL YOU CAN*

The second mandate of Mr. Wesley was "Save all you can." My Methodist parents were savers. They taught their children to be the same. On January 9, 1957 my father and mother opened a Magnolia Federal Credit Union savings account in my name. I was four years old. The initial deposit was $5.00. I have saved the savings passbook to this day. The tiny book records deposits of a dollar or maybe two each month. My first dividend was posted on January 28, 1958 in the amount of 27 cents. You have to start somewhere! For the first time in my life, I noticed in May 2019 the witty encouragement on the cover of the credit union passbook, "Teach your dollars to have more cents." That is both witty and wise!

As the years passed and the deposits increased in frequency and size, so did the dividends. A deposit of $8.00 on November 12, 1959 gave me a savings account balance of $100.00. I was rich! Or at least I was on track to saving for college a dozen years down the road. The passbook has columns for fees and fines, as well as loans. Fortunately, I was able to avoid all those detriments to saving. By the time college came, I had saved over $1,600 for tuition and books. That went a long way at a state school in 1971.

As far as a rule for saving and money management, I have always encouraged couples I marry to save ten percent of their income, give away ten percent of it and live happily on the remaining 80 percent. I have seen too many families across the decades living on 110 percent of their income. That seldom has a happy ending unless one wins the lottery. Fortunately, today there are payroll deductions which can go straight to IRAs and other savings vehicles to prepare for the future. Growing up I heard of the "miracle of compound interest." Sharon and I recall purchasing some very modest size certificates of deposit for our two very young children in the early 1980s. The CDs earned around 13 percent interest, locked in for 2.5 years. It was a good time to have a safe saving and growing tool for the future. The only valuable CDs we have now from that time are the Beatles, Beach Boys and Barbra Streisand. Saving money and music is good tonic for tired bodies and souls.

FIRST COMMITMENT: *GIVE ALL YOU CAN*

Hardly anyone has an issue with earning the max. Few are opposed to saving for a rainy day. How does one learn to give and to give generously? Role models, instruction, inspiration and invitation all brought me to be a giver in general and a tither in particular. My parents modeled for their three children

66

by giving money regularly and generously to God's work. Each quarter of the calendar year our family received a carbon copy from the church of our giving. The statement had our pledges made and amounts given in that three-month period. My parents pledged and gave $10.00 a week, a generous amount in the 1950s. My siblings and I each gave a dime a week, a tithe (10 percent) of our allowance. It was rewarding to see the totals accumulate through the year with each quarterly statement. The postage was three cents.

Giving was natural, normal and necessary. It was not a burden but a blessing, not an obligation but an opportunity, not a punishment but a privilege. Every year our church had a budget drive. Call it the stewardship campaign, the annual subscription drive, Loyalty Sunday or whatever, giving was necessary to support the work of God in the community and the world. Across the years of pastoring, I came to call these annual necessities "The Mission and Ministry of Christ through ABC United Methodist Church."

Some people cannot give large amounts of money. They are like the widow whom Jesus commended for putting in her two cents. He said she gave more than all the rich folks who were making their gifts to the temple treasury. In fact, she gave all she had. Read Luke 21:1-4 if you need a sleepless night. Amounts and attitudes both count in giving. We give with grateful hearts. Gracious and generous giving is essential to growing a soul. Across the years I have gathered these nuggets of wisdom which speak well to the privilege of giving all one can:

"God loves a cheerful giver, but accepts gifts from a grouch, too!"
"You can't out give God."
Q: "How much did he leave when he died?" A: "All of it."
"There are no hearses with luggage racks or trailer hitches."
"Will anyone rob God? Yet you are robbing me! But you say, 'How are we robbing you?' In your tithes and offerings! Bring the full tithe into the storehouse. See if I will not open the windows of heaven for you and pour down for you an overflowing blessing."
Jesus said, "Give and it will be given to you. A good measure, pressed down, shaken together, running over, will be put into your lap; for the measure you give will be the measure you get back."
Don't give until it hurts. Give until it feels good.

I am grateful for a home church which taught me to tithe. Giving 10% is not magic. Tithing, however, is biblical, accounts for inflation and is easy to figure. Like many pastor's families, Sharon and I have invested in capital and mission campaigns, doubling our tithe for a year or three. That is sacrificial giving, which is giving up something good for something better. We have never given an over-and-above commitment that we did not discuss, pray about and come to agreement. We always bought used cars, drove them for ten years when possible and took modest vacations with our family. Best of all, we felt good about what we gave. It is natural for Sharon and me to give 10% of the sales of this book to the Alzheimer's Association.

Several years ago, a contemporary Christian song had this convicting line, "Thanks for giving to the Lord. Mine was a life that was changed." Giving changes lives, beginning with the giver. In wise words of John Wesley, "Give all you can." Giving whispers love.

LAST COMMITMENT: *GIVING FOREVER*

Jesus told an offensive parable about a filthy rich individual who had everything: casinos, golf courses, tall towers, political power and all kinds of stuff. He had it all: trophy wife, the seeming Midas touch and his own television broadcast company. It was a 24-7-365 fantasy. He said to himself, "I have got so much stuff! What am I going to do? Tell you what, I will tear it all down and build bigger hangars for my jets and grander garages for my Jaguars and buy more property on the oceanfront for casinos and hotels. I will take it easy. I have years to eat, drink and party hearty!"

About that time God spoke to the man. What did God say? The Almighty spoke the honest-to-God truth. God has a way of doing that. God cut to the quick, "You fool! Tonight, you are going to meet your Maker. And all this stuff you have accumulated, whose will it be?" Then Jesus brought it home with a warning to the crowd, to his friends and to opponents, the Pharisees and the Publicans, the Democrats and the Republicans. The Master warned, "So will it be with all who store up treasures for themselves but are not rich toward God."

True, you cannot take it with you. True also, you can send it on ahead. You can give forever with an estate plan, a proper will or other appropriate document which lays out how you want to continue to do good for God by tithing your will or more. An anonymous author says of Abel, 'He died, but through his faith he still speaks."

Sharon and I are giving a significant portion of our modest earthly goods for God's work when we depart this temporary home for the house not made with hands. We will provide for our children and grandchildren, as did our parents. We have already arranged for our cremations upon death. No caskets, hearses, funeral homes or piped in music to send us off to the Grand Banquet! We are ready to go, though not ready to leave just yet.

As with many others, we plan to give forever through intentional estate planning. We are grateful for a church and faith tradition which provides tools, counsel and options for giving forever. We will die, but we will still be speaking. Imagine that. A preacher speaking forever! OMG! Actually, Sharon and I plan to be singing the resurrection song with all the saints in glory. No auditions required. All welcome. Look forward to seeing you there. Later. Much later, I hope!

MONEY WISDOM: *DOLLARS AND SENSE*

Not to beat this money thing to death, but yes, let's beat it to death! Most all of us have money issues of one kind or another. The pastorate has taught me that dollars and cents are often on our minds. No matter one's income, there is often anxiety about financial matters. Congregations across the land of all affiliations have found common ground in the call to educate, equip and empower folks about responsible money management. Grounded in biblical principles, these courses have transformed the lives of many individuals and couples in financial affairs.

The following resources have been taught and received well in many mainline and evangelical faith communities for decades. Visit the websites for more information: Good $ense, Master Your Money, Financial Peace University and Crown Ministries. They all have a fee, but the return is well worth the investment. I led the Good $ense course at Marvin Church in Tyler 14-15 years ago. One of the class members was the very discerning daughter of the senior pastor. Just out of college, she gave the class a thumbs up. She and I were impressed with the videos, materials and spiritual component of the package.

For better or worse we live in a culture which is most acquisitive. The messages on television and all other screens, magazines and billboards is buy, buy, buy. This product will make you sexy, suave and sophisticated. Or if you are more chronologically gifted, this device will help you hear, walk and feel better. If it is true that "Fools and their money are soon parted," there are countless ways to foolishly say goodbye to our financial resources daily, if we are not on our toes.

Here are a dozen practical, sensible suggestions to avoid financial struggles or crises in your life. These are the accumulated wisdom of 67 years of living, 45 years of being married and purchasing five homes in Texas and Colorado and living in five residences in the past year.

- Work for your money, then let your money work for you.
- Except for buying a home, avoid debt at all costs (cars might be an exception early on).
- Undergo free plastic surgery. Cut down to only two credit cards, one for limited purchases and one for backup emergencies only.
- Pay any credit card balances in full each month.
- Avoid impulse purchases.
- Be discerning in online shopping.
- Fast from plastic purchases for a season.
- Use bank drafts to pay monthly housing, utilities and charitable giving.
- Avoid overdrafts.
- Never buy a new car unless you are flush with cash. It depreciates nine percent when you leave the dealer and 19 percent in the first year.
- Build a savings account not to be used except for emergencies.

Final suggestion: If you are doing well in the financial arena, be thankful. Now buy ten copies of this book to pass on to friends, young families, kinfolks, students or anyone who may benefit from the needed guidance and encouragement in the financial arena and the whispers of love you may have received. You will bless them and their future!

Public Education Spaces

Launching a Love for Learning

Not all education comes from books and study. Some people learn from the school of hard knocks, the laboratory of life and the encyclopedia of experience. Pastor-turned author Robert Fulghum made millions declaring *All I Need to Know I Learned in Kindergarten.* His seminal work stayed on *The New York Times* bestseller list for almost two years.

The fact is we need schools, teachers, books, computers and classrooms. My daughter has taught kindergarten for fifteen straight years since graduating from college. As much as her students learned in that pivotal first public-school experience, every one of them needed to continue to the next level, first grade! Education is a foundation. Books are basic. We need to read.

But as the Bible says above, relentless reading and saturated study can beat you up and tear you down. The wisdom scripture notes the inadequacy of books to do it all. Gospel author John goes into hyperbolic theological overdrive in the last sentence of his own book, "If everything Jesus did were written down, I suppose that the world itself could not contain the books that would be written." I am deeply grateful for my formal public education from first grade through undergraduate school. School days for the Dent children were pleasant, positive and pivotal. Gilbert, Marilyn and I attended the same public schools in the Beaumont Independent School District between 1952 and 1971, and the same public college in our hometown. We were blessed to have many of the same excellent teachers. Our family lived in the north end of Beaumont, close to the campuses.

In 1959 my school education began, the only year the Dent children were on the same campus. As already noted, all of us had the same first-grade teacher, Miss Voyd Lee. She truly filled a void in her students' lives. She was an excellent teacher. She instilled in her students a love of learning, an appreciation of differences, and basic good manners.

Though six decades have come and gone since the first day of school, I clearly recall events, education, and experiences in those six years at French Elementary School:

- Enjoying daily outside recess to swing, climb the monkey bars, ride the merry-go-round, play chase, and run races.
- Learning to square dance in the fourth grade.
- Singing in music class in fifth grade *Dixie*

- Coloring world maps with what else, map color pencils!
- Paying three cents for a carton of milk at lunch.
- Valentine's Day Party in second grade when it snowed (a very rare event in southeast Texas)
- The best hot lunch of pinto beans and rice.
- Attending for six years a public school with an all-white student body and faculty.

While I loved school and did well in my studies, I suffered significantly in a critical classroom component. My "thorn in the flesh" was handwriting. I got an S (Satisfactory) or S+ in every other subject. In handwriting I earned an N, meaning "Needs improvement." I write in unknown tongues. Only when slowing down can I take notes which are legible later. "Take time to be holy," I sang in church. Take time to take good notes, my teachers taught me. It has been a lifelong struggle. Thank God for word processor and Spell Check.

MOVING ON UP

The next chapter was three years at James Bowie Junior High School, just a block from our home. The school was named for a Kentucky native who became a Texas hero when he died at the Battle of the Alamo in 1836 in the fight for Texas Independence from Mexico. Bowie was 39 and his legend lives on in the Lone Star State in the several schools of all levels named for him. For four years I served in a county in far northeast Texas named for the Alamo hero and my junior high namesake.

Junior high was a whole new world. Three elementary schools fed into Bowie. With 1,000 students and six buildings, there were many new faces, places and spaces to learn. I embraced the opportunity. My Top Ten List of junior high gifts were:
1. Having a locker for books
2. Parties with girls
3. Being able to walk home for lunch
4. Dances with girls
5. Sports teams
6. Phone calls to girls
7. Pep Rallies
8. Hayride with girls
9. Changing classes
10. Touch football with girls

Did I mention I discovered girls in junior high? I did play football for two years. My positions were end, guard and tackle. I sat at the end of the bench, guarded the water cooler and tackled anyone who came near it! Seriously, I played guard on offense and linebacker on defense. My only gridiron glory was gained in intercepting two passes in our ninth-grade season. When I split a bone in my finger in a spring practice scrimmage, I felt football was not in my future. Boy Scouts and girls were taking precedence in my moving toward maturity and not necessarily in that order.

One of my junior high football teammates went on to win a Super Bowl ring with the San Francisco 49ers. Shout out to fellow SMU grad and the original Bigfoot, Louie Kelcher. Louie was known for his immense size. Standing six-feet and five-inches tall, he once said his weight bounced between 280 pounds and infinity. Louie wears a size 17EEE shoe and has a size 16.5 ring finger. I hope to reconnect with the San Diego Charger Hall of Fame Player at our fiftieth high school reunion in 2021.

The junior high curriculum brought an expanded menu of classes. Beyond the basics, I took Spanish, speech and shop. Two of those were beneficial in mission and ministry in Texas and Colorado. Making a wooden napkin holder, welding a thingamajig and tearing apart a gasoline engine were not my calling. A blue ribbon in University Interscholastic League in eighth grade Number Sense certainly confirmed my call to ministry to be able to assist the church Finance Committee with the budget. Not!

Junior High was time of experiencing some almost requisite rites of passage – first date (chaperoned, of course), first corsage, first dinner, first dance, first kiss. I believe they all happened in one evening, but that was a very long time ago! Other things from grades 7-9 I recall with clarity include:

- Selling magazine subscriptions for $3-5 a year to raise money for the school library and for me to win a pair of not so high-quality binoculars.

- An all-school assembly to hear our U.S. Congressman Jack Brooks speak.

- A Friday Night Dinner, Talent Show and Dance. (You should have seen large Louie Kelcher as Little Red Riding Hood!)

- A Science Fair in which my project on Unidentified Flying Objects flew the coop and did not place.

- The beginning of racial integration of the public schools of Beaumont in the fall of 1966. I confess to calling a new student on the field by an epithet which was inappropriate and inexcusable. I was immediately convicted and apologized and begged James to slug me for my insensitivity and promising I would not strike back. He refused to take a free hit. James Ziegler was a far better, mature teenager than I that day. Some mistakes need to be learned from and never repeated. Repenting is not easy for any of us yet is necessary for all of us.

- Winning the slogan contest for the big all-school Friday Night Dinner, Talent Show and Dance. The award was two free tickets to all three events. I invited a special ninth grade classmate who was most attractive in my eyes. She accepted. I was elated. I could hardly wait! On Thursday night Becky let me know she was not able to go with me on Friday. I was stunned and stung deeply. Sometime puppy love did not whisper. It sucked. Time faded the pain. Rejection leads to dejection. I chose to stay home rather going dateless in Beaumont. Stuff happens. Move on. High school is less than a year away. A driver's license is on the horizon. All shall be well. Even junior high school. One broken date does not a crisis make. Easy for me to say now!

PREPARING FOR WHAT'S NEXT

As shared in my reflections on Coming of Age in the Sixties, 1968 was a weird, wild and wacky time on the planet. Assassinations and anxiety, protests and pain, rock and roll, pollution and poverty, athletes acting out and a seemingly forever war in Southeast Asia dominated the headlines. Despite the year's drama and trauma on both the national and international stages, 1968 was life empowering for me.

It was also the year I took Driver's Education in the spring while still in junior high school. French High School Baseball Coach Billy Poland was my driving instructor. Because I had a provisional driving permit, I could drive with an adult in the front seat. Coach Poland was a quality driving coach, baseball coach and human being. He encouraged a boatload of students in the class, behind the wheel and on the diamond.

He was a good gift to many students yearning to drive or striving to learn the intricacies of baseball. He was particularly so to me in my operating a 1954 four-door Plymouth coupe, stick-shift with 19 different shades of blue in the interior and three gear manual transmission mounted on the steering column. The "Blue Goose" was our family's second car and the one I first learned to drive. That was one hot/cool/lukewarm automobile! Coach Poland only offended me once when he nicknamed me "Lead Foot." As they say, if the shoe fits, put the pedal to the metal.

In the second week of September, I hit my sixteenth birthday and then hit the Texas Department of Public Safety to apply for, pay for and drive away with my first license to operate a vehicle independently and legally. Thank you, Lord! Guess what? I suddenly became very popular. Every sophomore guy wanted to double date. How many of my 400 sophomore classmates already had a license? Count them on one hand.

While I enjoyed the requisite studies, what prepared me most for the rest of my life were service and leadership experiences. My classmates trusted me enough to choose me to serve in some responsible, challenging, flattering offices, including Junior Class Vice President, Student Council Parliamentarian (Good to know *Robert's Rules of Order* at a contentious church council meeting), Sophomore Class Handsome (Don't be too impressed. There were six of us chosen by actress Patty Duke who played a blind girl in in a movie filmed near Beaumont), Good Sportsmanship League Representative (A nice tradition at the 50-yardline before each football game in which two-three representatives from each team exchange token gifts and then whisper not love, but something along the lines of "Were going to knock the living daylights out of your team tonight!")

My senior year I was blessed to serve as a Key Club Division Lieutenant Governor. Sponsored by a local Kiwanis Club, Key Club is a vital high school international service organization. Founded in 1925, Key Club International is the oldest service program for high school students. Often referred to as simply Key Club, it is a student-led organization whose goal is to encourage leadership through serving others. Its foci beyond leadership are character building, caring and inclusiveness. Serving as a division officer gave me many new experiences and opportunities, including:

- Flying for the first time (This was 1970 before smoking was prohibited on flights, and female flight attendants wore quite short skirts. All Key Clubbers aboard the flight from Houston to Chicago truly enjoyed one or both of those conditions which have since been wisely nixed.)
- Touring the Kiwanis International Headquarters in downtown Chicago, the Ford automotive plant in Dearborn, Michigan, as well as visits to Niagara Falls, Toronto, Canada and Cleveland, Ohio for the Key Club International Convention.

- Getting to meet and osculate Miss Teenage America. (Go ahead and Google "osculate"!)
- Attending state conventions in Galveston, Texas and Oklahoma City, Oklahoma.
- Learning valuable lessons, including do not throw objects from windows at surfers when staying at Galveston's USS Flagship Hotel. The seven-story 225- room hotel was built on the historic Pleasure Pier structure entirely over the Gulf of Mexico. The management will find you, confront you and not be nice to you. Several of us could have been locked up. Lesson learned!

Serving in the Key Club division position was a vital growth experience. It sharpened my skills in organization, supervision, and communication. These skills were essential in serving as a pastor for over four decades. Never in my ministry did I throw beer bottles at anyone surfing next to any hotel where I was residing. I swear on a stack of surfboards!

The historical and sometimes hysterical happenings of 1968 continued to some degree throughout my high school years. The musical festival near Woodstock, New York in August 1969 defined a generation at war with war. On a long and occasionally rainy weekend, over 30 acts performed outdoors in the fields of a 600-acre dairy farm. It is widely regarded as a pivotal moment in popular music history, as well as the definitive nexus for the larger counterculture generation. Over 400,000 souls showed up to share the songs, sounds, showers and the soul of a generation at war, yet yearning just to give peace a chance. Whispers of love echoed in the songs of a restless generation: *All You Need Is Love, Don't You Want Somebody to Love* and *To Love Somebody.*

While a generation was seeking such noble ends, I was continuing to enjoy high school classes, classmates and occasionally classy dates. The war was continuing, as was preparing for what's next. While our boys' teams never won any district championships, guess what? Our girls' volleyball team advanced to the Texas State Tournament in Austin. A group of us senior guys got off with good behavior and good grades to travel to the State Capital to witness volleyball history.

Indeed, each Buff was rough and tough and that was enough. We cheered with each serve, set, spike, and block. The girls brought home the gold. The senior captain Becky led the way. All is forgiven, Becky, for dumping me three years before just before our big date. Congrats again to you and all Buffalo gals who came out that day to serve, set and spike by the light of the Austin sun! All good things must end. High school days were diminishing.

Graduation invitations were being sent. Kind cards with cash or checks of $5-10 were appearing in our mailboxes. Our class of 410 students included five guys who went into the ordained ministry. Two of us were Methodists and three Baptists, a typical ratio between the big the boys of Texas Protestants. I was honored to offer the graduation benediction June 1, 1971, our final time to gather after three, six or 12 years together. By the way, the unofficial, unapproved and likely unacceptable to the school administration Class Motto was, *"Sin, sex, beer and fun. We're the Class of '71!"* Like so many other high school escapades, there was probably far more said than done. Speaking for myself here. If you want to know what was in the perhaps too long benediction, order online in early 2020 as many copies as you have friends of *Spirituality 2020: Public Service, Prayers and Proclamations and Public Service.* The timely tome will make a thoughtful gift for any Democrat, Republican or Independent on your Presidents' Day shopping list. In any event, the year ahead will be one of introspection, election and future direction determination.

PREPARING FOR THE FUTURE

High school was finished. The next public education space was Lamar University, founded in 1923 as a junior college. Known as Lamar State College of Technology since 1949, the school was renamed Lamar University at the time of my enrollment in the fall of 1971. The elevation to university status was not unwelcome. The new name recognized that the school offered many degrees far beyond engineering and technology. Business, education and nursing were and still are popular degree programs.

While there were dorms, apartments and fraternity and sorority housing options on or near campus, many students drove to classes. While commuting until my final year, I still felt a part of the university community through:

- Attending football and basketball games on campus. Enthusiastic cheerleaders led us in yelling repeatedly, *"Give 'em hell, Big L, give 'em hell!"* That was immediately followed by the bold echo, *"Damn right!"* Yes, high school was in the rearview mirror!
- Visiting the large Lamar library to peruse periodicals, do research for classes, and troll through treasure troves of microfilms to read articles about and see pictures from local newspapers over the past several decades. This was all pre-computer, of course.

- Hearing a variety of guests to campus including prominent atheist Madalyn Murray O'Hair, Watergate Scandal operative James McCord, the edgy Steppenwolf of "Born to Be Wild" fame, a performance by the smooth Fifth Dimension and a stunning performance of *Jesus Christ Superstar* written by budding composer Andrew Lloyd Weber in 1970. This was not your grandmother's gospel music!
- The best part of undergraduate school were the classes and professors.
- Taking an American Literature Class taught by Dr. Marilyn Georgas who duly criticized me for turning in an assignment composed on notebook paper she called "panty pink." She became an encourager in my discernment for ministry, as her father and brother were both Methodist ministers.
- Studying under Philosophy Professor George Wall who was a progressive Baptist (not an oxymoron) who wore a beard and bowties. He became a good friend. Dr. Wall came and spoke to the high school graduates in my first church. He was also the first person I knew to write a book. It was on logic, not the most scintillating topic but I was impressed.
- Taking courses valuable to pastoral ministry including Adolescent Psychology (youth ministry), Deviant Behavior (staff meetings), German (impressive to Lutheran clergy friends), Typing (too bad I dropped out), Race Relations (still a too timely issue), Marriage and Family (always relevant) and Experimental Psychology (Isn't life some big experiment?)

Several large issues were churning in my head and heart as I began college. What was God calling and gifting me to do and be in adult life? That is seldom clear as a teenager. Did I want to follow my brother and go to medical school? After all, I had applied and been accepted as a pre-med major. My parents would have rejoiced in that direction. Did I want to enlist in the military to avoid being drafted and serve on my terms? After all, I received a low draft number, 46, and was likely to be conscripted to service in South Vietnam. My future brother-in-law had no worries with the perfect draft number, 365. His mother was embarrassed to tell other mothers his good fate. She tried to change the subject when asked about it. Sadly, those who learned his supreme selective service slot tended to be resentful.

In the middle of my undergraduate education, I was summoned by Uncle Sam to catch a bus to downtown Houston with dozens of other young men, to take some terrifically easy academic tests, and to be checked from to toe. As expected, I passed all exams with flying colors. I was classified 1-H on my Selective Service card in September 1973, as I was pastoring a church, attending college and answering a call to ministry. I never asked not to serve and even considered enlisting as a Chaplain's Assistant. Uncle Sam left me alone as the true Commander-in-Chief had already called me into spiritual service. I continued in undergraduate school without a change in my Selective Service status, fully knowing that I could be drafted at any moment and prepared for military service in Vietnam.

But some other significant developments were happening. I had begun preaching the year I graduated from high school. The next year I delivered ten sermons. Several of those came while serving as a summer Youth Director at First Methodist Church in Orange, Texas. The pastor and people there were gracious, encouraging and kind. A call to preach which was literally a score of years in the making came to fruition on my twentieth birthday in mid-September when I "surrendered" to the call and committed myself to serve Jesus Christ as a minister of the Good News. You might say I was drafted into the Lord's Army! I am grateful to still be serving in retirement 47 years later.

Call is first. As did young Samuel (I Samuel 3:9), young Michael heard God calling. My call came over many years, but the commitment became concrete on the day I departed my teenage years. After the commitment came cultivation. Methodists are nothing if not methodical in their scrutiny of candidates for ministry. I adjusted my degree plan at Lamar, called my girlfriend Sharon in Tulsa, and began immediately working on the requirements for being approved for a License to Preach in The United Methodist Church.

First steps included an application sent to take a Course of Study through the denomination's Ministry Office in Nashville, and interviews with my pastor, Beaumont District Committee on Ministry and the congregation's Pastor-Parish Relations Committee. Not being a stranger to these folks, I was approved at each level after due conversation and deliberation. Once the Course of Study was completed, the church called a special Charge Conference to consider approving me to receive a License to Preach. By secret ballot, the members of the North End Methodist Church approved another one of its sons to answer a call to ministry. The process took several months to complete.

My calling first voiced in the fifth grade was officially confirmed with the issuance of the license on November 25, 1972. Life would never be the same.

My time of complete cultivation would take another eight years. Everything happening in my university years seemed to be preparing me to be a love whisperer.

Rookie Sent to the Beach

Within a few weeks of being licensed to preach at age 20, I received a telephone call from Beaumont District Superintendent Jack Shoultz. He asked to meet as soon as possible. We met and he asked if I would consider serving as an undergraduate student pastor at St. Matthew United Methodist Church in the tiny town of High Island on the Texas Gulf Coast. Known around the world for its bird sanctuaries, ironically, High Island is neither high nor an island. The small coastal community of about 500 residents was built on a salt dome a mile from the Gulf of Mexico. Just several dozen feet above sea level, the town can resemble an island when a tropical storm or hurricane hits and raises the sea level substantially.

Though only 45 miles from Beaumont on Interstate 10 and State Hwy 124, a drive to or from there might take well over an hour. There was a drawbridge two miles north of High Island which had to be opened several times each day and night for tugboats to guide one or more barges loaded with valuable petroleum products headed to Galveston or Port Arthur. This intracoastal canal is still a valuable means of transportation, but the drawbridge was eventually replaced several decades later with a bridge over the waterway high enough to accommodate the tallest tugboats.

This invitation to serve St. Matthew's was a timely gift. I did not take long to give an answer after Dr. Shoultz shared a little bit about the congregation: 120 or so members, a variety of ages, a Sunday School program and education building with a kitchen and restrooms. The worship space was an old Army Chapel moved there sometime after World War II. There was a small parsonage (home for the pastor) with one bedroom, one bathroom, kitchen, a sleeping porch on the back, living room, study, detached wooden garage, and many mice. It was fine for me. The annual compensation was $4,200.

Though the appointment began January 1, 1973, I did not preach my first sermon until January 14 because of a previous engagement – my first ever snow ski trip. Fortunately, I came home from Ruidoso in one piece after more than a few falls. From beginning to end, our ministry of 29 months at High Island was a time of mutual learning, growing, and blessing, with no broken bones.

Lead, Listen and Love

I did my best to follow Paul's call to Timothy, "Let no one despise your youth, but set the believers an example in speech and conduct, in love, in faith, in purity." If I was to lead this flock, I had to listen to them and love them to the max. My goal was founded in my experience and learning as a Boy Scout to "to do my best to do my duty to God…" and to be a healthy example of faith, service, speech, purity, love and service.

Speaking of love, I had on-the-job lessons in negotiating being a single, young pastor in a setting of several unattached females seeking to become attached. That challenge subsided significantly when I announced my engagement to Sharon eleven months into my pastorate. Nonetheless, being tall, dark, and holy can have an upside and a downside. Dating or being pursued by a member of one's flock can lead to a myriad of unintended consequences. The rumor mill can crank into overtime in no time. Jesus calls us to love our neighbors, but boundaries are wise and welcome friends.

I believe one's first extended experience in any field – education, sales, healthcare, manual labor, management, law, engineering, or ministry - will shape, shake, make or break his or her career or call. One's initiation in any industry or enterprise is critical. I am grateful to have had some special experiences in my first ministerial appointment which shaped the next 42 years in fulltime pastorates. The experiences of leading, listening and loving were mutually beneficial.

FIRST FUNERALS

My first funeral came six weeks into ministry. Having attended only a handful of funerals in my life, I was unsure what to do. A veteran clergy colleague coached me long distance by phone in the important steps of meeting with the family of the deceased to decide the day, time and place of the service. Other questions to answer in the planning with the family included what hymns to sing, scriptures to read, liturgy to use, recipient of memorials and burial details. By the way, funeral directors are wonderful people. After all, they are the last ones to let you down!

The service was in the church and went well. Hard to go wrong when you read and preach on Psalm 23 and sing *How Great Thou Art*. Though the deceased seemed quite advanced in years, my pastoral record reflects he was only 69 old, two years north of me in 2019. Though I have planned, participated in and/or preached in over 500 funerals, memorial services, and graveside rites, I was initiated in grief ministry and the promise of the resurrection firsthand in February 1973 when I was 20 years old. The saints at

St. Matthew Church were kind and gracious to initiate me into the fellowship of the grieved, yet not as those who grieve without hope.

Five more times in the next two years I would go the High Island Cemetery with families in the community to commit their loved ones to the earth and their spirit to God. Sometimes it was easy. One service was for Laura Meynig, known to all in the community as "Grandma Meynig." Born just five years after the War Between the States ended, she was 103 years young when she departed this world. The only tears came when her 84-year-old son leaned over into casket at the church to kiss his mother goodbye. The tears were mine as I witnessed this tender farewell.

Contrast that farewell with that of the young couple whose infant daughter was dead on arrival in late September 1974. The only note I have from that graveside service is a scripture, John 13:7. I have never read that passage since at a funeral, but it must have made sense at that time and place. Jesus speaks there about his own death in his extended Farewell Discourse. Jesus says, "What I am doing you do not know now, but afterward you will understand." Forty-five years later I cannot explain how a 21-year-old chose that verse. My best guess it was an effort to say such unjust sorrowing is simply inexplicable.

A bumper sticker in the movie *Forrest Gump* summed it up this way, "_ _IT HAPPENS." I prefer and have often quoted from seminary days the wisdom of theologian Paul Tillich. He framed suffering in these cogent words which I have tweaked ever so slightly, "God created the word finite and free. Physical evil such as hurricanes and cancer is the natural implication of a finite world. Moral evil such as murder and war is the tragic implication of a free world."

I have never been comfortable hearing a pastor, priest, president, or parent say in the face of an inexplicable tragedy, "This was God's will." My initiation into ministry at St. Matthew Church confirmed that it is always better to weep with people in pain rather than try to explain their pain.

COMMUNITY SERVICE

Community service became a delightful calling in this first pastorate, setting a pattern which continued over 40 years in multiple ministry settings. The High Island community embraced a pastor who was willing and wanting to do more than preach, teach and hang out at the beach. My gold colored Dodge Charger was welcome to visit the homes of church members and nonmembers alike.

Anytime I did cold calling, I learned to ask first at the door, "Is this a good time for a brief visit?"

Only one time did I not ask at the door if it was a good time for a visit. After turning 21, I walked into the Babineaux Tavern on Hwy 124 near the High Island Beach. It was owned and run by St. Matthew member Eva Babinaux. Though I never had been in a beer joint, I felt a pastoral call was in order. You can guess the Methodist minister was greeted with more than a few quizzical looks from those shooting pool, listening to the juke box and partaking of a favorite adult beverage. I do not recall staying long or saying much. Sometimes just showing up as a non-anxious presence in a non-church setting is valuable.

A nontraditional holy communion is shared and can bestow a needed blessing. Jesus of Nazareth modeled that truth in several conversations and interactions with "outsiders."

Fond memories flowing from this special peachy, beachy pastoral initiation include these diverse community services opportunities:

- Delivering the high school commencement address to the 12 graduates, two of whom were pregnant
- Serving on the volunteer ambulance corps, transporting emergency patients to John Sealy Hospital 32 miles away in Galveston
- Announcing the high school home football games
- Attending the high school girls' basketball three-on-three games
- Umpiring behind home plate for the Little League baseball games (Note to self: Don't do this just before your honeymoon!)

PRESENCE AND PRESENTS

Surely the most significant personal event in my time as a student pastor was entering the covenant of Christian Marriage with Sharon in July 1974. The service was held at our home church in Beaumont on a Saturday afternoon. We rejoiced to welcome many guests from St. Matthew Church to this holy rite and the reception. They blessed us greatly by their wedding presence and presents. The church gave me time away for a honeymoon to New Orleans to enjoy the sights, sounds, and seafood of the famed French Quarter. I do not recall going to church there, but we did have a heaven of a time in the Big Easy.

New York Theologian

Another unique highlight in High Island came when some visitors showed up unannounced on a summer Sunday morning. A retired Methodist pastor from nearby Crystal Beach, Bill Conerly and his wife Virginia, came to worship with us. They brought their adult daughter and son-in-law with them. Thank God that I did not know until after the service who their son-in-law was. His name was Walter Wink, a distinguished Associate Professor of New Testament at Union Theological Seminary in New York City. Google Walter to learn more about this internationally known lecturer, pastor, author, scholar, Bible teacher, theologian and activist. Colorado author Philip Yancey references Walter frequently in his work. I would have been more than slightly intimidated had I known of Dr. Wink's presence beforehand. Nonetheless, I preached as usual and Walter was most gracious in his commentary on the service and sermon.

A pastor never knows who may be in the congregation on a given Sunday. I learned later to imagine that Jesus is present (he is, of course) and to pray that my message is pleasing to him. With many other pastors across the world, I learned to pray aloud in each service before preaching, "Let the words of my mouth and the meditations of our hearts be acceptable to you, O Lord, our Strength and our Redeemer. Amen."

Humanity at Its Best – and Worst

My first pastorate introduced me to the rhythms of a small-town congregation. Nothing in the community brought folks together better than church events, Sunday and otherwise. From annual to weekly to occasional gatherings, the saints came marching in for:

- Wednesday Night Covered Dish Suppers
- Domino and "42" Game Nights
- Spring Cleaning of the Sanctuary
- The "Flowering" of the cross on Easter Sunday
- Senior Dinner honoring high school graduates
- Summer Vacation Bible School
- Promotion Sunday
- Revival Services
- Guest speakers from the Gideons Bible Society
- Meals at the church following a funeral

All these traditions, large and small, came together to create Christian community and camaraderie. There is a spirit in a small town that unites its citizens in congregations and other gatherings to pull together in hard times. Such a time came to High Island in my first summer there.

Over a period of several years dozens of male teenagers and young adults had disappeared in the Houston Heights area, victims of a hideous torture-murder ring. On August 10, 1973, perpetrator Elmer Henley, an accomplice of depraved criminal mastermind Dean Corll, accompanied police to Lake Sam Rayburn in East Texas, where two bodies were found buried close together. As with the two other bodies discovered the previous day, both victims had been tortured and severely beaten. That afternoon, both Henley and accomplice David Brooks went with police to High Island Beach, leading police to the shallow graves of two more victims.

Then on Monday, August 13, both Henley and Brooks again accompanied the police to High Island where four more bodies were found, making a total of twenty-seven known victims over three years -- the worst killing spree in American history at the time. What I recall most vividly from that day in our tiny town of 500 on the beach of the Gulf of Mexico was the swarm of news and law enforcement helicopters hovering above, and airplanes circling the circus crime scene. National networks ABC, CBS and NBC all had boots on the ground and aircraft above the boats in the water. Local television and radio news anchors and reporters from nearby Beaumont and Houston telecast and broadcast from the beach for hours on end. The whole event was surreal, sorrowful and sad.

I wish this terrible, traumatic, tragic crime which devastated dozens of families in Texas had never happened. I had blocked it from my mind for 45 years until writing this account. It could have been worse. George Leger, a 30-something oilfield pump truck driver, husband, father of two young children and active member of St. Matthew Methodist Church, was driving along the High Island beach one evening that summer when he came across two young men who appeared to be burying something in the sand. George asked them if they were okay or needed any help. They said nervously they were stuck in the sand, could get out on their own and declined his offer of assistance. A couple of days later George recognized the pair when their faces made newspapers across the country.

My initial pastorate was nothing if not inclusive of being in touch with humanity at its worst, and at its divinely intended best. This time as a rookie at the beach confirmed my call and prepared me well for the seasons of cheers, tears, fears and jeers which would come my way in pastoral ministry over the next 40 years. Love can whisper, mercy can echo, and grace can abound even in the best and worst of times.

A SURPRISE PHONE CALL

While I planned and was approved to stay at St. Matthew though the summer months before heading off for seminary, something strange and marvelous happened in late spring of 1975. The phone rang in our tiny married student apartment on the Lamar University campus. Sharon was there and I was feeling a little silly, giddy and loosey-goosey. Perhaps it was because I was just a few days from graduating from college on time and with High Honors. For whatever reason, I answered the call with these flippant words, "Dent's Pool Hall. Eight Ball speaking."

Not a smart move, of course, for the caller was a prominent pastor seeking to fill an attractive, short-term position on his staff. He immediately replied to my smarty remark with a wisecrack of his own, "Eight Ball, this is the Hustler. I'm trying to hustle me a man to come work for me this summer." Rev. Doc Klingle of the First United Methodist Church in Orange where I had been the Summer Youth Director in 1972 was calling to invite me to serve as his Interim Associate Pastor and Youth Minster for three months before starting seminary. The three-month deal was soon sealed. We laughed for years over the crazy content of that call out of the blue and Doc's immediate retort to my wisecrack. Our paths would cross again and again.

This surprise opportunity to return to Orange after three years was a great gift. While it meant departing High Island sooner than expected, the three months in Orange were full of blessings. The gracious congregation put us up in a nice apartment, paid us a generous salary for the three months, and provided me the opportunity to preach six Sunday mornings across the summer. What an amazing pastoral experience to have under one's belt before ever stepping into seminary for formal training for ministry in the local church.

After almost three years of pastoral service, I felt well prepared for what was ahead, while knowing there was much yet to learn. One lesson already learned, however: Be careful how you answer the phone. It may not be someone so gracious and kind as Doc was. The whispers of love to a rookie at the beach were good gifts of a gracious God to a green guy getting going on the path receiving and sharing whispers of love.

Expanding Education and Empathy

The United Methodist Church requires an educated clergy. Methodist movement founder John Wesley was an Oxford don. Candidates for ordained ministry are required to meet much more than minimum measures before being fully credentialed as a pastor in the church of Jesus Christ. While an approved part-time course of study over some five to nine years may be a route to eventual ordination, attending graduate school for three-four years is the norm for candidates aspiring for ordination. Seminary is the route most taken by candidates preparing to serve in the ministry, priesthood or rabbinate.

While some prospective seminarians may apply to several schools of theology, I chose to put all my eggs in one basket. In early 1975 I applied to Perkins School of Theology, a graduate school at Southern Methodist University in Dallas, Texas. While there were over 100 theological schools in the country, I knew this was the best choice. Perkins had these ten attractive assets:

1. Five hours from Sharon's and my parents in Tulsa and Beaumont
2. Location in the growing Dallas Metroplex
3. Location on the attractive SMU Campus
4. A renowned faculty, library, and quadrangle commonly called "the God Quad"
5. My brother was in Dallas completing his medical internship and residency
6. Sharon's brother and family lived in nearby Garland
7. The school's significant endowment to provide Student Financial Aid
8. Most pastors in my home Methodist Conference had attended Perkins
9. SMU was a member of the Southwest Athletic Conference.
10. The Dallas Cowboys were perennial Super Bowl contenders!

MAKING ENDS MEET

Sharon completed her degree in Elementary Education at Lamar in August, and we moved our meager possessions to a one room campus housing unit. As I was a full-time student, we hoped she could land a teaching position in the Dallas area. None was available, so she took a job with Manpower for $2.30 an hour. She was able to put her professional skills to work at Sun Energy Development in Dallas plotting and coloring topographical maps of coal deposits in faraway Gillette, Wyoming. The men in the office were amazed at her proficiency with a set of colored pencils plotting wells in the pre-computer era. They affectionately called her "PW", meaning "Preacher's Wife"!

Sharon occasionally carpooled to work with a woman who lived nearby. Mary Sue was glad to have a friend whose husband was preparing to become a pastor. She attended a fundamentalist church. One day Mary Sue told Sharon that her pastor always preached on one of two things on Christmas and Easter. It was either tithing or hell. Why in the world did he do that? Because that is when the attendance was the largest. By the way, tithing and hell are the same thing for some folks.

I did my little part financially that first year taking a part-time position at Skillern's Drug Store in nearby Snyder Plaza northwest of the SMU campus. When I was not sweeping the floor or unpacking merchandise, I was occasionally called to work a register at busy times. Three items I seemed to sell the most were the three C's: cigarettes, cosmetics, and condoms. I guess you can say I contributed to people's beauty, death and wellbeing. Everyone should work in retail at least once in his or her life.

Another source of income for the two years in Big D was housesitting. SMU is in University Park and adjacent to Highland Park. The Park Cities are highly affluent neighborhoods, as are several other enclaves of North Dallas. When these well-to-do folks traveled on the weekends and longer, they wanted their opulent homes to be occupied. So, they called Perkins to secure names and phone numbers of seminary couples who could always use some money. Who was more trustworthy than folks studying to serve God? The going rate was $20/day, sometimes more when there were children. That was good money in the mid-seventies.

What a gift to hang out in a family's Highland Park home eating their food, watching their color television, swimming in their pool, and sometimes driving their luxury car to chauffer children to weekend commitments. One home came with three active children. Fortunately, there was also a cook. If we needed anything at a meal, we had only to push a button under the table to summon her from the kitchen. Sharon advised me not to create any expectations about buttons in our future dining rooms!

One Highland Park family gave us their tickets to the 1976 Cotton Bowl game. What a thrill to be at Fair Park on a cold New Year's Day with 77,500 red-clad fans of the Universities of Arkansas and Georgia. The Southwest Conference Co-Champion Razorbacks defeated Southeast Conference Co-Champion Bulldogs, 35-10. We were delighted to be a part of a New Year's

Bowl football game, despite a kick-off temperature of 30 degrees. We were in the top of the world as we began the Bicentennial celebration of our nation!

My kind parents sent us $95 a month to pay our rent in Moore Hall, the married student housing in the God Quad. We regularly shared covered dish meals with other young seminary couples, literally sitting on the second-floor hallway. It was a Holy Communion of sorts. Our diverse dorm neighbors came mostly from across Texas, as well as Louisiana, Arkansas, New Mexico, Kansas, Oklahoma, Nebraska and Missouri. These eight states comprise the Southcentral Jurisdiction of the United Methodist Church. Legally, the SCJ of the UMC owns SMU. OK?

EXPANDING DIVERSITY

Other seminary students came to Perkins from the U.S., as well as South Korea, Australia, South Africa, Argentina, The Netherlands, India, Indonesia, and Thailand. While United Methodists comprised about 75 percent of the student body, the seminarians also included Episcopalian, Assembly of God, Baptist, Unitarian, Lutheran, Nazarene, Presbyterian, Christian Methodist Episcopal, Latter Day Saints, and United Church of Christ students. Most students were in their twenties or thirties. The school enrollment of 425 was approximately 90 percent male, 80 percent Anglo, and 75 percent under 30 years of age. Being a young white male, I was in the majority in classes, study groups, and the seminary softball team which competed well against the law school, fraternities, and resident hall teams. Perkins power at the plate prevailed profusely!

EXPANDING THE HEART AND MIND

While classes, lectures, extensive reading and writing were the major focus of seminary for the students, our souls were fed with winsome worship in two weekly worship services. The lovely Georgian architectural Perkins Chapel was filled with students, professors, staff, and community guests each Tuesday and Thursday morning at 10:15 for a half-hour preaching or communion service. Professors, visiting preachers and occasionally students led worship and witnessed to the Word. The organ music by Robert Anderson and the anthems of the Seminary Singers directed by Roger Deschner were antecedents of the Heavenly Hosts!

Classes in theology school were no walk in the park. While we students enjoyed the exposure to new and important fields, we worked hard to stay up with rigorous reading and writing assignments. My favorite fields of study were Moral Theology (ethics), Homiletics (preaching), Pastoral Care and Counseling and Worship. I also benefited greatly from courses on the Book of Revelation, Introduction to the Old Testament and the Book of Psalms. These last two were taught by Bill Power, an Episcopalian priest, who made the first testament stories come alive like nobody's business. No Perkins student can forget his line about Jonah's refusal to go to Nineveh, as God had commanded him to do. In Dr. Power words, "Jonah took the noon balloon to Rangoon," seeking to escape Yahweh's call.

The most passionate and profound professor I studied under at Perkins was not a Christian. Yet he influenced for God and good a generation of Methodist preachers. American Reform Jewish Rabbi Levi Arthur Olan was a progressive social activist, author, and professor. Born in Ukraine in 1903, he grew up in Rochester, New York. The diminutive Rabbi Olan served Temple Emanuel in Dallas from 1948 to his retirement in 1970. He was one of the most prominent liberal voices in Dallas, which was a predominantly conservative city. His views on poverty, war, civil rights, civil liberties and other topics were disseminated largely through his popular program on WFAA radio and earned him the moniker, "the conscience of Dallas."

He also had a longstanding visiting professorship at Southern Methodist University and published numerous works on Judaism, process theology, and contemporary social issues. He died in 1984. Rabbi Olan's passion, knowledge, and deep faith in Yahweh brought many Methodist and other seminarians to a much-needed appreciation for the First Testament and our shared roots of a monotheistic faith. Google Rabbi Olan to learn more of this twentieth-century prophet.

FOOTBALL AND FAITH

My major project in our Moral Theology class was a research paper on "The Ethics of College Football Recruiting." I chose this topic for several reasons: my lifelong interest in sports, the intense focus on high school football in Texas and the rabid recruiting competition among college coaches to get the most athletically gifted high school students. The competition was fierce to get commitments from teenagers from across the Lone Star State and beyond to attend an institution to block, kick, run, or catch for the next four years.

Much was at stake and sometimes alumni, boosters or coaches discreetly dispensed gifts to an athlete and/or his family. Under-the-table disbursements of cash, clothes, cars, and female companionship were not unheard of in recruiting wars. I was able to interview an SMU football team player, a coach, and the Faculty Athletic Representative in my research. The latter was Dr. Douglas Jackson, a Perkins Professor of Church and Society. He was most gracious in contributing his knowledge of the budgets, pressures, and cutthroat competition in recruitment of college football players. Fortunately, the 20-page paper was well received by Dr. Fred Carney, my Moral Theology professor. Unfortunately, SMU became a major violator of the rules of college football in the next decade.

Campus Life

Being a student at the university afforded us some fun and welcome benefits. These included attending SMU football games at the Cotton Bowl and basketball contests at Moody Coliseum, access to Fondren Library, Friday Night Movies in the Student Center, University Worship in Perkins Chapel on Sundays and hearing renowned speakers on campus. Persons we heard speak included Presidential candidate Jimmy Carter, poet and civil rights activist Maya Angelou, Secretary of State Henry Kissinger, Reverend Cecil Williams, Professor Martin Marty, Fred Rogers from the neighborhood and President Gerald Ford.

Talking Football with the President

In September 1975 President Ford was scheduled to speak at the Opening Convocation for the fall semester. Just seven days before, the President had been shot at in Sacramento, California by Charles Manson cult member Squeaky Fromme. His appearance in Dallas was suddenly uncertain. Sharon and I had never seen a U.S. President and were excited about the prospect, then disappointed his trip might be cancelled. President Ford's visit was cleared, and the day finally arrived.

We walked across campus early that warm day from our apartment in Moore Hall. The crowd was large, and the President finally entered Moody Colosseum with much fanfare. After the usual preliminaries, Mr. Ford spoke, was awarded an Honorary Degree from SMU and the session was soon over. The student crowd felt a great sense of satisfaction and joy at having seen in person the most powerful man in the world. A previous president visiting Dallas a dozen years before had not been welcomed so well.

As Sharon and I started our leisurely stroll back across campus, we noticed some commotion in front of the Meadows Fine Arts Building. There were several black limousines with men in dark glasses attending them. The word spread quickly that President Ford had stayed on campus to watch part of a ballet in the SMU Meadows Fine Arts Center. Realizing that the presidential party would have to pass the seminary quadrangle to leave campus, we ran and stood along Bishop Boulevard right in front of Perkins Chapel. In less than a half hour, the presidential party emerged, got into the limos and proceeded south to where we and dozens of others had gathered.

Some students were waving and taking pictures as the motorcade approached, but the President could not be seen. However, just before his car got to the spot where we were standing, the bulletproof sunroof was rolled back. President Ford stood up through the roof along with Texas Senator John Tower to wave to the students along the way. Senator Tower was rather diminutive in stature and President Ford was a good size man, so it looked like Mutt and Jeff side-by-side. Tower, the son of a prominent Methodist pastor in the Texas Conference, used to say, "My name is Tower, but I don't."

In just a matter of seconds the presidential limousine would pass right in front of us, ten feet away. I thought of what I might say to get the President's attention. Before I could really think long and hard on the options, the President of the United States of America was right in front of us! Suddenly I cupped my hands around my mouth and shouted to Mr. Ford two words. What two words would you choose? I shouted, "Yea, Michigan!" Immediately, the President turned and looked this 22-year-old seminary student in the eye and said, "Thank you, I hope they win today. I hope they don't do like Alabama." Alabama had lost the previous Monday night in a special Labor Day season opener.

Why did I yell, "Yea, Michigan"? I remembered that Mr. Ford had played football for the University of Michigan and that he was still a big fan of the Wolverines. If he would respond to anything, that would get his attention. Over 40 years I have shared that story on Christmas Eve in every church I have served, most recently in 2017, my final December 24 services as a pastor. At Christmas God speaks in a way which gets our attention. The word becomes flesh. Incarnation. Emmanuel. God with us, or as Calvin Miller says, *"God with a zip code."*

MEETING MR. ROGERS

The visit by Fred Rogers to Perkins was a low-key event. I stumbled on this seminary convocation in the Kirby Hall Lounge when it was in process one afternoon. Growing up in a community without Public Broadcasting, I had never heard of Mr. Rogers. That afternoon introduced me to a true, gentle spiritual saint.

Fred McFeely Rogers was born in 1928 in Pennsylvania and grew up to become a television personality, musician, puppeteer, writer, producer and Presbyterian minister. He was the creator, composer, producer, head writer, and host of the preschool television series *Mister Rogers' Neighborhood* which mesmerized children for a third of a century, beginning in 1968. The show featured his kind, neighborly persona, which nurtured his connection to the audience. Mr. Rogers would end each program by telling his viewers, "You've made this day a special day, by just being you. There's no person in the whole world like you. I like you just the way you are."

When my precious preschool-trained teacher wife learned I had met Mr. Rogers, she was incredulous! Sharon was elated I met him yet deflated I did not know who he was. If I could somehow go back in time and take Sharon with me, we would return to that fall day in seminary when a Presbyterian pastor in a sweater and a pair of sneakers dropped in and blessed the Perkins community in the name and spirit of the One who taught, *"Let the children come to me. Do not get in their way. For to such children belongs the kindom of God."*

Fred Rogers was accompanied that afternoon by Johnny Costa, his musical director, arranger, and keyboardist for the children's program debut until his death in 1996. Before his own birth into eternal life in 2003, Mr. Rogers received the Presidential Medal of Freedom, 40 honorary degrees and a Peabody Award. He was inducted into the Television Hall of Fame and was recognized in two congressional resolutions. The Smithsonian Institution displays one of his trademark sweaters as a "Treasure of American History." Both our son and daughter grew up magically captivated by the gentle and genuine goodness of a Presbyterian pastor sharing the grace of God for all. Thanks be to God for gentle Mr. Rogers. He graciously, gently whispered love to generations of the nation's children.

THE LANGUAGE OF THE BIBLE

Some seminary classes were intense. Studying Greek was Greek to me! Learning to translate the language of the Second Testament was no walk in the park. I learned enough to throw in an *agape* and an *ecclesia* here and there to lead a Bible Study or preach a scholarly sermon. Today there are many Bible translations available. I like the child who preferred his Grandmother's version. He said, "She translated the Bible into the language of love." Hard to top that. A love whisper *par excellence.*

THE LANGUAGE OF FAITH

At the core every Perkins seminarian's study is the writing of his or her credo. The Latin word *credo* means "I believe." In our second year we had to create our concise, complete, cogent creed of the Christian faith in a maximum 30 pages. No fair photocopying the Apostles' or Nicene Creeds! Thirty pages may sound like a lot, but when you begin professing and giving credence to the existence and attributes of the Creator, the life and salvific work of Jesus of Nazareth the Christ, the person and work of the Holy Spirit, the Church as the Body of Christ, the nature and number of the Sacraments, and the understanding of death, judgment, resurrection and return of Christ, you may wish for far more pages. Meaningful faith is not as easy as, "God said it, I believe it, that settles it."

Creating a credo called us to wrestle with the angels, dig deeply into not only what we believe about these historic confessions of faith, but why we believe what we do. The first stab at this for many of us may have been in a Confirmation Class when we were around 12 years old. Faith, of course, is forever changing, growing, maturing, sometimes questioning, even doubting at times on the journey. Frederick Buechner observed, "Doubt is not the opposite of faith. It is an element of faith." He calls doubts "the ants in the pants of faith."

I am grateful that seminary called me to reflect and ruminate on the depth and power of the words of the Christian faith tradition uttered sometimes quite glibly in our faith families, *"I believe in God...Jesus Christ...the Holy Spirit...the communion of saints...the forgiveness of sins...the resurrection of the body..."* Professing our faith, possessing our faith, practicing our faith and being possessed by our faith, all have a daily and lasting impact on our lives as love whisperers.

EXPANDING EMPATHY AND EXPERIENCE

Not all seminary education took place in the classroom. In a Pastoral Care and Counseling class we could choose one of several diverse sites to visit and write a reflection paper for discussion. Options included the Emergency Room at

Parkland Hospital, Sparkman-Hillcrest Funeral Home and the Metropolitan Community Church, a congregation serving primarily the gay community in central Dallas.

Having been in pastoral ministry for years before seminary, I had considerable experience and comfort in ERs and mortuaries. I chose to go with some classmates to the MCC congregation. We had never been to nor even heard of a church which was openly embracing of homosexual individuals and couples. We were not sure what to expect, but guess what? Though it has now been 44 years, I remember everyone was filled with the joy of the Lord! There was spirited singing, a faith testimony, Bible reading, an offering, a strong sermon, and inclusive invitation to Holy Communion. Did I take the sacrament in the gay church? You bet I did. The people of God present that Sunday evening came to praise God, pray to God, give to God, practice hospitality and listen to God's word.

GETTING READY FOR THE END

The most intriguing course I took at Perkins was on the Book of Revelation. Being raised in the Bible Belt, I had seen many bumper stickers with the messages including *Jesus Is Coming Soon, In Case of Rapture This Car Will Be Unmanned* and *Honk If You Love Jesus.* I was fond of the sticker which retorted, *Tithe If You Love Jesus – Any Fool Can Honk!*

End-of-time movements have come and gone over the centuries. Diverse interpretations of the sections of the Book of Revelation, Daniel and the little apocalypses in the synoptic gospels have stirred hopes and fears in the heads and hearts of people of faith in times of persecution. When the course on the Apocalypse was offered, I knew it was a timely gift. Rather than running away from the Book of Revelation, I wanted and needed to embrace it as a pastor serving in Texas where there are many very conservative congregations. The benefit of studying Revelation in depth in seminary soon began in my pastoral internship.

Dr. Virgil Howard, a New Testament and Preaching Professor, opened our eyes and hearts to apocalyptic literature and the historical context in which it originated. The Book of Revelation was never intended to scare people into faith, but rather to comfort and encourage them in tough times of pain and persecution. The promises of God for the future are sure in the pain of the present. So many times, I have had the pastoral privilege of proclaiming these powerful promises and whispers of love at the graveside with a family:

"God will wipe away every tear from their eyes…

Blessed are the dead who from now on who die in the Lord…

They rest from their labor, for their deeds follow them…

Behold, the home of God is among mortals.

He will dwell with them;

they will be his peoples,

and God himself will be with them;

he will wipe away every tear from their eyes.

Death will be no more;

mourning and crying and pain will be no more,

for the first things have passed away.

Behold, I am making all things new.

I am the Alpha and the Omega, the beginning and the end.

I will be their God and they will be my children.

(Revelation 21:4-7)

YEAR TWO IN THE GOD QUAD

By the time we got to our second year at Perkins, things changed for us. The good news is Sharon received a fulltime teaching position in the Dallas School District. The less than good news is it was in a challenging diverse section of South Oak Cliff where she had 36 kindergarten students. Some spoke no English. With minimal support from the administration and parents, she did her best to whisper love and to instill a firm foundation for future success. We moved off campus to a small apartment across from the seminary. We also adopted a cute, crazy kitty we named Asbury after the Methodist movement leader in America. We still participated in the Perkins Food Coop by going to the downtown Dallas Farmers' Market monthly.

I had a new job in the fall of 1976 serving as Editor of the weekly Perkins *Newsletter*. In addition to announcing worship services, community lunch menu, convocations and speakers on campus, I authored a brief weekly column. In writing editorials, I learned a male editor should probably refrain from writing on demythologizing childbirth. Editorials and sermons have at least two things in common. One is they are sometimes too long. Two is usually someone will disagree with you. If a sermon or editorial moves us to reflect and to be challenged in our comfort zones, something positive has happened. While Jesus often comforted the afflicted, he also afflicted the comfortable.

A MATTER OF DEGREES

While most Perkins students were studying for a M.Th. degree (Master of Theology for service as pastors), others had different pursuits. Some seminary students were in the M.S.M. (Master of Sacred Music) program, planning to serve as professional church musicians. Others were enrolled in the school's M.A. or Ph.D. programs, seeking to become teachers or professors of religion or theology. Rumor has it some students were on campus hoping to receive an MRS.

I would not change my two fulltime years on the seminary campus for anything. Perkins prepared me academically, socially and spiritually to serve the church and the world. And I was only halfway with my seminary education. A very special year of internship was on the horizon. Armed with the knowledge of two years of graduate school, I was ready to explore and experience ministry in a vibrant congregation 240 miles south of Dallas. My learning was soon to grow exponentially.

Pastoral Internship

If pastoral ministry is anything, it is a partnership. Pastor and people, shepherd and sheep share ministry in tandem. Paul praises God with gratitude for his sharing the Good News with the saints in the church at Philippi from Day One. The pastoral internship at Perkins School of Theology was a new program in the mid-1970s. Formerly called Field Education in seminary training, the introduction of a formal internship was a major step forward in preparing persons to serve as effective pastors upon graduation and deployment in professional ministry.

While a minimum of one semester, about four months, was required, nine and twelve-months placements were also available. Students with family or financial considerations often chose the shortest terms. Students might request a placement to be near family or home conference. Many churches in the Dallas-Fort Worth area had interns every year. The purpose of the ministry internship was to provide a positive pastoral experience in a setting where one was supervised, supported, and shared in congregational leadership and ministry. Just as my brother was supervised in his medical internship at Baylor Medical School in Dallas 1974-1975, I would soon be assigned to a ministerial internship for twelve months beginning in June 1977.

WORKING WITH WALTER

When it came time be placed after two years on campus, I did not choose a placement. It chose me. Dr. Walter Underwood, the Pastor of First United Methodist Church in Fort Worth, moved to St. Luke's United Methodist Church in Houston in late 1976 to replace Dr. Kenneth Shamblin who had been elected a Bishop. Dr. Underwood was a creative, dynamic, visionary leader and pastor. He served St. Luke's with vitality, vim, and vigor for eight years before being elected to Episcopacy in 1984. Bishop Underwood would die in his sixties from illness after only three years in office.

When Dr. Underwood was assigned to St. Luke's, he hit the ground running. He wanted the church in the plush River Oaks area to grow in membership, attendance, mission service, outreach and all areas of ministry. The church had a large, attractive Georgian architecture sanctuary with balcony, adjacent chapel, education space, fellowship hall, parlors, professional kitchen, shop, garage, ample parking, and an outdoor swimming pool (for immersion baptisms, of course!). The Sunday services were televised live on

Channel 2, the local NBC affiliate station.

In addition to these assets, St. Luke's had a most capable staff with professional leadership in pastoral, music, children, youth, financial, administrative, maintenance and food service areas. Begun 1945, the congregation reached 6,000 members in 1977. In 2019 the church has an active membership of 8,000. It also planted a dozen more new congregations.

Soon after hitting the Holy Ground of Houston in late 1976, Dr. Underwood contacted the Perkins Seminary Field Office requesting a ministerial student be assigned to the church for a year beginning June 1, 1977. Being a Perkins graduate and the new pastor of a high steeple church, Walter's request did not go unnoticed. St. Luke's had never had a seminary intern. Getting a student placement would be a mutually advantageous arrangement, not to mention the benefit to the intern. In the strange and marvelous ways of Providence, I was chosen in the spring to go down to Houston to interview with Dr. Underwood. He took Sharon and me to the Confederate House on Westheimer Drive for lunch and conversation. That evening we met with a group of lay leaders and church staff.

Very soon the deal was sealed. Sharon and I would spend a year in the Space City interning at one of Methodism's great churches. I am eternally grateful for the opportunity to learn in a setting which to this day has blessed us with friendships, opportunities, lessons, memories, ministry experiences and an addition to our family.

ROCKING WITH THE YOUTH AND THE SHRINK

Guess where my summer was primarily invested that summer? I had the joy of working with the youth in their busy Sunday School, Bible Studies, trips and mission projects. This was a wonderful gift, getting to meet the parents of the kids, being in their homes for studies and fellowships, gaining appreciation from the staff and making friends with these teenagers who affectionately called their new minister-in training, "Rev Junior." However, I did not join these creative adolescents in referring to the Senior Pastor as "Underwalter Wood" nor "Walter Underwear"!

As in any professional internship, there was significant supervision put in place for my time at St. Luke's. The seminary required three areas of continual connection: an ordained pastor on staff as my direct overseer, an Internship Committee of diverse, capable, committed lay members and a psychotherapist who was employed by the seminary to meet monthly for several hours with the five Houston-area ministerial interns. Therapist Virginia Austin facilitated our gatherings of checking in, sharing any issues for group processing, individual counseling and assignments, as needed. She was a down-to-earth woman in her late fifties who provided the all-male group a safe place to vent, share, celebrate, seek counsel and get away for a day of reflection and inventory. Knowing that "Every priest needs a priest," Perkins was wise to include this component in our training for ministry.

REVEREND RILEY ROCKS

St. Luke's put together a diverse, competent committee to meet with me monthly, as well as individually at their or my request. Men and women of diverse ages, religious backgrounds, places of origin, marital status, professions and economic and social standing made for a strong group. One was a PK, or "Preacher's Kid." Another, Rev. Ron Sunderland, was an ordained pastor from Australia, serving at the Texas Medical Center's Institute of Religion. The chair and his wife invited the committee for a welcome reception for Sharon and me in their River Oaks home early in the summer. When the adult beverages were served, we were surprised and made an immediate decision that to decline the wine would be fine.

The monthly meetings were well run, well attended and quite productive. After a prayer opened each meeting, I reported on my ministry experiences in the previous month, received feedback from committee members on any events they attended and a heard a report from Associate Pastor John Riley. Though only four years older than I, he was an excellent intern supervisor, son of a distinguished pastor in the Texas Conference and a competent and respected associate pastor on the St. Luke's staff. The seminary provided John and each intern supervisor professional training for their roles. The Internship Learning Covenant I signed in the spring with the church stipulated John and I would meet weekly to review the past seven days, as well as sneak a peek at the next week. The core learnings in those sessions came in our analysis and reflection on either a verbatim or Process Note I wrote and submitted to John a day or two before our weekly conference.

A verbatim is a word for word recounting of a conversation. Reviewing the content of a conversation enabled me to reflect on what I said, how I said it and whether it was helpful or not to a parishioner. John's role was to identify conversation components which were very helpful, helpful, not-so-helpful, or "You said what?"! He had an amazing ability to ask helpful, probing questions to assist improving my pastoral care and counseling skills. John would later serve for a score or more of years as a chaplain in the Department of Pastoral Care at The Methodist Hospital in Houston.

The Process Note tool consisted of a two-page summary of a ministry event, encounter or experience resulting in recording and reflecting on what transpired. The note included an introduction of who, where, what and why. John and I took ample time to discuss how a Bible Study, hospital visit, pastoral prayer, funeral, church meeting, baptism or church visitor phone call went. This evaluative method was highly intentional and a valuable component of the Learning Covenant.

John was most helpful in orienting me to the vast Texas Medical Center just south of downtown Houston. Home to two medical schools, the world-famous M.D. Anderson Cancer Center, a half-dozen major hospitals, a dental school and The Institute of Religion, this world-renown center has treated presidents, kings, movie stars, athletes and destitute patients since opening in the fall of 1945. During my three pastoral assignments in the Houston area, I made many hospital visits to the medical center. My sister was treated for her brain tumor at Methodist Hospital, as well as both of our children were born there. In 2018 the TMC had 106,000 employees, 60 institutions and a $25 billion GDP. Everything seems bigger in Texas!

A medical learning highlight on my internship was getting to see Dr. Michael DeBakey, a premier world cardiovascular surgeon, perform open heart surgery at The Methodist Hospital. Rev. Riley somehow arranged this special opportunity. Born in Lake Charles, Louisiana, Dr. DeBakey was the Lebanese-American scientist, medical educator, chancellor emeritus of Baylor College of Medicine and Director of The Methodist DeBakey Heart & Vascular Center. We witnessed arguably the best-known heart surgeon in the world perform a double valve replacement on a man from Italy. I was amazed there were as many as 14 persons in the Operating Room at one time, including the patient's Italian physician who had traveled with him from home. John and I with a couple of other guests sat above the operating suite and had direct view of the operation.

Fifteen years later this experience came to mind when watching an episode of *Seinfeld* in which zingy Cosmo Kramer drops a Junior Mint from the theatre opening above the operating room. The tiny mint descends delicately in slow motion and somehow comes to rest in the exposed gut of the patient. Google the March 18, 1993 episode for some healthy laughs.

Reverends Riley and Dent had no Junior Mints in the operating observation opening at The Methodist Hospital. Maybe a Tic-Tac or two though!

During my internship whenever I taught, prayed, preached, conducted, a funeral, joined a couple in marriage or had some visible pastoral role or responsibility, it was not unusual to have one or more Committee members attend with or without notice. Each would offer constructive comments, ask any questions and offer me the opportunity to ask questions of them. This process was a positive path to sharpen my pastoral leadership and skills in a mutually beneficial process. Their words were always whispers of love.

LEAVING A LEGACY OF REVELATION

Two significant opportunities took place in the fall of my internship. Knowing I had studied the Apocalypse at Perkins, St. Luke's Director of Christian Education Joe Zink invited me to teach a course on the Book of Revelation in the church's Community Continuing Education Classes. This was the era of the apocalyptic *The Late Great Planet Earth* book and *A Thief in the Night* movie, both fundamentalist interpretations of Revelation. Joe thought a series on Revelation would attract folks from the church and community. He was quite right as the high enrollment forced us to move to a larger space. The ten weeks went fast as we shared the historical setting of the book, the nature of apocalyptic literature and the powerful promises of Providence.

Dr. Underwood was a pioneer in church television ministry from his time on the staff of First Methodist Church in Dallas in the 1950s. Following the positive response to the Revelation class, he asked me to do a video series on Revelation. We taped six 15-minute segments with props, plants, books and maps to enhance the presentation. The church's volunteer video team did an excellent job with patience, kindness and professionalism in producing the VHS Revelation package which was used for several years. I think my residual revenue for the Revelation revelations got lost in the mail. Seriously, what a grand opportunity to share some seminary studies with the saints at St. Luke's for some years to come. BTW, does anyone today know what VHS is?

TO PREACH OR NOT TO PREACH?

The second special opportunity came on very short notice. Dr. Underwood called me on late Saturday afternoon, October 22, 1977 to invite me to preach at both services the very next morning. He was under the weather and was not improving. As much as he wanted to preach, he could not do so. Would I be willing to preach on such short notice? He could have asked the district superintendent or one of the several clergy staff to preach. I was deeply honored and accepted immediately, though Sharon and I had long ago purchased tickets to a John Denver concert that very same evening. This was likely and logically to be my lone opportunity to preach from St. Luke's lofty pulpit.

Denver concert, or Dent sermon?

Rocky Mountain High, or Mountain High Pulpit?

Poems, Prayers and Promises, or Pulpit, Prayer and Proclamation?

The answer, of course was -- both! We would go to the nearby Summit on Saturday night, and St. Luke's on Sunday morning. Next question. What does one preach on less than a day's notice? No time really to carefully, prayerfully prepare from scratch a message with which God and I would likely be pleased. So, I did what other pastors have done for millennia under similar dire circumstances. I dug in my files for a sugar stick, a sermon I had previously prepared, preached and received at least a modicum of praise. I had preached only once in the past year, however. That was at Pollard UMC in Tyler where good friend, Bill Scales, was the pastor. That sermon was the last, best and only sugar stick I could find, refine, and feel fine preaching.

I did not sleep well Saturday night. In fact, I am not sure I slept at all. First, John Denver was awesome. Unfortunately, the man behind us knew every word to every to every song. More unfortunately, he sang every word to every song. Most unfortunately, he sang every word to every song offkey! We raced home so I could prepare to preach live to a congregation of 1,200 souls in the pews expecting to hear Dr. Underwood and countless semi-awake souls in their pajamas asking, "Where is Walter today? Who is this kid preaching?"

My only two questions were, "Will Walter be healthy enough to watch from home?" And, "Will my mother's outdoor television antennae 90 miles away in Beaumont be able to pick up the KPRC telecast of the service?" The true gravity of those two inquiries over 40 years ago is that I cannot remember the answer to either one!

The two most important questions on any Sunday morning are, in large measure, "Will God show up?" and "Will the preacher let God show off?" In the words of a question in the Good Book, "Is there any word from the Lord?" I did my best to witness to the word. The message that morning was *The Great Invitation*, from Matthew 11:28-30. In the text a gentle and humble Jesus issues a timeless, universal invitation and precious promise about labor and rest, yokes and burdens, as well as a gift of soul peace.

The response from all parties present or accounted for was positive. The thing about ministry is that as soon you finish something – say a sermon – you are thinking about Monday's three meetings, Tuesday's funeral and a dozen other important pastoral and personal priorities just ahead. If you are the primary preacher, you always have five to six sermons germinating in your head and heart. I will forever treasure the measure of trust Dr. Underwood placed in the hands of a 25-year-old seminary student to whisper love to tens of thousands of Houstonians on a fall Sunday morning in 1977 in the senior pastor's first year at St. Luke's.

I learned much from Walter, John and other staff members observing their ministries, asking questions and participating hands-on in answering the calls on the church switchboard, putting the weekly newspaper together, planning worship as a team six months ahead and managing finances in a large congregation. The values which surfaced repeatedly in these conversations and observations were teamwork, quality, prayer, trust in one another and common goals. Many of those staff colleagues for a year were much older than I and have preceded us to glory. Through the grace of God, I look forward somehow, some way, some day to catching up with them for another St. Luke's staff meeting, retreat or party led by Dr. Underwood's winsome wit and wisdom.

BUMPS ON THE ROAD

Not everything in my internship went so smoothly. As the church was entering its annual finance campaign to fund the 1978 budget, I was assigned delivery of the Children's Moment, a brief message to the children who come forward to the front of the sanctuary early in the service. I decided to try to teach a lesson in tithing. Tithing is giving 10 percent of one's income. Trying to keep it simple, I had ten dimes and told them if you give one dime to God through the church, that is tithing. If you have ten dollars, you give God one dollar. And if you have ten million dollars, you honor God by giving one million dollars. I thought the lesson was simple, timely, and biblical.

That week Dr. Underwood received a letter from a well-to-do-member who was offended. Walter shared the critical letter with me, as well as the gracious one he wrote in my defense. I will always remember and be grateful that Walter stood up with integrity to a grouchy giver on behalf of his low-ranking student intern. That lesson stayed with me for the over thirty years as a senior pastor. Whenever possible, stand with and have your staff member's back.

The year was filled with a variety of other opportunities to interact with the with the congregation in a pastoral capacity. These included Sharon's and my going on the Youth Ski Trip to Winter Park, Colorado where it was 25 degrees below, and we all had to get out of the bus for it to make it up treacherous, icy Berthoud Pass. The only persons on the bus besides the driver were a youth with a heart condition and a preacher's pregnant partner. All went well with no ski injuries and no skiers left behind. We got back to Houston in time for the Christmas Eve Services.

Crazy Christmas Eve Communion

Christmas Eve worship is a magical, mystical, majestic and mysterious experience in most churches. With carols, candles and a creche, who could want anything more? We wanted one more thing at the 5:00 p.m. service. Why not have Holy Communion? Why not have the Minister-in-Training, an ordained deacon, assist Rev. John Riley, the ordained elder, in consecrating the bread and cup for the 800 folks including many children at the Family Service?

John and I shared the Prayer of Consecration. He broke the bread, led the congregation in The Lord's Prayer. I lifted the cup and gave the invitation for all to come. As John and I moved from the altar to the communion rail, he with a plate of bread and I with a tray of 30 cups to begin serving, something unexpected and unwanted happened.

This was the time before cordless microphones for worship leaders. I had a small, yet strong microphone hanging around my neck and plugged securely into an outlet in the floor of the chancel. There was probably 18 to 20 feet of cord available for me to move about and be heard in the sanctuary. After offering the invitation, I took the tray of cups and walked toward the chancel to start serving the sacrament.

No one could have guessed what happened next. As I moved with authority and anticipation on this august occasion, suddenly I was jerked backward by the neck when the cord connected to the chancel floor came to a sharp end. The tray of cups spilled in every direction, embarrassingly baptizing with grape juice my program, robe, and the chancel floor! My gut reaction was "I'm going to flunk internship." My grace reaction was, "All shall be well."

Grace prevailed. Love whispered. Mercy echoed. We all had a good laugh later. All was well. Grace is amazing. Lesson learned. One of many in a year in an internship and true partnership with the scores and scores of beloved saints at St. Luke's. We look forward to a reunion in the sweet by and by. The spring of my internship year continued to be filled with meetings, missions and ministries of various kinds.

Sharon continued to grow great with child toward the June 21 due date. Our pregnancy forced us to move from an apartment in the all-adult West Creek Apartments near the church to a two-bedroom unit, eight miles west on Westheimer. It gave us room for all the accoutrements required when the baby arrived. The youth led by Ruth Penton had a shower for "Baby Dent" in May. The generous group gifted us with every item a newborn could possibly need.

A Funny Farewell from a Fantastic Flock

In early November of our internship year, Sharon and I had rejoiced to announce to our families and that were going to have a baby. A child would arrive in June. Monthly Church Board meetings are a big thing. Dinner is served. Attendance is in the hundreds. Reports are given. Finances are reviewed. Ministries are celebrated. Prayers are offered. God is praised. A good time is had by all.

At the May 1978 board meeting, I was called on by Chairman Nat Rogers to give a report on my activities as the church's first pastoral intern. After I completed an accounting of the many ministry experiences in the past twelve months, Mr. Rogers asked Sharon and me to stand and be recognized. After commenting on my very busy year of ministry, he looked at Sharon who was well into her ninth month of pregnancy. This distinguished Houston civic leader who was President and CEO of First City National Bank of Houston paused and then shared an observation, "And from the looks of things, Mike's been busy at home, too!" His gentle wit was a benediction on an amazing year.

Sharon was able to complete her year of teaching in the St. Luke's Day School just before a bouncing baby boy arrived June 1 by C-section, three weeks before the due date. Our mothers were gracious to come to Houston to assist for several days each while Sharon recovered and I left to begin a student appointment in Edom, Texas. She and our son joined me in East Texas as Edomites at the first of July. The year at St. Luke's had been memorable for all the right reasons. The year at Edom would be memorable for not all the right reasons.

My Year of Living as an Edomite

Thus says the Lord God concerning Edom:
We have heard a report from the LORD,
And a messenger has been sent among the nations:
"Rise up! Let us rise against it for battle!"
--Obadiah 1:1

Have you ever heard of Obadiah? I did not think so. Most normal people have not. Even pastors skip over it. Obadiah is the shortest book in the First Testament, only 21 verses. Obadiah's vision for Edom is not a pleasant one. The Edomites reaped what they had sown. I became an Edomite for one long year. Every pastor has a pasture that is his or her least favorite. My time in the land of Edom began and ended in strange and funny ways.

As a seminary student pastorate in the Texas Conference, Edom was at or near the top of anyone's list of such appointments. The congregation had been served by a series of strong student pastors over the years. The church had a long history, dating to before the War Between the States. The present beige brick building was erected in 1955 and includes an inviting sanctuary, classrooms, kitchen, fellowship hall and restrooms. A large, comfortable brick parsonage built in 1974 sat on a double lot next door to the church. The annual compensation package in 1978 was $9,300 for salary, travel, business expenses, health insurance, and utilities.

The town of Edom was 20 miles west of lovely Tyler, the Rose Capital of America, and 80 miles east of Dallas. The town developed a strong arts and crafts community in the early 1970s which continues today. The annual Edom Arts Festival and the monthly First Monday Trade Days in nearby Canton bring many guests to the growing community in the Free State of Van Zandt County.

THE POOPY PARSONAGE

Strange and funny, indeed, was my advent in the land of Edom. Because of the early arrival of our son on June 1 (he was due June 20), I did not pull into town until Saturday afternoon, June 3, less than 24 hours before preaching my first sermon. When I entered the parsonage, I could not believe my eyes. Never had I seen a sight like this in any home. The house was filled with bird poop, bird feathers and dead birds! I felt as if I had wandered on to the set of an Alfred Hitchcock movie. It was unbelievable!

Obviously, no one from the church had bothered to inspect and clean the parsonage before the arrival of the new pastor. Apparently, the previous pastor had left the flue on the chimney open and the birds found a safe place to defecate at will. Strange and funny at best. Repulsive and revolting at the worst. I did not have the intestinal fortitude to call Sharon and tell her our new home for our new baby was poop city, filled with feathers, and containing the stains and remains of big black birds.

> *Thus says the Lord GOD concerning Edom:*
> *We have heard a report from the pastor*
> *And a messenger has been sent among the Edomites:*
> *"Rise up! The parsonage is filled with feathers and bird poop!"*

Strange and funny to say the least! Forty years later we can laugh, but it was not quite so funny then. I preached my first sermon twice the next day after arriving, first at the tiny Sexton Chapel at 9:00 a.m. and then at Edom at 11:00. The title was "New Life," celebrating our beginning in a new pastor-parish partnership, the arrival of our new baby and the Sacrament of Holy Communion. For the first month I commuted from Houston to Edom a couple of times a week. That gave the church time to clean and restore the reverend's residence from the ravages of the ravens.

Our precious newborn son was doing his own fair share of contributing to the presence of poop in our apartment. One of the best baby gifts Sharon says our son received at his April shower by the St. Luke's youth was a month's diaper service. A delivery person would bring an abundant supply of clean cloth diapers several times a week and pick up a pail of soiled ones. What a practical gift!

Sharon and our son moved from Houston at the first of July and officially became Edomites. The church was composed of married folks primarily, along with a fair share of widows. As in many congregations, the females outnumbered the men about 2-1. The church family had several interconnected families and almost everyone was someone's second or third cousin.

The folks in small towns of East Texas are hard workers and serve their communities well. Edom church members taught school, farmed, hung wire for the light company, ran the printshop for Tyler ISD, worked in sales, served at the café, cleaned houses, raised and sold livestock and ran a lumber yard. One couple lived in Irving where they owned a florist shop. After closing Saturday afternoon, Ted and Juanita drove to their country home near Edom. Every Sunday morning, we had fresh flowers! Blessed with a strong baritone voice, Ted led our Sunday night hymn-sings.

A Serpent Was Cast Out of Edom

Bill Faulkner was a traveling salesman. He drove a station wagon with samples of products he sold to hardware stores. His vehicle was filled with boxes of various tools and toys, gizmos and gadgets, items and innovations. One day as Bill was driving down the highway, he felt something slowly moving in his pants leg. He carefully pulled off the to the side of the road, cautiously got out of the car and began to shake gently his left blue jean pants leg. Almost immediately a baby copperhead snake fell from his britches. Bill called on the name of the Lord in no uncertain terms and without hesitation helped the Lord Jesus call that poisonous little reptile to its resting place for eternity.

Grave Cleaning Sunday

Tradition is very strong in places with over 125 years of history. I learned that painfully in my first month in the land of Edom. As we approached July, I was told by church leaders that on the first Sunday of July we would not be having worship on Sunday morning. Say what? No church? The explanation was that it is the annual Cemetery Day in the community when all the congregations cancel morning services to meet at the graveyard to clean the graves. As Tevye sings in *Fiddler on the Roof,* I can tell you why Edomites clean graves every first Sunday in July: "Tradition!"

So, who do you think won this spitting contest? The 25-year-old seminary student pastor weeks on the job from big Houston? Or the 125 years of tradition in the tiny town of Edom? I pleaded *nolo contendere.* While the graves of the dead were properly tended to July 2, 1978, some few souls showed up in the church house to receive Holy Communion, celebrate Independence Sunday and share in worship and the message. Tradition is the living faith of the dead. Traditionalism is the dead faith of the living. I hope there were no losers that day. Certainly, there was none in God's eyes.

Standing on the Promises, Sitting on the Premises

Sexton Chapel United Methodist Church was the second station on the Edom appointment. Five miles up the road from Edom, at the intersection of Farm

112

to Market Road 314 and Van Zandt County Road 4905, the congregation was small, yet faithful. Every Sunday 10-15 saints assembled to praise and pray, sing and share, listen and learn, and give and go. The average age of the attendees was around 70. That is including the teenage pianist. Go online to see a picture of the chapel. The congregation had two significant challenges. First, the young lady who played the piano had a very limited repertoire. I mean 3-4 hymns tops. After singing *Amazing Grace* (the Methodist national anthem!), *The Old Rugged Cross,* and *Sweet Hour of Prayer* every other Sunday, you may wish for more.

The other challenge was taking care of business before bowing on bended knee in worship. While the Sexton Chapel was a nice facility built in 1961, the budget must have been quite tight. The good news is the church had restrooms. The not-so-good news is that the facilities were external outhouses. That is why it was wise to take care of personal business before taking care of the Lord's business of praise and worship. I came away from my year at Sexton Chapel believing it is much better to be standing on the promises of God rather than sitting on the premises of God. The church might have experienced a significant membership expansion had it been willing to tweak its name. Just remove three little letters. Take out a "ton." Can you imagine the "Sex Chapel United Methodist Church"? Well, I cannot either. But...

HAPPY, HOLY WHISPERS OF LOVE

Preaching two times on Sunday, learning to be a father, and preparing for my final year of study at Perkins kept me busy that summer. Several significant sacramental celebrations in our family were soon to be shared in September. On my 26th birthday, our three-month-old son was baptized, named and claimed by God. Sharon and I promised to rear him in the Christian community, to be an example to him, to exercise Godly care over him, to teach him Biblical wisdom, and to move him to owning and confirming the Christian faith for himself. Dr. Bill Scales, our close family friend and pastor, administered the sacrament. Almost 35 years later our son traveled to Boerne, Texas on his own initiative to celebrate the life of the pastor who baptized him into the family of God, an ever-expanding family whose bonds cannot be broken by time or space, nor even death.

Less than a week after our son's baptism, the Dent clan congregated again, this time in Dallas for the sacramental service of Christian marriage. What a joy for me personally and pastorally to tie the knot for my beloved brother and his beautiful bride. Though it has been 40 years, I must not have celebrated too long or hard that night. I drove home to Edom to preach twice on the next morning on *Ahab's Lessons in Living.* Though it was not one of the lessons learned by King Ahab, I learned early in my ministry that we are to rejoice greatly with those who rejoice, as well as to weep with those who weep. Less than three years after rejoicing in my brother's wedding, our family gathered again in Dallas. This time it was for his funeral.

ON THE ROAD TO BIG D

I commuted to Dallas several days a week with Perkins classmate and friend Bob Long to complete our fourth and final year at Perkins. He did most of the driving for two good reasons. First, he and Marsha had two cars. Sharon and I had one car and one baby. Do the math. Second, Bob had a church member who gave him a gasoline credit card (remember those?) to help him with his travel between Asbury UMC in Tyler and SMU. We student pastors used our time in the car together to reflect on current recreational and religious issues.

In addition to chewing the fat about the Oilers, Cowboys and President Jimmy Carter's challenges, we discussed the current events in our churches and the world. One of those issues was the depressing mass suicide of 909 followers of Pastor Jim Jones of the Peoples Temple cult in mid-November. Over 300 children were among the dead ordered by Jones to drink the cyanide-laced, grape-flavored drink. Religion and delusional leaders never have healthy outcomes. This one was particularly grim.

Bob and I let ourselves dream as we drove to and from Dallas. When we traveled past the Little Hope Baptist Church near Canton 2-3 days a week, we could not help but wonder how the congregation got that name. Can you imagine wanting to affiliate with a congregation called "Little Hope"? What about a "Meager Methodist Church"? Or a "Puny Presbyterian Parish"? Or a "Diminutive Disciples of Christ congregation"?

We soon-to-be possessors of sheepskins from Perkins professors proclaiming us Masters of Theology dreamed about the future. Bob and I wondered, "What's next? Where will we be appointed when we complete our studies?" Students graduating from seminary were probably not at the top of Texas Conference Bishop Finis Crutchfield's list, we hoped. He had bigger fish to fry for sure. Several months later we learned our futures would be in nascent places of pleasant parish ministry.

New Life among the Edomites

As the 1979 spring term unfolded, so did new resurrection life among the Edomites. I had the great privilege as a young pastor to lead a youth confirmation class at the church on Wednesday afternoons for several months. On Palm Sunday, April 8, four teenagers publicly professed their faith in Christ. Two of them were baptized, one by immersion in nearby Callender Lake early that Holy Week morning. Why is it always unseasonably cool when you dunk a new disciple?

The year of living as an Edomite wound down with some renown. I was pleased as punch and as pastor to conduct only two funerals in twelve months. The death rate is 100% of course, but it slowed down for those dozen months. In Tyler 25 years later, I presided over and preached three funerals in a five-hour period one January Saturday. That is two too many in a day, but such comes with rescuing the perishing and caring for the dying.

The pastoral joys of the year in Edom were several, including marrying three couples, baptizing four folks, and welcoming 18 new members. The addition of a garage door at the parsonage was also a victory. The clothes washer had been in the open garage for all to see as Sharon carried our clothes to and fro. With a garage door, no longer could passersby see what color underwear the preacher and his family wore. Our chronologically gifted neighbor across the street was not in favor of the garage door. Why? Sweet Saint Lois complained, "I can't see what's going on over at the parsonage!" There was no dryer, but fortunately, the clothesline was in the backyard making our colorful undies less exposed to inquiring minds which wanted to know.

Going South and Going Home

The call came from the 713-area code sometime in late April 1979. The pastoral appointment season in the Texas Conference was in full swing. All of us graduating from seminary in late May expected a phone call from the District Superintendent telling us where to go. That is, the DS was sharing the news of a new ministerial assignment made by the Bishop and his cabinet. That group prayerfully and carefully discerns gifts and graces of prospective pastors and seeks to place them in congregations where pastor and parish can function and flourish in mutual ministry with maximum benefit.

While there were several somewhat attractive opportunities open, I was delighted to be chosen to "interview" for a new position. A congregation in the Klein community of North Harris County was seeking its first associate pastor. Founded in September 1977 under the strong, steady leadership of Pastor Wayne Day, the church took off like a rocket.

The toddler church flew me down from Tyler on tiny Texas International Airlines. The commuter plane made stops in Nacogdoches and Lufkin before arriving in Houston. I was impressed to be recruited by air, but the air sickness was no fun. Wayne and the church's committee hosted me for dinner, conversation and a tour of the church. That night I called Sharon and said, "I will pray about it while you start packing!" The quick decision to accept the appointment to serve at Klein deeply determined the direction of our ministry for the next 40 years.

Our twelve months in the land of the Edomites was not insignificant. Our baby boy had to have surgery in Tyler that year. He also survived being accidentally locked in our tiny 1976 tiny white Datsun B-210 along with the car keys in the heat of summer in nearby Brownsboro by one of his parents. I will not say who, but it was not me. All's well, ends well. We enjoyed living in East Texas and dreamed of perhaps returning someday. We were impressed by the roses, rolling hills, and religious spirit alive in the Tyler area. If we ever got the chance, we knew it would be a lovely place to land, perhaps more than once.

GOODBYE TO SEMINARY – UNTIL WE MEET AGAIN

As we prepared to complete our student assignment in Edom, I had one more task to complete: Graduate! As my final semester was winding down at Perkins, Registrar and Director of Academic Procedures Wayne Banks invited me to meet with him. He had some good news and some bad news to share. "The good news is you are graduating with a GPA of 89.45." "Wow! That's great!" I replied. "So, what's the bad news?" Winsome Wayne winked with a wicked grin, shook his head and said, "Mike, I hate to tell you that you missed graduating with honors by .05%. If your average was 89.5, we could round it up to 90 and you would be an Honor Graduate." I smiled, shook my head and said, "Dr. Banks, if that is the worst thing that happens to me, I will be a most blessed man." Wayne had a wonderful wit and wisdom. He replied with a grin, "When you die and go to heaven's door, just hope and pray you don't get that close and not get in!" Wayne was a love whisperer.

Much later I heard a wise preacher remark, "God grades not on the curve, but on the cross." By the grace of God, we are all forgiven, accepted, redeemed, saved, washed, and won. By the way, no one in the past 40 years has ever asked about my seminary GPA. God does not care about much we know. God cares about how much we care.

I cared that my mother and father were able to drive from Beaumont to Dallas to attend with Sharon the commencement exercises held on campus in Moody Colosseum. The graduation was filled with the normal circumstance and pomp. What every one of the 9,000 persons present will forever remember was a promise by the commencement speaker, none other than SMU President James H. Zumberge.

Dr. Zumberge, a former Antarctic explorer, concluded his address to the Class of 1979 with this promise to the several thousand degree recipients – future engineers, scientists, teachers, preachers, business executives, healthcare professionals, professional golfers, attorneys, and financiers – "Always remember, graduates, that wherever you go in the future, whether to the North Pole, behind the Iron Curtain, into the jungles of Africa, or even into outer space – wherever you land in the future – the SMU Alumni Association will find you!" (Can I get an "Amen"?)

Several times over the years I have shared in sermons President Zumberge's assurance. Only it is not only the SMU Alumni Association which will not let us go. No, it is likewise the gracious love of God which goes behind, beside and yes, before us. Go online and read "The Hound of Heaven," a poem written by Englishman Francis Thompson. Divine love will pursue us all the way home and then some. The whispers of love are eternal.

Now it was time leave the land of Edom, to say goodbye to some good friends and move forward in faith. I preached my final two Sundays before packing all our earthly goods in the small Datsun and a medium U-Haul truck in the first week of June. As our year as Edomites began in a strange and funny way with a poopy parsonage, so it ended. No, there was no physical poop nor feathers this time. However, as Sharon drove out of the parsonage driveway, a neighbor waved to my wife and said, "Goodbye, Debbie!" Debbie? Who was Debbie? She was the popular previous pastor's wife. No poop! Strange and funny was a year as an Edomite. We were ready for a new pasture in which to witness and whisper love.

From Old to New

Whereas the Methodist Church in Edom began in 1860, Klein United Methodist Church was birthed over 115 years later in the Klein High School ninth-grade school cafeteria on a September Sunday morning in 1977. The key to any church launch is a visionary leader who can inspire others to invest in something which can be seen only with the eyes of faith. Such was the one chosen to birth a new congregation in North Harris County in Spring, Texas.

Only in his early thirties, Reverend Wayne Day brought a compelling vision, charm and charisma which attracted hundreds of hungry hearts to commit themselves to a dream, desire and determination to build a vital community of faith which would bless all who came into its orbit. That challenging invitation was echoed in Wayne's winsome words which bookended each service. The weekly worship opened with a challenging echo: "There is a God who is calling out." *"Let us not be afraid to answer that call to preach the gospel, teach the word, nurture children and bring youth to maturity."* Each service ended with this challenge, commitment and blessing: "Our gathering will soon be over. Where will we go and what will we do?" *"We will go out to be God's people in the world."* "May grace, peace, love and joy forever accompany you." Lost and found saints and sinners found a place of grace, whispers of love and a contagious call to build a new faith community in an old German farming community a score or more miles north of the hustle and bustle of downtown Houston. Hundreds of new and settled residents came to the school campus each Sunday morning to study, sing, pray and be challenged and inspired by the understated charisma of Wayne's practical, positive preaching.

PIONEERS, PLANTERS AND PAYERS

People and pastors who plant churches are pioneers who pay a premium price. They sacrifice time, energy and effort in meeting, praying, listening, discerning and determining where, when and how to make a vision a reality. A fair number of new church plants die on the vine. Others struggle for years before gaining traction. Klein UMC was an extraordinary exception. Its founders also paid the price financially. Within 13 short months, the congregation raised money and built an attractive, functional cross-shaped metal facility on a five-acre plot on a major Farm to Market road in a growing area of new subdivisions. The building included a multiuse worship space with seating for 400 in portable chairs, a kitchen, restrooms, classrooms, nursery, offices and a concrete parking lot for 200 cars. The facility had visibility, flexibility and accessibility.

Worship attendance doubled when the congregation moved into its new home. Married with two young children, Wayne was working long and hard. The congregation voted to request assignment of an associate pastor. That is when I was wined, dined and designed to be assigned as the first associate pastor at the young church. The church raised the money to provide support for a second pastor. My compensation was set at $12,000. We felt rich! The church planters were willing to pay the price to provide for a growing ministry.

"BEHOLD, I MAKE ALL THINGS NEW"

The operative word for the Dents was "new." We moved with our one-year old son to a new church, new community, new home with new furniture, new neighbors and a new challenge. Soon we met new folks in the new church who would become forever friends. Though we served at Klein Church for less than three years, we had three couples from the congregation show up and share in our retirement service in Denver 36 years later in 2018. Not only did they show up for worship and the reception, they came to our home and helped us pack our U-Haul truck for new next chapter in our lives. One of those couples, Paul and Renee, have been vacation compadres over the years. It was my pleasure to join Wayne and Paul's pastor-uncle in uniting this couple in their early thirties in the covenant of Christian Marriage. That was in 1981 and they are still going strong, as is our friendship.

Sharon was invited to assist in choosing some of the new furnishings for the new parsonage in the young Willow Forest subdivision off Kuykendahl Road. I told you it was a German farming community! The previous residents of the church's property were a herd of cows who grazed the pasture for close to a century before residential real estate ran rampant in north Harris County.

Another new and most memorable experience Sharon and I shared in our short time in the new Klein UMC was a ride in the Goodyear Blimp. The blimp base was on Interstate 45 in Spring, less than ten miles from the church. Blimps have been around for centuries. Goodyear made them an American icon with a fleet of lighter-than-air aerial ambassadors beginning in 1917. Pastor friend Bill Scales and his wife Janet were gifted with four tickets which are rarely, if ever, available to the general public. They graciously invited us to join them for this amazing aerial adventure on the blimp America. We spent an hour in the air floating freely, quietly and effortlessly in the lighter-than-air airship.

Captain Larry Chambers graciously guided us over the church and our home while we shot rolls of pictures of both.

The highlight of the one-hour flight came when Pilot Larry turned to us and asked, "Would you like to fly the blimp?" Are you kidding me? Fly the Goodyear Blimp? Of course, we would! At least Bill and I did. The ladies just wanted to be backseat pilots. We learned to go left and right with the rudder pedals, and up and down with the elevator wheel. What a super Texas high! Two Methodist ministers were like little kids on Christmas morning, or a pair of pastors preparing to proclaim the Easter good news, "He's up!" All good things of this world must end. Our ride was over after 60 memorable minutes.

After 23 years in Houston, Goodyear moved its airship operations in 1992 to Ohio, the home of Orville and Wilbur Wright, sons of a bishop in the United Brethren Church, a direct antecedent of The United Methodist Church. The pair of pastoral progenies pioneered human flight in 1903. While recently cleaning out folders in retirement, I came across the Aerial Ambassadors brochure and the Goodyear Blimp Club membership card signed by Captain Chambers in 1980.

Those faded blue cards mean nothing in what's to come, but they are glad reminders of a novel, uplifting experience provided by a pastor friend. Bill's generosity to experience a one-hour ride in the blimp may well one day be erased from my memory by my MCI. However, Jesus' generosity in inviting us to all share what's next will forever be etched in eternity. It will not be grounded after an hour of flying high in our beautiful balloon, blimp or Boeing Dreamliner 777. The Good Book has more than a good ending. It has a mighty assurance. After promising all things new in the verse above, the last chapter of the last book assures in the last verse, "The grace of the Lord Jesus Christ be with all the saints." That is a love whisper which includes you and me.

CRAZY THINGS IN A NEW CHURCH

You cannot expect everything to be just right in a church, especially in a new one where folks are learning on the job and not always completely on top of things. One summer we took 80 kids to church camp for a week at Lakeview Methodist Assembly near Palestine, Texas. There were two busses filled with kids, suitcases and pillows for any sleep that might be had or fights which might break out. The Summer Youth Director and I did our best to keep our fifth-twelfth graders happy, healthy and holy, though not necessarily in that order. Camp was awesome as always. Put 600 campers, counselors and staffers from Houston in the piney woods of East Texas and anything can happen and often does.

The week was wonderful, however. Kids made new friends from other churches. We played fun games, swam, hiked, sang camp songs, had altar calls, celebrated dedications, rededications and re-rededications to the Lord. Nobody was stung, sick, snake bit nor beamed up by satanic aliens to outer space. Everyone left with the joy of the Lord in his or her heart.

But something strange and scary happened. I can hardly believe this took place on my watch as associate pastor overseeing the Youth Ministry. When we pulled into the Klein Church parking lot after three hours on the buses sleeping, singing and sharing memories of the week, we began to unload bags of dirty clothes, sleeping bags and bags of candy. Parents and siblings ran to their short-lost children to hug and kiss them. Soon we realized there was a family waiting for their son to get off one of the buses.

When the buses were both empty, these parents stood with an empty stare and anxious heart. "Where is our son?" They asked. I was aghast, for I had apparently left a camper at camp! We called Lakeview Camp. They had no missing child. I knew that I must jump in the car, drive three hours back to Palestine and search 1,200 acres for Matt, the missing camper. This was 1981. There were no emails, cell calling, texts or instant messages in that ancient time. I was responsible for a missing child. Not a good way to be in the news. My short ministry might be over in short order!

As it turned out, Matt had somehow thought his parents were going to pick him up at Lakeview to begin their summer family vacation. His bad. Perhaps their bad. Nonetheless, Matt did not bother to get on one of the Klein buses to go home. My bad. Big bad! When his parents did not show up to pick him up at Lakeview, he hitched a ride with a new friend from another Houston area church. Matt anxiously called his anxious parents who called their very anxious young associate pastor that all was well. Lessons were learned and there was laughter at the end of the day. Youth are awesome. Young associate pastors can make mistakes and make amends. We all got a good laugh at the end of the day. Names have been changed to protect the guilty, except mine. Lessons learned. Time to move on.

Another crazy funny incident was at the Texas Annual Conference 1980 Ordination Service at the historic First United Methodist Church in downtown Houston. The sanctuary was packed for the for conference with 2,000 members and guests of the two dozen mostly men being ordained as Deacons and Elders. As I was being ordained, several members of Klein UMC drove in for the special Wednesday evening service to see their young associate pastor be ordained by Texas Conference Bishop Finis Crutchfield.

Apparently, there was a shortage of ushers for the full house, so several worshipers were tapped on the shoulder and asked to help take up the offering in the middle of the service. After all, where two or three Methodists gather together, they shall eat and take up an offering! One of the persons asked to pass the offering plate that evening was Jack Paige. Jack was a guest that evening, not even a Methodist. His wife Barbara was the Klein UMC secretary. So, here is this Roman Catholic guest taking up the offering at a United Methodist sacred ordination service in the heart of downtown Houston. Awkward as it was, Jack answered the call to serve by his Protestant brothers and sisters. We laughed for weeks at the church about the Catholic layman conscripted to collect the cash, checks and coins at the Protestant ordination service! Jack enjoyed the whole thing and relished the memory for years to come.

WORKING WITH WAYNE

Wayne Day was wonderful to entrust significant pastoral responsibilities to his young associate. Having been an associate pastor himself early in his ministry, he respected the role and its importance. He assigned me responsibility for youth, evangelism and teaching. The church grew exponentially in our thirty months, going from 600 to 1,400 members. We welcomed an average of seven new members each week. I learned from Wayne how to make prospect phone calls, visit homes and send notes to prospective members inviting them to commit to Christ and the Klein Church family.

One year we had 50 youth join on Confirmation Sunday. How do you pronounce l-o-n-g s-e-r-v-i-c-e? It was awesome! We started a new young couples class using cassette audio tapes from Focus on the Family. The Seekers Class is still going strong with 100 active members, though the average age has moved from 30 to 70 years young. One of its founding members was Rod Canion, cofounder of the Compaq Computer Company. Wayne had a large effect on Rod's highly successful entrepreneurial career.

Wayne graciously shared many prominent pastoral responsibilities with his young associate pastor. In my 30 months at Klein I preached 28 Sundays or special services, married 29 couples and preached or participated in eleven funerals or memorial services. The toughest thing to do as a pastor is to bury young adults and children. We did that way too much from car crashes, a plane crash on Easter Sunday evening, a homicide and sudden illnesses. One was a triple funeral. Eleven of the 13 deceased were 33 or younger. Suffice it to say we shared many tears and much faith together in our young congregation and community.

Wayne was an excellent pastoral role model for me in taking a day off during the week, going on a vacation each year, having a sport to play and having a non-anxious presence in challenging times. Prior to his appointment to launch the Klein Church, Wayne served a much more traditional church in East Texas which still had worship services Sunday morning and evening.

One first Sunday night at Troup UMC when Holy Communion was to be served, he uncovered the elements of grape juice and bread left on the altar table from the morning service. The pastor had a surprise. An army of ants had quietly invaded the gifts from God for the people of God. They were everywhere! The servant of God did not flinch, fail nor fold. Wiseman Wayne invited the hungry saints and forward and whispered in a low, loving voice, "The body of Christ given for you. Watch the ants. The blood of Jesus for you. Watch the ants." Perhaps Wayne winked with a wicked grin as he warned of the protein addition to the Last Supper. Remember this story the next time you come forward to receive the Eucharist. Smile as you receive the bread of life, the cup of salvation and perhaps some other good gifts of God. Maybe you will be blessed with some echoes of mercy and whispers of love.

RECEIVING PASTORAL AND CONGREGATIONAL CARE

We had just begun our third year of service at Klein when the call came on a Thursday afternoon. Our youth staff had been working all week to get ready to leave early the following Monday morning for summer church camp at Lakeview. I was set to serve as senior high co-director with good pastor friend and youth ministry guru Wayne Middleton from Kingwood UMC. The call was from my parents. They told me my brother had been in a serious car crash in Dallas. They were unclear on the details but asked me to travel the four hours to Dallas with them to be with Gilbert, his wife and their young son. Waynes Day and Middleton blessed my leaving immediately to make the four-hour drive north ASAP to be with family and a fatal date with fate.

As we later learned, my brother had been T-boned by a fugitive being pursued by two Dallas Police Department officers who had the man stopped on suspicion of trying to pass a forged prescription. Failing to follow proper

124

police procedures, the cops carelessly allowed the suspect to drive off and evade arrest. That is until the high-speed police chase needlessly began and suddenly and unbelievably ended when my physician brother had the life knocked out of him as the fugitive's car broadsided Gilbert's Mazda. My brother never regained consciousness. A week later, Friday August 7, our family chose to take him off life-support and give him back to God. Easy? Hell, no! Necessary? Heavens, yes! Earth has no sorrow which heaven cannot heal.

Love more than whispered when Pastor Wayne Day, his wife Marta and dozen or more members of the Klein Church family showed up to attend the service of death and resurrection for Gilbert in North Dallas. I only pray the blessed comfort of their powerful presence never ever fades from my declining memory. That prayer has already been answered, come to think about it. After all, the Great Physician promised, "I will not leave you comfortless."

We returned to our home very soon, as well as to the Klein church community. In April we had welcomed a precious daughter at Methodist Hospital in Houston. A three-year-old and a baby brought endless joy and loads of wash to our parsonage. Birth and death had both come our way in a few short months in 1981. What could possibly happen to our young family now to change things our life in a most profound way? Did someone say the "M" word? Bingo! Though we did not know it at the time, an unexpected move was coming our way at the end of the year. The Methodist method of moving ministers was about to make its mark.

A Call from the North

In early December 1981, I received a most surprise call from my former boss at First Methodist Church in Orange. He had given me my first God job in the summer of 1972, as well as inviting me back to serve as his summer associate, sans seminary, in 1975. "The Hustler" was calling to hustle me again! Rev. Walter "Doc" Klingle, now the Texarkana District Superintendent, needed a pastor to serve a strong historic church in his district beginning January 1982. Mid-year pastoral changes often mean one of several things, none of them good. The parting pastor has died, divorced, misbehaved or become disabled in some way. Stuff happens. Pastors are human. Fortunately, none of these was the case. Though Pastor Joe M. Wilson had been in his appointment for only six months, he had trained to become a hospital chaplain. When an opening came at a major medical center in the Dallas-Fort Metroplex, this pastor was accepted and appointed to the position.

Enter the Hustler again asking me to leave a young church which was happy and growing and where my family was happy and growing, to move to a congregation which was begun the year the Republic of Mexico defeated the Republic of Texas at the Battle of the Alamo. For non-Texans, the year was 1836.

I do not remember the exact process of making the decision to accept the surprise opportunity but do remember consulting with wise Wayne who had to make a similar decision to leave an associate position and pastor his own church full time. While it was very painful for Sharon and me to part the vibrant Klein Church family and move far from my still grieving parents, we made the move without many tears, fears or jeers. Bottom line: It was hard to say yes, yet impossible to say no. God told Abram to relocate to the Promised Land, "Go from your country and your country and your kinfolks. I will bless you and be with you." And that is the gospel truth, whispered in love across generations of God's people.

From New to Old

Moving from Harris County to Bowie County in far northeast Texas at the beginning of 1982 was akin to relocating from New York City to Mayberry, USA. Upon arrival in DeKalb we noticed the slower pace of talking, walking and living. We loved it! One hears more whispers of grace when not having the pedal to the metal most waking hours. No one seemed to hurry, worry or scurry about as if being busy was a virtue. Waiting in line at the post office, bank and grocery was a time to visit with neighbors, discuss the weather and comment on last Sunday's sermon or next Sunday's Cowboys game.

FAMILY TIES

In a town the size DeKalb, everyone seems to be related in some way to scores of others. Whether in-laws or out-laws, there were generations of folks who stayed home, came home after college or retirement or built a house down the street. One learns quickly not to speak disparagingly
of anyone, lest she or he be the second cousin of your hairdresser. That connection contributed to a sense of community, camaraderie and collegiality. Blacks and whites, old and young, rich and poor, old-timers and newcomers to DeKalb and its Methodist Church quickly learned to speak well of the living and the dead.

The ghosts of pastors past can also be a stumbling block. One previous popular pulpiteer came back to visit DeKalb on several occasions. I will call him Brother Billy. Everyone loved Brother Billy and he loved everyone. His frequent returns to his former parish were cut short one day when he a met a lady on the street. He asked with her great gusto, "Mrs. Jones, how is Mr. Jones doing?" The shocked woman stopped and stuttered, "Brother Billy, don't you remember? You buried him two years ago." Pastors, beware, especially if you have MCI!

CHURCH TIES

Congregations in small towns are tight. Members care for one another, visit one another, call one another, encourage one another and pray for one another. They do these things because they love each another. While those tasks are primary in a pastoral portfolio, sometimes it is the shepherd's family who is on the receiving end of congregational care. As the title of a book I was required to read for my elder ordination, *They Cry, Too* notes, pastors and their families are eventually wounded by pain or grief.

Indeed, that happened in our time in DeKalb. Sharon's father, a highly decorated U.S. World War II pilot, worked for Sun Oil Company for 37 years. He retired in the fall of 1983. Soon after retirement he began having pain and blackouts. Eventually he was diagnosed with a malignant brain tumor. Dennis died three months later in a Tulsa hospital on December 21. We had a five-year-old and a two-and-a-half-year-old at the time. I was planning to lead worship Christmas Eve and Christmas Day Saturday and Sunday services in DeKalb prior to getting the word of his unexpected passing.

When Noble and Robbie Bates, father and son lay leaders in the church and local funeral directors, learned of our loss, they came immediately to our parsonage and said, "You take the church van so you can carry and cover the Santa gifts and get to Beaumont to plan and prepare for the funeral. We will take care of the Christmas services here." What a welcome gift! That is what we did. It all seemed like a dream as there was snow and ice on the roads. The love, thoughts and prayers of the Bates family and the DeKalb Church family surrounded, supported and sustained our grieving family in that surreal seasonal experience of a timely birth and an untimely death. After the Christmas Eve funeral and burial in Beaumont, we went to our home church to light candles, receive communion and sing, "All is calm, all is bright…Christ the Savior us born." His birth whispered love, peace and hope when we needed those gifts most.

A week later when we returned to DeKalb, six inches of snow was still on the ground. The Bates family invited our young children to join theirs in sledding down the U.S. Hwy 259 overpass embankment near their home. After seemingly hours of laughing, careening down the icy, snowy paths and crying happy tears, we adjourned to the Bates home for hot chocolate and a warm fire. What a fine, fun way to begin the new year 1984! Church ties are ties which bind forever, echoing mercy and whispering love.

METHODIST TIES

The year 1984 marked the bicentennial of Methodism in America. The Methodist movement migrated from England to the colonies in the eighteenth century and was spread through the tireless efforts of young circuit-riding pastors. The frontier was a rough place to preach, teach and do outreach. The average age at death of these bearers of good news was 26 years. Inspired by the evangelical messages of John Wesley and the spirited hymns of his brother

Charles, Methodism spread, even amid the political revolution taking place in the colonies. The Methodist Church in America organized itself into being at a Christmas Conference at Lovely Lane Chapel in Baltimore, Maryland in 1784.

The DeKalb UMC celebrated the first 200 years of the Methodist Church in America by inviting John Wesley to come to its sanctuary to address the Texarkana District on a cold Sunday night in January 1984. Over 260 souls packed the place to welcome Wesley to America. Also known as Bill Vance, a commercial airline pilot and member of a Dallas-area United Methodist congregation, Mr. Wesley stilled and stirred the souls of all the saints who gathered that memorable evening. In honor of ten score years of American Methodism, Mr. Wesley was gracious to stay and share the unofficial social sacrament of coffee and cookies before departing by horseback or plane or both.

Four months later the DeKalb Church sent Sharon and me by plane to be official observers at the 1984 Bicentennial Methodist General Conference in Baltimore. What a blessing to attend the grand pageant of 200 years of Methodist mission and ministry in the United States. Both Methodist Democrats and Republicans have served as U.S. presidents. Visits to Fort McHenry, the National Cathedral, the Capitol and the National Mall with all its monuments and memorials inspired our gratitude for spiritual and political freedoms. On top of all that, we were introduced to Maryland lump crab cakes. If they are not on the menu for the heavenly banquet, we will be not a little disappointed!

COMMUNITY TIES

The DeKalb Church was closely connected to its community. The United Methodist Women prepared and served at the church a lovely breakfast each spring for the graduating seniors of DeKalb High School. The congregation hosted a Community Vacation Bible School each summer for all children in the town. A Friday Night Fifth Quarter was held in the Church Fellowship Hall after all home football games for all high school students to have a safe place to gather.

The congregation participated in a Community Crusade at the high school football stadium one year. A popular, polished Baptist evangelist was brought in to rid our homes of drinking, smoking, dipping, chewing, cable TV and having lustful thoughts. Most all the churches in town promoted participation so everyone could get saved or saved again. I am not sure how successful it was, as another revival was already being discussed for down the road. Even if the faith being served was not totally healthy, the food and fellowship were always sweet gifts.

Another ecumenical experience shared with friends from DeKalb days was a road trip to New Mexico. What made this outing was the diversity of people and professions. We had a Methodist funeral director, pastor, pharmacist, farmer and bank president. Add to that an Episcopalian judge and a Catholic district attorney. Sounds like a joke on the way! The Methodists topped the high church folks five to two. We ecumenists shared the driving to and from Angel Fire. I do not remember anything about the skiing but will never forget witnessing a highspeed wreck occur just ahead of us on U.S. Highway 82 near Gainesville, Texas. It happened in a moment as suddenly a car went airborne and flipped on its top on the divided highway.

Praise God the undertaker and preacher were not needed to prepare the body and soul of the crash victim for what's next. The judge was the first out of our two vehicles and ably assessed the accident was not life threatening. It could have easily been a fatal accident. I have had two young adult young cousins die in car crashes. Too many ties to life have been severed too soon by driving too fast, without seatbelts or under the influence. Listen to the whispers of love to buckle up, slow down and stay sober. Bless be tie that bind our hearts and lives in the love of community, Christ, family and friends.

DEATH TIES

Death is the great leveler in life. The death rate is 100%. Even in small towns tragedies take their toll. In our less than four years in DeKalb it was my pastoral responsibility to conduct services for four families whose loved ones were gone too soon by any measure. While giving thanks for the lives of persons aged 100, 94, 90, and 89 years, I also presided over services of death and resurrection for precious children of God aged 45, 20, 12 and three years. Those are tough, tough. The deep gratitude for these young lives is sometimes surpassed by the deeper grief when the passing is sudden. I can testify from personal experience that it takes time to heal from any profound loss. The good news is that death does not have the last word. God does and it is a good word.

Two deaths of well-known persons brought national attention to DeKalb before and just after my service there. The first was that of popular actor Dan

Blocker who portrayed the affable Hoss Cartwright on the long running television series Bonanza (1959-1973). At six-feet four-inches and 300 pounds, Blocker was a commanding yet beloved presence in his character and in real life.

Prior to Bonanza he had served his country in the Korean War and was awarded a Purple Heart for being wounded in combat. He earned both bachelor's and master's degrees and taught school before his acting career. His life ended suddenly at age 43 in 1973 from a pulmonary embolism during a routine surgery. Blocker came to Beaumont when I was a child for a celebrity appearance at a major charity rodeo. I was thrilled to get him to sign a small green piece of paper. He wrote one word, *Hoss.* That was enough. I still have it after almost 60 years. He was a good guy on television and in real life. Born and buried in DeKalb, Blocker's life still echoes mercy and whispers love.

It was my pastoral privilege to visit and play dominoes with his mother Mary while pastoring in DeKalb. She loved to bake yeast rolls for her pastors. In addition to losing her son, she also lost a daughter who was twelve years old. One day on a visit at Mary's home, I asked how she could go forward so well with grief in losing two children. She took me over to the piano bench and had me sit down beside her. Then she began to play and sing these hopeful words "Count your blessings, name them one by one. Count your many blessings, see what God has done." Mary Blocker lived to be 98. She had a bonanza of faith and hope in the Lord.

The country's spotlight shone on tiny DeKalb again six months after our departure. On New Year's Eve 1985, a small DC-3 airplane crashed six miles west of town in a field belonging to the grandparents of our son's first grade classmate Dustin. Seven of the nine onboard died in the fiery crash. One was Ricky Nelson, a popular recording artist from the '60s and '70s, who with his parents Ozzie and Harriet and brother David starred on radio in the '40s and on television in the '50s and '60s. Their TV show, *The Adventures of Ozzie and Harriet,* was truly must-see TV. Ricky Nelson was posthumously inducted into Rock-and-Roll Hall of Fame and given a star on the Hollywood Walk of Fame. He was 45 years old.

FRIENDSHIP TIES

One of the great joys of serving in a small community is making new friends of all kinds, all of whom are wonderful gifts of God. These beloved saints and servants were stained-glass windows through whom God's light passed daily and generously to bless others and whisper love constantly. They included:

- Ancient church organist Hazel Mac who had been playing the instrument since God was young and could creatively conflate a church classic with a jazzy vaudeville tune to praise God in a scary good way.
- Retired County School Superintendent J.C. who served as Church Treasurer. J.C. did not mean *just cash, just checks,* or *just coins.* He would gladly receive your offering at any time, in any form for any good work in God's world.
- Lois who had a toenail ministry at the Sunny Acres Nursing Home. She went from room to room regularly to clip and care for the nails of the aged residents, reminding us of Jesus' serving his disciples by washing their feet.
- Eileen, a bank teller M-F and serving as our son's Sunday School teacher on the first day of the week.
- County School Superintendent Bob who followed J.C. in that position, and as Church Treasurer. He had a stern countenance yet accounted accurately for every good gift for God's good work.
- Martha, the church historian who did the legwork for over a year to enable the church to receive a Texas State Historical Marker celebrating its sesquicentennial year in 1986.
- Walter, husband of Martha, who built dulcimers when he was not assisting her on all things historical and hysterical. We still have a dulcimer he crafted for us.
- Nola and Art who were chronologically gifted church members, neighbors and onsite grandparents, affectionately called by our three-year old daughter, "Noah and the Ark."
- The Bates Family, pillars of the church and community, taking care of families compassionately for generations when death sooner or later came home.

You cannot buy friends such as these for any amount of money in the world. They are gracious gifts of a good God who first befriended us in his Son. In fact, Jesus called us his friends. He sticks to us tighter than family. (Proverbs 18:24) What a friend we have in Jesus. Somebody should write a song about that! That would be a true whisper of love.

From Old to New 2.0

The zigzag of my pastoral path was again pronounced when I learned while on a mission trip in Haiti in April 1985 that new Texas Conference Bishop Ben Oliphint was appointing me to launch a new congregation in the Houston North District. Can you say, "Scared spitless!"? My family was doing well in DeKalb. We loved the community, church and parsonage. I was writing a weekly "Parson to Person" column in the *DeKalb News* community newspaper. Sharon was teaching children of migrant workers in a rural school district. Our son was headed to second grade and our daughter to preschool. All was well.

Then the appointment came. We would be leaving a congregation with 149 years of history, vital mission and ministry, a strong cadre of leaders and teachers, a staff of five, a significant presence in the community, strong financial resources and a group of God's people who loved the Lord and their pastoral family. What, me move? Yes, we would be moving June 1 to launch a new congregation with no building, no members, no staff and no big stash of cash to make a splash! On top of that, Sharon and I had committed many months before to co-lead with three other clergy friends and their wives a 16-day Holy Land Tour and six-country Mediterranean Cruise with DeKalb Church members and friends in mid-June. Not the best timing!

LAYING THE FOUNDATION WITH ICE CREAM

Methodists have been whispering love and starting new congregations in this land for almost 250 years. It is not an exact science, however. Some new church plants are dead on arrival or struggle for years. Others strive, thrive and are alive for decades and centuries. After returning from the Holy Land and visiting its millennia-old faith communities, I attended with three dozen other new church pastors a Methodist Church Training Conference in Dallas, determined to learn how to plant and grow a thriving baby congregation which would endure.

The gurus who taught us included Methodist evangelist Eddie Fox and highly successful church planters Steve Sallee, Jeff Spiller and Jim Cowell. Their personal stories were inspiring and informative. Never did I dream in a few years I would speaking to groups of new church pastors in New Orleans and Chicago on how to start and grow a new church. My fine time at Klein certainly was very valuable, yet the experience of planting is unique, just like everyone's else's!

The five-acre plot in northeast Harris County for the planned Atascocita United Methodist Church was purchased in June 1984 by the Houston Methodist Board of Missions at a cost of $360,000. The new church was expected to repay the cost of the land in the future. The mission board provided funds for salary, housing and expenses for me for a year, as well as other start-up expenses.

I was most fortunate to have a creative colleague and co-conspirator in the bouncing baby church business. Rev. Charles Anderson, 30, was launching a new congregation 35 miles away in the Houston suburb of Katy at the same time. We chose to hold our first worship services on September 8, 1985, the first Sunday after Labor Day. For the next five years we talked every Sunday evening comparing attendance, offerings and new members. In our friendly competition and cooperation, we gained much from one another's ministries, methods and occasional miseries.

So how do you gather a nucleus of committed, called, caring folks together to sacrifice, serve and share their lives? Well, we tried Coffee Fellowships. Who wants to drink coffee in the hot Houston summer? We tried home Bible studies. Only a handful raised a hand for the Word handed from the Holy One. Then the word of the Lord came. Actually, two words. Ice cream! More specifically, Bluebell Ice Cream. The Little Creamery in Brenham, Texas had a distribution center in nearby Humble which sold the sinfully delicious Homemade Vanilla and other tantalizing flavors in three-gallon containers. We placed an ad in the local weekly paper inviting anyone interested in a new Methodist congregation to come to a Backyard Ice Cream Party at a home in the Atascocita community on August 18.

Fortuitously, the home of key lay leaders was adjacent to the Oaks Elementary School where Sunday services were to begin September 8. Guess what? Seventy-four persons showed up to learn about the new church and eat Bluebell ice cream. Not necessarily in that order! The best news is ten families committed to join the church. From then on, the new Atascocita United Methodist Church had an alternative name – Blue Bell UMC! "Miss Blue Bell" (AKA Carla Hopkins, supreme special education teacher) would later show up at AUMC anniversaries with her special southpaw scoop, Blue Bell costume and carton hat to serve children of all ages. Ice cream whispers love for many souls and stomachs, then and now almost 35 years later.

THE FOUR-SHIP CHURCH

Ice cream will get you only so far. Even popular Blue Bell proved its product could be dangerous. In 2015, Blue Bell issued its initial recall in its over 100-year history. The company called in an assortment of items produced in its creameries due to five cases of listeriosis in Kansas believed to be caused by products from its Broken Arrow, Oklahoma creamery. Three persons with listeria died. The business recovered and is going strong. With or without ice cream, new churches need four ships to launch, stay afloat and expand in service to its Spiritual Commander-in-Chief. Atascocita Church invested heavily in these ships to become an effective vessel for the spiritual voyage of over 900 adult passengers committed in its initial seven years.

THE SHIP OF FELLOWSHIP

The first ship is Fellowship. The fancy Greek name is *koinonia.* Fellowship is the gathering of God's people simply to be together in community, conversation and likely coffee. Though not a coffee consumer myself, I am a habitual eyewitness to the sacramental role of Sanka and the faith component of Folger's in your cup. Like the woman at the well, many Methodists get their cups filled physically and spiritually when they come together in beloved community.

Fellowship is inclusive, welcoming the up and in, the down and out and all in between. All churches are comprised of mixtures of saints and sinners. Fellowship in the church is a ship of fellow pilgrims on a faith journey. Wherever one is on the pilgrimage, he or she is welcome to come aboard. Fellowship at Atascocita UMC flowed around coffee pots, in parking lots, at New Member Fellowships in our home, in United Methodist Women gatherings, as well as adult, youth and children's choirs. Jesus had a way showing up, so to speak, when fellowships formed (Matthew 18:20).

THE SHIP OF WORSHIP

Ship two is Worship, ascribing glory to God in praise and thanksgiving for who God is and what God has done, is doing and will do for the children of God. Acts of worship often include praise through various musical instruments, singing, praying, kneeling, standing, lifting hands, bowing in humility and giving offerings of time, talent and treasure. Like nautical ships, worship will usually be smooth sailing, shared with others, and move us forward in a helpful way. The biblical Book of Psalms is a worship guide packed with songs of praise and adoration, petition and confession, repentance and renewal, liturgy and love. Fellowship is a part worship, yet worship goes deeper with spiritual transformation and regeneration.

THE SHIP OF DISCIPLESHIP

The third ship is Discipleship. Followers of Jesus are called disciples. Disciples are formed, grown and nurtured in Sunday School classes, small groups, choirs, Bible studies, prayer teams and accountability partners. It was exciting to see folks of all ages grow and mature in their faith. Jesus commanded his followers to make disciples from all kinds of folks.

In southeast Texas, not the most progressive place in the land, we welcomed, baptized and discipled black, brown, yellow and white folks. We received many people by profession of faith and reaffirmation of faith, as well as by transfer of membership. Ten Sunday school classes for all ages were launched within a month after the first public service. Volunteer teachers did their best discipling with all ten classes meeting in two large rooms, the gymnasium and cafeteria of an elementary public school. They did pretty darn well, as at least five members from the school days heard and answered a call to ordained ministry.

THE SHIP OF STEWARDSHIP

The fourth and final ship is Stewardship. Atascocita UMC could not meet in a school forever, even though the rent was a bargain at $100 a week. We needed money also for modest salaries, programs, publicity and rental office space. We wanted to be involved in outreach in the community and in Methodist mission work in the state, nation and world.

Inviting persons to give generously, many of them young families, was no small task. The concept of stewardship is a biblical one which teaches that we are not owners, but stewards or caretakers of our money, possessions and even our bodies. Stewardship is summed up in four single syllable words, "God owns it all." With that foundation, inviting new members to give generously to a new congregation with no building was done regularly and unapologetically. We wanted to grow and be good stewards from Day One!

LAUNCHING THE NEW SHIP

Our seven-person Steering Committee ran ads in the local paper. We prayed. We rang doorbells took brochures to over 500 homes in the community. We prayed some more. The week before the first service we mailed a newspaper to every home in the community inviting all to share in a new beginning. The choir of six prepared an anthem. A small nursery with three playpens was set up in the corner of the gym. Bulletins were printed. Greeters and ushers were trained. We had commitments of at least 50 folks to attend.

Would they bail out at the last minute? Would anyone show up on the second Sunday of September 1985? A few days later I would turn 33. Would it be a happy birthday? My mother and father were driving over from Beaumont. Would they be embarrassed? I know they were worried few folks would want to worship in an elementary school. The seven members of the Steering Committee and their families were sure to be present. The District Superintendent was all in and would attend. We were hoping and praying to have a hundred persons present to launch the newest ship in the fleet in the Lord's navy.

The launch was memorable for all the right reasons. Over 300 persons attended! We were late launching as folks flowed in and filled the cafeteria. Some skateboarders outside breezed by, curious about the crowd inside. The weather was perfect. The sky was Houston Oiler baby blue. The District Superintendent, Bill Jones, brought episcopal greetings from Bishop Ben Oliphint. In true Methodist fashion a Covered Dish Luncheon - something of a Methodist sacrament in the South - was set to be served. The meal was hijacked by a miracle. When I gave the invitation to Christian Discipleship and Church Membership, 153 persons came forward to join the new church. My amazed mother declared, "It looked like an altar call at a Billy Graham Crusade!" Whispers of love flowed and filled a school cafeteria one sunny September Sunday morning. Lives were redirected and changed forever by an amazing church launch. Love did not just whisper. It shouted, "All are welcome."

CRAZY STUFF HAPPENS

Funny and strange things happen when a congregation worships in a school. One Sunday morning the piano on the stage was locked. Used to accompany the choir and the congregation, the instrument was essential. There was no custodian on hand that day with a key to help. In a moment of brute strength and frustration, a choir member ripped open the piano lock to the cheers of the choir director and members. Destruction of school property is not normally nice and accepted behavior. In this case, however, the destroyer was Dr. Michael Say, the Humble School District Superintendent and member of the church choir!

On another Sunday when the service was over and designated families were completing the cleanup and setup of the cafeteria, a man entered the school with a gun. He meant business. He was surprised to see us, and we were surprised to see him! After a moment of awkward and anxious confrontation, we were relieved to learn he was an off-duty deputy who happened to be driving by and was suspicious of folks in the school on a Sunday afternoon. We were all relieved we were on the same team to serve the community. No harm, no foul.

A weekly challenge we endured for 39 months in an elementary school was the location of the bathrooms. The only restrooms available to us opened directly into the worship space. We had lots of children each Sunday. When nature called, the kids answered, flushed and flew back to their seats with the residual sounds and smells of the restrooms not whispering love and peace during the pastoral prayer or sermon! Nonetheless, the Oaks Elementary School was home. So much so that the first memorial service of a member of the new church was on a Friday evening in the cafeteria. Jesus said, "Where two or three are gathered together up my name, there I am in among them."

SERVING THE COMMUNITY

Congregations do not exist for themselves. Long before it had a permanent home, Atascocita UMC was making a difference in the community. We launched a highly successful Boy Scout Troop 56. We expanded our physical presence by renting space for offices, meetings and choir practice. The building was small, drab and behind a carwash. Best of all, it was inexpensive. Lamar Smith, our second District Superintendent jokingly called it "St. Michael's at the Car Wash." Shortly after the church began the energy industry went in the tank. Many folks were laid off. Soon we began a Job Loss Support Group in the community with a job bank, counseling and support group.

Our Methodist Men initiated a monthly Saturday morning trash cleanup along Farm to Market Road 1960, a busy four-lane highway bisecting the community. We learned a lot about humanity by the items trashed intentionally or inadvertently. The fellowship was fantastic, and the garbage was ghoulish.

The church family held its first annual Fall Fun Festival in the Atascocita Town Center on its third anniversary in September 1988. Games, food, entertainment, celebrity athletes and more highlighted the fundraiser benefitting the church and community. Several of the men and women in our

138

congregation served in the Atascocita Volunteer Fire Department. They kindly invited me to serve as their chaplain. Many of them were professionals in the Houston Fire Department. Others went for training and drills on weekends. Being a chaplain on a fire or car crash scene is grim work. Our calls often involved children and youth. Growing up in church we often sang, "Rescue the perishing, care for the dying..." That is what is what fire and emergency teams do. I will always treasure the Atascocita Volunteer Fire Department Badge they gave me to keep when I was transferred in 1992. It was a genuine honor to serve the community with those almost 100 men and women volunteers for six years.

The new congregation joined a small local number of congregations in launching an interfaith coalition to provide food, clothing, medical care, job training and other support. Known as HAAM for Humble Area Assistance Ministries, the mission of help and hope was launched in 1986 and is still going strong. Google to get the latest good work by God's guys and girls. The infant church received its initial mission offering on October 9, 1985, giving $250 for earthquake relief in Mexico. It was the first of many second-mile financial asks in the next seven years.

BRINGING IN THE BIG BOYS

How do you bring in big crowds when the newness subsides? One way is to invite special guest speakers. Promote a special occasion with a big name. Who was more special to preach at our Charter Sunday Service in January 1986 than our resident episcopal leader, Bishop Ben Oliphint? When he came to preach, the cafeteria was packed, 19 persons joined the church and the Charter Membership closed with 180 full members and 84 preparatory members. On our second anniversary we invited Dr. Charles L. Allen, retired Senior Pastor of the fabled First United Methodist Church in downtown Houston to preach. Dr. Allen authored more than 40 books, including the best-selling *God's Psychiatry,* conducted more than 30 tours of the Holy Land and preached on five continents. Over 400 souls shared his sermon in the Oaks Elementary School cafeteria.

A couple years later we welcomed Dr. Allen's popular successor, Dr. Bill Hinson, also a Georgia native. Bill was a compelling communicator for the cause of Christ. We rejoiced to welcome another prominent Bill to our pulpit in our Lenten series. He was not a pastor, but a highly successful college football coach. Bill Yeoman led his University of Houston teams to eleven bowl games and four Southwest Conference championships, as well as being elected to The College Football Hall of Fame and Texas Sports Hall of Fame. He would be the first to tell you that his chance to glorify Christ was far more important than any football glory.

BUILDING A HOME

Not many congregations last long without a permanent place to call home. The church continued grow in the early years, but we knew a building would was necessary to reach the community significantly for decades to come. Our goal was to complete plans, raise money and finish the facility within three years, an aggressive yet achievable accomplishment. A Long-Range Planning Committee met for nine months. Its report was adopted in September 1986. After several interviews with three Houston architectural firms, one was chosen to do a Campus Master Plan with an attractive building, parking, outdoor attractions and all the normal public spaces.

To erect such an edifice was more than we could likely raise from a congregation of our size. Planning, patience, prayer and putting piles of provisions in the plate would all be required. And one more thing: a Baptist brother named Wimpy. We interviewed several capital campaign consultants and choose Wimpy Smith to assist us in moving our members' money from their pocket, stocks, bonds and bank accounts to build a new mission station in the community.

Working with Wimpy was a wonderful way to go. He led us, challenged us and encouraged our congregation to give generously. We set three goals in early 1987: a $250,000 Challenge Goal, a $350,000 Victory Goal and $450,000 Hallelujah Goal. That is the one you shout "Hallelujah" if you make it. We prayed. Members gave testimonies. We gave sacrificially. The Together We Build campaign in the spring of 1987 yielded over $550,000 in gifts and commitments. Fellow new church pastor Charles Anderson declared we hit the "Shazam Goal"! The word miracle comes to mind. It would be another sixteen months before the construction was complete.

We wept at a disappointing delay when we were just a couple of weeks from opening. Late one night a group of neighborhood boys unconnected to the church broke into the building and defecated on the newly laid carpet, drew satanic symbols on the walls with spray paint and destroyed the tools of the construction workers. A Houston TV news channel carried reports of the vandalism, including footage of the demonic defacing of the dwelling place of

140

the Divine. All four gospel accounts reflect Jesus was not happy when God's house was misused. I can promise you some church members were quite unhappy when God's new house was abused. It is good the authorities apprehended the offenders before some of God's unhappy children did. Repentance, restitution and rehabilitation followed, not necessarily in that order.

Finally, after 39 months of meeting in the school, the Atascocita UMC family held its first service in its new home on December 11, 1988. Over 600 saints shared the celebration, overflowing a worship space designed to hold 400. How do you spell S-R-O? Sixteen new members joined on that historic Sunday. A month later Bishop Oliphint retuned to preach at the Building Consecration Service and Community Open House. Cornerstone membership closed that day with 41 persons joining the church when the invitation was given. The growth continued after the building was opened. Membership reached 500 in April 1989.

A year later at Easter over 1,000 souls shared the joy of the resurrection in three services. The church added an associate pastor, Cub Scout Pack and Parents Day Out ministry. On the fifth anniversary of Atascocita Church we welcomed renowned Bishop John Wesley Hardt to celebrate that milestone. He was a prominent pastor and role model for 18 years in my hometown of Beaumont. Bishop-in-Residence at the Perkins School of Theology, he was warmly welcomed at Atascocita Church in September 1990. The heavenly hosts welcomed him into the Church Eternal in June 2017 at age 95. He was a spiritual hero to me and many. Go online to learn more of this winsome servant of Christ who still echoes mercy and whispers love to countless souls.

TERMINAL DEGREE: ALCOHOL AND METHODISTS

What does a pastor do after investing heavily for four years in a new church plant? Some move on after construction is complete. I chose to stay and simultaneously enroll in a new a minimum three-year Doctor of Ministry degree program at SMU's Perkins School of Theology. Sharon was teaching and our children were in school. Why not go back to grad school? The DMin (not DEMON!) degree could be earned in three to seven years by attending three weeks of intense study in the first summer on campus in Dallas, fall and spring classes in Houston for two years and completing a minimum one year-long approved project in one's ministry setting.

My parents were generous and gracious to invest in my further graduate education. The Atascocita UMC leadership and my bride also blessed my entrance into a challenging new chapter. All of us would be invested and stretched for at least three years.

Being in school in Dallas was not all bad. While there the Boston Red Sox came to town for a three-game series with the Texas Rangers. I called Rac Slider (what a great baseball name!) who was a member of DeKalb UMC and third base coach of the Beantown team. His wife went with us to the Holy Land in 1985. I asked Rac if he could get me a couple of tickets to one of the games. "Which game?" He asked. "Any of them," I replied. He immediately said, "How about all three?" "Are kidding me? That would be awesome!" So, for three warm Texas nights I sat along the third baseline in baseball heaven enjoying the entire series. It beat the heck out of reading a Practical Theology textbook. Besides, I invited my professor, Dr. Stan Menking, to attend one of the games!

I loved being back in the classroom but living in a college dorm for three weeks in my mid-thirties was not the highlight of my life. What a joy to get home to my wife, kids and pulpit. I missed them all three. The two years of group study met monthly for a couple of days of classes, conversation and contemplation in a Houston church near Hobby Airport. The professors flew in from Dallas. We students drove in for the gatherings three times each fall and spring for two years. The accessibility of the faculty members, the comfortable church setting, investment of the students and the extended time together made for holy conversations and deep reflection and growth.

The key to completing the doctoral degree was the selection and approval of a proper professional project. For years in church and society I had witnessed and wrestled with the conflicted professions and practices of people regarding alcohol consumption. From abstinence to moderation to inebriation, I had witnessed and experienced a range of beliefs and behaviors in the Methodist faith community. Under the approval and supervision of my doctoral committee comprised of theology professor Dr. Leroy Howe, clinical psychologist Dr. Ron Hopkins and prominent pastor Dr. Bill Scales, I planned, executed and analyzed an extensive project entitled *Identifying, Measuring, and Seeking to Modify Actions and Attitudes about Alcohol in the Life of a Local Suburban United Methodist Church*. With the major assistance of a ten member Project Task Force from the congregation, the effort was completed on time and awarded with distinction.

An average of 225 adults and youth joined together in seminars in the sanctuary on seven consecutive Sundays in the fall of 1991 to listen to a variety of speakers, share personal experiences and complete pretest and posttest surveys. The timely themes in the presentation and discussion sessions included:

A Look at Alcohol in History, the Bible, Church and Today

Physical and Psychological Factors in Alcohol Use, Misuse, Abuse

A First-Person Account of Alcoholism, Recovery, and the Church

Moderation and Abstinence as Faithful Witnesses for Christians Today

Alcohol and the Family: Parent and Youth Attitudes About Alcohol

Key Learnings about alcohol and the church from the 156-page project were:
1. Education makes a difference.
2. People will participate.
3. There is a need for such seminars.
4. Resources are available.

The Final Word from the 156-page, 12-month professional project: All key learnings have been encouraging. My own knowledge and comfort level regarding alcohol and related issues have increased greatly as a result of this project. What the people of God called the church must never lose sight of is this reality: We are called to minister with compassion, concern and care, and provide hope, healing and help for the abstainer, the moderate drinker and the problem drinker all three.

On May 16, 1992, I was hugely honored and humbled to have my parents, wife, children, church members and friends come to Dallas to share the joy of graduation. We were blessed to have longtime Texan and sitting President of the United States George H.W. Bush speak. I will never forget that the most powerful man in the world quoted from the New Testament, calling on the graduates and all present, "Let us love, not in word and speech, but in truth and action."

Love whispers do not always come with words and promises. Love is let loose in action. No words necessary. Two weeks after graduation, time was up. After seven amazing years in Atascocita, I was being sent by Bishop Oliphint to a 50-year-old congregation. It did not seem right. It was not fair. I was just learning to spell and pronounce A-T-A-S-C-O-C-I-T-A. How many nine-letter words do you know which have five syllables? That's I thought. By the way, do you even know what "Atascocita" means? How about "boggy land"? Look it up. We did move to a new ministry in June 1992. It was hard to leave friends, founders and faithful souls. They blessed us to invite me back to preach on several significant Anniversary Sundays across the years. We look forward to the fiftieth anniversary in 2035! Go online to Atascocita UMC to get a glimpse of God's girls and guys doing good stuff to and whispering love to this day.

From New to Mid-Century

My next pastoral assignment was only 34 miles from Atascocita, yet it was a major change for our family and the congregation to which we were appointed. Change can be good, and change can be hard. This one was both. Bellaire United Methodist Church was an early Baby Boomer, born September 22, 1946 in the Condit Elementary School, probably in the cafeteria, I am guessing. The congregation moved in 1948 into a home of its own, a surplus World War II army chapel purchased from Aloe Field in Victoria, Texas. The military Methodist meeting place served for ten years before a large modern sanctuary was built in the heart of Bellaire, a small island community founded in 1908 and surrounded by Houston and adjacent to West University Place. Mainline Protestantism peaked in America in the sixties. Bellaire UMC's membership exceeded 3,700 at its apex with an average weekly attendance of 1,100. A pipe organ was installed in 1963.

Despite strong clergy and lay leadership over the next several decades, the congregation dropped in attendance and membership by 50%. With the Vietnam War, assassinations, student protests, Watergate and the rise of religious and poll conservatism, mainline Protestant congregations suffered sharp declines. The Bellaire church was no exception. In 1992 its pastor decided after four years there he was ready to retire. He was none other than Doc Klingle, my former boss whom I served under for two summers in 1972 and 1975. Doc was now in his mid-sixties and I was still in my thirties. Change was coming. Change can be good. Change can be hard. Yet love whispers hope in transitions, turmoil, teenagers and teams.

TRANSITION: *CHANGE IS NECESSARY, MISERY IS OPTIONAL*

The move from a member of the Silent Generation to a Baby Boomer in the pulpit brings change. When a new pastor walks around, wears a costume (even a biblical one), speaks fast, tells funny stories, cries in the pulpit, or has moments of silent reflection, it can be disconcerting to some saints. Every preacher has her or his style and methods of communication. It took the Bellaire saints a little time to adjust to a faster pastor in the pulpit. Some Sundays a preacher has a 30-minute message and only 20 minutes to deliver it. However, I did learn in 44 years of preaching no one complained about a sermon being too short.

Our very capable associate pastor was ten years younger than I. Never will

I will forget the Sunday Scott remarked to me after the service, "You were smoking today!" His comment had nothing to with "cigars, cigarettes or tiparillos," but the sizzling sentiments in the sermon, now long forgotten. A prominent preaching professor pushed his students to do three things in the pulpit: "Rise high, strike fire and sit down." Enough said.

Transition was occurring not only in the church, but also in the community. Bellaire was becoming the hot spot for young urban professionals (yuppies) pouncing on properties convenient to downtown Houston, the Texas Medical Center, the Galleria Shopping mecca and major sports venues. Physicians, attorneys and business executives were buying small, older homes and "popping the top" (adding a second or third floor) or building "McMansions," expensive edifices stretching as close to the lot lines as possible. A star member of the Houston Rockets lived a block from the church. His son attended our School for Little Children. Lot values skyrocketed, as did taxes.

Church founders were moving away to live with children, in nursing homes or with God in priceless houses out of this world (II Corinthians 5:1). As the community upgraded its residences, so did the church recognize the need to prepare for the future with additional facilities, parking and egress. Transition is threatening to a few folks in the family of faith. Fortunately, they were few. Unfortunately, a few folks outside the family but not outside the neighborhood created and contributed to craziness and turmoil in the community. As love whispers, sometimes the opposite of love shouts. Never in my zaniest moments in ministry did I ever expect to be engaged with angry neighbors shouting, strutting and sarcastically seeking to shut down the building plans of the church I was leading.

TURMOIL: *RELIGIOUS RIGHTS FIGHTS IN CITY HALL*

As BUMC lay leaders, architects and senior pastor brought the church's plans to the city officials for routine required review in November 1995, we learned we had opposition from a handful of nearby neighbors (particularly one) regarding a proposed building, parking lot expansion and accessibility to our property. What seemed like a routine request soon evolved into a tense, tumultuous turmoil. The controversy expanded exponentially when the local weekly newspaper serving the southwest Houston area made it front page news and the local cable system televised the Bellaire City Council and Planning and Zoning Commission meetings. Talk about "Must See TV"!

146

A front-page article in the *Southwest News* began with this quote from one of our church lay leaders and an attorney. "You would think with all this hoopla, we were trying to put in a gentleman's cabaret." The story reported over that 200 members of the church crowded into the council chamber and stretched into the city hall lobby on January 22. The show of support was for a request for a permit in response to a process which had dragged on for over two months. Who said church life is boring? Merry Christmas and Happy New Year!

The article stretched on to three pages, included a picture of my holding plans for the construction and called the turmoil a "good drama." The curtain came down on the show after four months when Bellaire City Council approved the construction permit. All is well which ends well. The concerns of the eight protesting neighbors were heard, addressed and satisfied. I should have picked up a law degree at SMU.

TEENAGERS: *TRANSITION, TRIBULATION, TRANSPORTATION*

One of the challenges of being a PK ("preacher's kid") is being compelled to move from to time. There are blessings from moving, as well as staying in put. In the spirit of Psalm 16:6, "The boundaries have fallen for me in pleasant places," our son and daughter relocated in 1992 when each was at a time of transition. Our son was beginning high school and our daughter middle school. Both would be in grades where many other students would be discovering new friends, faces, campuses and classes. Their transition was eased further by their new friends in Sunday School and Youth Group for three months before the first bell rang.

Bellaire High School became our son's academic home the next four years. Nicknamed "Hebrew High" for the large Jewish population in the community, BHS was the language magnet school for Houston ISD. The school taught classes in Mandarin, Hebrew, Russian, Latin, German, French and Spanish. Our son studied Spanish, but confesses he learned more of the language from the cooks in Jax Grill in Bellaire than he did in the classroom.

As with many high school boys, our son's major rite of passage was the purchase of his first set of wheels, a shiny red 1984 CJ Jeep. I must confess I enjoyed taking a spin in it from time to time! The only difference between men and boys... He did learn a painful lesson of the human condition one afternoon when he discovered his pride and joy had been keyed by an unkind classmate. His words about the perpetrator were stronger than mine.

Our son did survive one life-alarming tribulation in our time in Bellaire. Early one morning his ritual of getting ready for school was suddenly interrupted and reversed. Immediately he appeared with a stunned look on his face. He had encountered a small poisonous copperhead snake coming up of the bathroom tub drain as he was turning on the water to begin his shower. By that evening you can bet that the church handyman had come to the parsonage to ensure no reptiles would be baptized in the Bellaire parsonage henceforth and forevermore.

Our young daughter had her own transportation tribulation soon after beginning her Houston ISD education at Johnston Middle School. One afternoon when riding her bicycle in our Meyerland neighborhood she was struck by an automobile operated by an apparently distracted driver. We were alarmed as our dear daughter was transported by ambulance to the Texas Medical Center where she required emergency care. Thankfully, she recovered quickly, and all ended well. It was a tough way to get a new bicycle. We were relieved. The driver's insurance company issued a very modest settlement check for the bicycle and our daughter which went into her college savings account. We were grateful to move on but knowing what we know now about billionaire insurance companies, perhaps we should have sought a more significant settlement sum. All's well ends well.

Being students in the Houston ISD and at Bellaire High School gave our children important exposure to diversity at all levels. There was respect, inclusion and appreciation for students of many colors, languages, customs, diets, religious expressions, native lands and socioeconomic levels. Their public education in those four years were formative in preparing them for higher education at Emory University, Texas A & M University and Texas Tech University Law School.

TEAMS: *CHAMPIONS IN SPORTS AND LIFE*

What a time to reside in Bellaire-Southwest Houston! The venues for the four major Houston professional sports teams were all ten miles or less from our home. Tickets for the Astros (baseball), Oilers (football), Aeros (hockey) and Rockets (basketball) were often not too hard to come by.

Sports in major American cities and other countries are good tonic for community *esprit de corps,* often providing entertainment, escape and existential engagement. Competition, courage and camaraderie show up when athletes show up. Though paid to play, many athletes are motivated by more

148

than the money. The drive to do one's best, play as a team and advance in the playoffs is occasionally achieved. Yet, to win a championship is an elusive goal for many athletes.

No major Houston professional team had won two consecutive championships until the Rockets did so in the National Basketball Association in the 1993-1995 seasons. Our family went to the Astrodome to celebrate the Houston team's victories. Over 50,000 of our most close personal friends from across the city came to share the cheers, chants, shouts, videos and the parade of players and politicians. Star Hakeem Olajuwon could have been elected Houston mayor and Coach Rudy T was a shoo-in for police chief. In 2017 the Astros won the World Series and city of went bonkers again.

Although the Houston Texans football team has never won a Super Bowl in its almost twenty years of history, no one can forget the efforts of its All-Pro defensive star player J.J. Watt to raise $37,000,000 dollars for Hurricane Harvey relief efforts after the monster storm flooded the Houston area. It is good to be a champion in sports. It is even better to be life-enhancing hero in the game of life.

BTW, the Bellaire High School Cardinals won the Texas State Baseball Championship in 1994. Two of their star players were active members of Bellaire United Methodist Church. They were champions on the field, in the classroom and in their faith journeys. Thanks, Garrett and Taylor, for bringing it home!

One more team from our time at Bellaire Church merits mention without question. Though it made no headlines in the community newspaper nor had much mention in congregational communications, the church launched an AIDS Care Team during our ministry together. Few congregations were jumping on the bandwagon to care for the sick, and often the dying. This team, and later another, was trained by personnel from the Institute of Religion in the Texas Medical Center to walk with persons in the community living with AIDS. While there was some fear, anxiety and judgment of persons living with the condition, Bellaire UMC believed in caring for persons in pain, be it physical, emotional or spiritual.

A select group of church members were vetted to receive their training by personnel from the Institute of Religion at the Texas Medical Center. The need was significant, and another team was vetted, trained and deployed in the community. The compassionate service rendered by these teams was life-enhancing for all it touched. These AIDS Care Teams followed the command of Jesus to care for the sick. Team members offered whispers of love to children of God, some abandoned by their birth families.

I am certain some of our AIDS Care Team folks may have heard remarks from a few church members about the care ministry such as, "I would not do that for a million dollars." And those who did it would not do it for a million dollars either. But for love they would, and for love they did. And Jesus said, "When you did it to one of the least of my brothers or sisters, you did it me." These teams truly echoed mercy and whispered love.

BELLAIRE BONUS BLESSINGS

Several special surprises came our way during our years in Bellaire. Almost immediately after our arriving in our parsonage on Ferris Drive, our new next-door neighbor came to greet us. Rabbi Moshe Cahana brought us a bottle of wine and a loaf of bread, signs of friendship. He was a retired reformed rabbi at a Meyerland neighborhood congregation. Moshe's wisdom, passion and moral fortitude reminded me of Rabbi Olan from seminary days. Over many years Rabbi Cahana was a progressive voice who graciously taught classes on Judaism at Bellaire United Methodist Church. His kindness, faith and wisdom were rich gifts to our family, church and the community.

His wife was a Nazi concentration camp survivor as a teenager. Alice Lok Canaha used her artistic gifts to interpret her Holocaust journey in a redemptive manner. Her work has hung in museums across the globe. Steven Spielberg paid tribute to her art in his documentary *The Last Days*. Go online to learn more about the blessed Cahana family.

On a much lighter note, on a very rainy night in Texas, I joined friend, neighbor, Bellaire church member and engineering professor John Glover at an outdoor rock concert in 1994 with 40,000 other baby boomers at the Rice University football stadium. In a lottery drawing for ticket purchase priority we hit the jackpot. The professor and preacher were pleased to plop down our plastic for a pair of tix on the fifth-row center stage for a show by two aging solo performers with biblical names. From the Bronx and the UK, Joel and John were piano men who played their and our songs that night. Thank you, Billy and Elton.

Methodist ministers move. Some move by choice of the pastor, and some by the choice of the congregation. Other times a move comes as a surprise to the church and pastor. I was completing my fourth year at Bellaire Church when a move rumor became a reality. I have never asked for an appointment to another congregation. In April 1996 Bishop J. Woodrow Hearne announced he was appointing me to serve as senior pastor of Marvin United Methodist Church in Tyler, Texas, effective June 1. Since I seldom give credence to rumors, I was surprised to be assigned to the prestigious pulpit of such a prominent congregation. It was not an unhappy surprise.

A WEALTH OF HISTORY

Moving to East Texas after more than a decade in the Houston area was a pleasant transition for our family. A new resident to Tyler is immediately attracted to its wealth in many areas. Founded in 1848, the city has a treasure of history. Tyler was named after the nation's tenth president, John Tyler. He presided from 1841-45 in the sad season of slavery in the South. The era of racial divide brought the United States to a most uncivil Civil War. The new state of Texas, born in 1845, seceded from the Union with other southern states in 1861. The Lone Star State returned in 1870 and Tyler with it.

In the next 125 years the city expanded exponentially and became the economic, educational, financial, medical and cultural hub of East Texas. Red brick streets laid over 100 years ago still provide an attractive charm all around downtown. The Methodists established the first church in the infant community in 1848. The brick second-floor sanctuary in which the Marvin family worships today was erected in 1891. The church was named for Bishop Enoch Mather Marvin who was elected to the episcopal office in 1866.

Three Marvin pastors have been elected to the episcopal office. Most recently were Bishop Joe Wilson (1992) and Bishop Ben Chamness (2000). An excellent history of the first 150 years of the church was written in 1999 by Bishop John Wesley Hardt, a lifelong friend. The volume is entitled *Forward in Faith: The Ministry of Marvin United Methodist Church 1848-1998.* Marvin member Marilyn Hardy chaired the ambitious undertaking and wrote in her acknowledgments, "A church must always look forward in faith, but this brief glance back into the history of this great congregation provides strength and inspiration for the challenges of the future."

A Wealth of Economy

The new economic wealth was literally grounded in the East Texas Oilfield discovery in 1930. The find was the second-largest oil field in the United States outside of Alaska, and first in total volume of oil recovered. Covering 140,000 acres and parts of five counties and having 30,340 historic and active oil wells, the East Texas Field has yielded over 5.42 billion barrels of oil in its almost 90-year history. It was often said that the Sears store in Tyler was the only one in the national chain to turn a profit during the Great Depression. The wealth of history and oil had contributed to make the Tyler metro area an attractive place to call home when we arrived in 1996. We soon discovered why.

A Wealth of Generosity

There was not only a wealth of economic resources, there was also a wealth of great generosity in the city. Yes, the well-to-do built stately mansions with manicured gardens, servants and elegant landscapes. Yet they also established foundations, gave scholarships and built buildings for community services. I was amazed and grateful to witness the generosity to the community from its citizens in gifts of time and talent, as well as treasure.

The many worthy nonprofit organizations in the city were the beneficiaries of the abundant wealth of generosity from many Tyler citizens. They included Red Cross, Stewart Blood Bank, Salvation Army, PATH (People Attempting to Help), Tyler Literacy Council, East Texas Food Bank, St. Paul's Children Clinic and Foundation, the Bethesda Medical Clinic, Alzheimer's Association and the Junior League. The wealth of money and the wealth of the willingness to share abundantly replicates the ministry of the first-century faith community who lived with "glad and generous hearts."

A Wealth of Beauty

The wealth of natural beauty was another bounty of Tyler and Smith County. The soil and climate are conducive to healthy and abundant flora and plant life. Azaleas, dogwoods and oak trees thrive in the mild weather. By the 1920s the rose industry had developed into a major business and by the 1940s more than half the U.S. roses were grown within ten miles of the city. In the late 1950s over 250 nurseries with 1,500 employees grew and shipped 20 million rose bushes.

Though the numbers have declined since that peak, everything is still coming up roses in the Rose Capital of America. Go online to see the Tyler

Rose Museum, tour the Rose Garden and its 14 acres, 35,000 bushes and 600 varieties. Admission to the garden is free. The beauty and bounty of Tyler Roses are celebrated each October with a festival, parade, rose queen coronation, art shows, parties and a vesper service. Four times in my ten years in Tyler it was my privilege to preach at the Rose Festival Vesper Service. I am glad be part of a beautiful community which celebrates with two billion friends every spring that Jesus from the dead rose.

A WEALTH OF MEDICINE

The wealth of the medical community was an amazing asset to Tyler and all East Texas. Three major hospitals were primary employers, performed major surgeries and competed in friendly ways, most of the time. There seemed to be quite a spirited competition among them over who had the most ambulances, helicopters, specialists and convenient parking. We had over fifty physicians in our congregation, ranging from psychiatrists to podiatrists, and neurologists to urologists. We were covered from head-to-toe, and everything in between! Sharon and I both had surgeries in Tyler. When your surgeon and anesthesiologist are both members of your congregation, you feel you are in good hands and God's hands.

While I visited and appreciated all the hospitals, I connected primarily with Mother Frances, a faith-based institution founded by the Sisters of the Holy Family of Nazareth in 1937. Many church members worked there. The institution was gracious to invite me to serve on its Foundation Board and chair the hospital's Ethics Committee. It was an honor to serve in these community capacities. The rewards were rich in relationships, responsibilities and reverence for life and the end of life.

My across the street neighbor for ten years was a devoted Marvin member and prominent surgeon who operated tirelessly to mend bodies and save lives. Sunday was the only day he did not beat me out of the driveway to work. Dr. Andrews was a community servant, typical of the thousands of healthcare givers in the city. The blessed healer is now in his mid-80s and still operating and serving the Great Physician. The healing touch of this wonderful doc over a half-century will whisper love through eternity and then some.

A WEALTH OF EDUCATION

The educational wealth was another outgrowth of great generosity in the community. Public and private schools, as well as three colleges, have all been beneficiaries of abundant generosity for 125 years. Texas College was established in north Tyler in 1894 by the Christian Methodist Episcopal Church to educate area African American students. Over the years the monetary wealth of community benefactors has kept the school afloat in some hard times. The college is still going strong with over 1,000 students enrolled in a dozen diverse degree programs.

In 1926 Tyler Junior College kicked off and has won over 60 junior college national championships in 10 sports. The school has a 145-acre main campus and multiple degree programs, including bachelor's degrees. The school has long been famous for its high-kicking Apache Belle Drill Team. Warning: Do NOT try their rigorous routine at home. You may be making a trip to the ER! Begun in 1947, the precision high-kicking shows have entertained millions across the globe at Super Bowl halftimes and before three U.S. Presidents.

More than a dozen campus buildings are named for generous Tyler benefactors. Perhaps TJC's best known alumnus is multiple Grammy, Golden Globe and Academy Award-winning composer Will Jennings. He wrote the love lyrics to "Tears in Heaven" sung by Eric Clapton, "My Heart Will Go On", the theme song for the film *Titanic* and "Up Where We Belong" from *An Officer and a Gentleman*. Will's sister was our across the street neighbor and Marvin Church member for a decade. Will occasionally attended worship with Joyce at Marvin in our time there. His spiritual lyrics gently whisper love in our hearts that we will one day end up where we belong in a tearless and timeless holy house where our hearts are at home (II Corinthians 5:1).

The third institution of higher learning arrived in 1971. The University of Texas at Tyler has grown to over 10,000 students on its 200-acre wooded campus. The school is a part of the well-endowed UT System and offers masters and doctoral degrees, as well as many undergraduate offerings. The young school's endowment has grown to over $26 million.

It was my privilege to pray at several UTT commencements over a decade and at the dedication of the school's new baseball and softball complex. How do you connect baseball and God? Look soon for *Spirituality 2020: Public Service, Prayers and Proclamations* to find out! The Cowan Center Fine and Performing Arts Center hosted lectures, concerts, musicals and other community events. Educational wealth is present in the quality Tyler public schools, as well in at least six private, faith-based school systems with college preparatory campuses. Enrollment fees, tuition, uniforms and chapel are standard at these popular choices. Wealthy benefactors invest in these campuses with gifts for buildings, bell towers, classrooms, endowments and athletic facilities.

A WEALTH OF SPIRITUALITY

The wealth of spirituality is a vital element in community life. There are over 300 congregations in greater Tyler. The city is the buckle of the Bible Belt. There are churches on every other corner. Billy Graham preached in Rose Stadium in 1953. The church I pastored 50 years later helped sponsor his presence in Tyler. Major evangelical national and international ministries and missions are in or near Tyler. These include Mercy Ships, Youth With A Mission (YWAM) and Pine Cove Camp. The Last Days Ministries and Evangelist David Wilkerson were both nearby before deaths and other relocations took them from Texas. A year before my arrival in Tyler, the community's churches united for a spiritual crusade at the Oil Palace led by Argentine-born Evangelist Luis Palau.

There was a lot of spirit and spirits in the same fabled Oil Place setting a few years later when Sharon and I went hear Methodist Willie Nelson on a Saturday night. We saw a lot of Baptist and Methodist friends in the spirit on that occasion. How can you tell a Methodist from a Baptist? Methodists speak to each other in the liquor store! Smith County was the wettest dry county in Texas, according to many. Willie soothed the souls of saints and sinners alike with his playing and singing of "I'll Fly Away" and "Just As I Am." He was whispering love in his gospel solos. It does not get much more spiritual than that.

The spirituality of the Tyler community encompassed more than evangelical Christian. Spiritual leaders from Catholic, Jewish and Islamic congregations shared fellowship, friendship, food and faith on a regular basis. The Tyler Ministerial Alliance planned and led the annual MLK March and Worship Service at the Roman Catholic Cathedral in downtown Tyler each January. It was always a full house and almost always quite cold.

One of the best speakers we ever had was not a priest, preacher, imam or rabbi. He was a trauma surgeon from Trinity Mother Hospital who put people's parts back together after a car crash, shooting or other major mishaps. One night at the hospital I saw a large Anglo-American family embrace at length the skilled African American physician who literally saved their loved one's life after a severe accident. That surgeon was a member of Marvin Church. I asked Dr. Errington Thompson if he would speak at the upcoming

Tyler MLK Community Service. His poignant, personal, powerful message of serving one another touched a full house. A Jewish rabbi taught, "The greatest among you is the one who serves." Dr. Thompson is still serving and saving the lives of God's children of all colors with whispers of love through his skilled hands and sharp mind fifteen years later.

A WEALTH OF GUESTS

The wealth of guests who traveled to Tyler to visit, entertain, speak or raise money was abundant. In our decade there we were pleased to cross paths with prominent public servants, award-winning athletes, spiritual leaders, authors, musicians and an Olympic Gold Medalist. They included these who spoke or worshiped at Marvin Church: First Lady Laura Bush, Rabbi Harold Kushner and CMA Female Vocalist the Year Janie Fricke. Others we met at various venues were Hank Aaron (the true baseball home run champion before steroids), figure skating star Peggy Fleming, Masters Golf Champion Justin Leonard, political commentator Bill O'Reilly, Astronaut Buzz Aldrin, English author and social critic Os Guinness, Governor George W. Bush, First Lady Barbara Bush, Governor Rick Perry and Texas First Ladies Rita Clements and Anita Perry.

Though we did not meet them personally, Sharon I laughed until we cried at a performance by the Smothers Brothers at Caldwell Auditorium in downtown Tyler. Cain and Abel had nothing on Tom and Dick Smothers when it comes to sibling rivalry. Go online to learn more on some of these nice folks who passed through Tyler for a day or two. Maybe they heard some love whispers as they drank a cup of coffee and stopped to smell the roses.

A WEALTH OF QUALITY OF LIFE

The wealth of the quality of life was visible in a variety of valuable nonprofit venues which dot the cityscape. The Caldwell Zoo opened its gates in 1953. Located on 85 lush acres in North Tyler, the nonprofit is home to 2,000 animals of all types from all over the world. Beyond the fabled Rose Museum, the city attracts many guests to the Discovery Science Place, Historic Aviation Memorial Museum, Goodman Museum, Tyler Museum of Art and Cotton Belt Railway Museum. Restaurants serving all fares abound. Three country club thrive.

When it is time to check out, turn in the keys and head for the nineteenth hole, several rosy resting places are ready to receive your remains. Go online to see Dr. Madge Ward's Piano Grave and how to go out with flair. I bet you have never seen a grave marker eight feet tall and which weighs twenty-five tons, with another twelve tons of concrete in the foundation. Dr. Ward's casket lies under the piano's legs in Rose Hill Cemetery. Her music goes on. Her love for the keys whispers in the memorial she created. The Bible indicates there will be music in the world to come. Count SMU grads Madge and me in. She can play the keyboard and I can make a joyful noise!

The Children's Park of Tyler is a special place to celebrate the lives of all children. Begun in 2001 by a couple who lost an infant, it is a unique park which provides opportunities for both natural play and quiet meditation. Dozens of families have chosen to engrave along the park's meandering pathway the names of children who arrived early in eternity. As a member of the founding Children's Park of Board of Directors in 2003, I with Sharon was pleased to donate two bronze plaques in memory of my beloved siblings. The small park is in an historic niche near downtown and operates under the public-private partnership between the City of Tyler and the Children's Park of Tyler. Visit online the passive park of waterfalls, memorial stones, lush landscaping and footbridges. You will sense the whispers of love.

A WEALTH OF COMMUNITY SERVICE OPPORTUNITIES

The wealth of quality community service opportunities was another vital attraction of Tyler. Individuals served in Junior League, Rotary Clubs, nonprofit boards, PTA, baseball and softball coaching, scouting and dozens more contributing to the common good. I always believed my pastoral appointment was not only to a church, but also to a community. Living in the Rose City offered many meaningful settings to serve. I was pleased to speak annually at the Leadership Tyler Quality of Life Day, serve on the Regional East Texas Food Bank Board, sit on the Executive Committee of the Hospice of East Texas and serve two years as President of the Tyler Ministerial Alliance. One of those was 2001 when America was attacked on a September morning.

Everyone born before 1995 remembers the shock, numbness and fear of the day. It was incumbent on the spiritual leaders of the community to offer hope, assurance and faith in the face of the unfathomable assault on our nation and our senses. Our clergy alliance hastily met and planned a service for the city. The other officers appointed me to preach. We asked the biblical question that evening in the service in the auditorium of the First Baptist Church, "Is there any word from the Lord?" The local television and radio helped get the word of the service out. Nearly 1,200 folks from all or no religious affiliations showed up, shared tears and fears, hymns of faith and assurance, prayers of lament and confession and scriptures of hope and trust.

I have little memory and no notes from the service, but I do know the Holy One showed up and shared assurance and confidence. We read the timeless word of God for the people of God, "God is our refuge and strength, a very present in trouble. Therefore we will not fear... The nations are in an uproar, the kingdoms totter... The Lord of hosts is with us; the God of Jacob is our refuge" (Psalm 46). This was, is and always will be the word of the Lord.

The most interesting community service I shared with a score of fellow Smith County citizens was being summoned to serve on a Grand Jury for six months. Once a month we met in the basement of the courthouse for eight hours, hearing 90-100 cases presented and deciding whether to indict the accused or not. This experience reinforced my belief in the doctrines of original sin and original stupidity.

One case involved a suspect accused of hiding a stash of illegal drugs between his buttocks. A quiet, pudgy older male member of the jury surprised us all when he wryly asked in a southern drawl, "Is that what you call crack cocaine?" The room exploded in laughter. We had to call a recess to recover.

A most interesting experience came when I was invited to serve on a U.S. Magistrate Judge Selection Panel for the Eastern District of Texas. There were 50 applicants for the position. Five were members of my congregation. I was the token non-attorney on the panel. Deliberations were confidential. I do not recall our recommendation nor who was chosen, but I was grateful for high quality candidates willing to seek justice and resist evil in whatever forms they present themselves.

THE WEALTH OF MARVIN HISTORY

The wealth of Marvin United Methodist Church is impressive at all levels. As with Tyler, the Methodist faith community has a rich history. The congregation's birth overlapped the city's beginning in 1848. In June of that year the Trustees of the Methodist Episcopal Church South made the top bid at public auction for a lot at the southwest corner of Erwin and Bois d'Arc Streets. Over 170 years later the saints are still marching in and out, singing and serving, preaching and praying, and marrying and burying. The 1891 sanctuary is one of few houses of worship erected in near frontier times still in service over 125 years later. The second floor sacred space seats 800. Over the next century, the church added property for building, parking and ministry.

THE WEALTH OF MARVIN FACILITIES

The wealth of facilities has grown over the church's history to support ministries to all ages. The 1891 sanctuary, pipe organ and stain glass windows still serve the congregation with beauty and strength. The addition of an education building in 1923 and a large chapel a few decades later expanded worship and classroom space. In 1987 the church dedicated a $4,000,000 Family Ministries Center which included 62,000 square feet for a new kitchen, Pirtle Fellowship Hall, Fair Gymnasium and Herd Auditorium.

In my ten years at Marvin we had two $5,000,000 capital campaigns. Renewing God's House provided for significant deferred maintenance, refurbishments, landscaping, playground, new youth center, upgrades to three parsonages and Wesley Missions Center. Building for All Ages invested in renovation and expansion of Children and Youth areas, conversion of the racquetball courts to a new and significant investment in the long-awaited Meadow Lake Methodist Retirement Community. That nonprofit facility was to be erected on 90 acres given by generous Marvin member many years before. The late James Fair and Bob Irwin, along with Quinton and Billie Chamness, donated the 90 acres of prime property. As did many other Marvin families, Sharon and I stretched to make a sacrificial gift to the goal. We were pleased to designate our investment for the Administrative Area of the campus in memory of my parents. Generosity begets generosity. Love whispers from one generation to another.

THE WEALTH OF MUSIC AND WORSHIP

The riches of music and worship have long been staples of Marvin Church. Handbell, Chime, Children, Youth, Chancel or Grown Ups (chronologically gifted) choirs have all provided quality music for Sunday services and special worship occasions for 17 decades. Harps and other musical instruments have blessed the ears and souls of saints sitting in the sacred space of God's house. The powerful pipe organ is a staple in the service of God in the sanctuary. Music is about fifty percent of most worship. While silence is essential for coming into God's presence, so is praising God with voice and other instruments.

During our tenure at Marvin we introduced a new service in a new setting with new songs, new instruments, new leadership and new ways to worship.

With drums, guitars, tambourines, keyboards, and raised hands, the progressive Power Praise service attracted hundreds of God's children of all ages each week to experience the presence of Providence in praise, prayer and presentation of provisions. Yes, there was an offering! The lighting, screens, stage and tiered seating in cozy Herd Auditorium made it the perfect place to gather for the good and glory of God. The most fun and challenging thing for me on the Sundays I preached in Power Praise was stripping off my clerical robe and stole, putting in a golf shirt and sprinting to Herd in time to get in the flow of the service in progress, all the while greeting parishioners and guests along the way.

Several special services took place in the sanctuary and chapel on a regular basis. Weddings, funerals, baptisms, Holy Communion, Christmas Eve Candlelight and Holy Week Services happen each year. We hosted four Rose Festival Vesper Services during our decade in the Rose City. The annual service is conducted in the home church of the Rose Queen. One year just before the processional began, I asked the queen's father what he did. I did not know him well. It was an appropriate question. He answered, "I own three businesses." "Wow!" I replied impressed. Then he looked his pastor in the eye and confessed wistfully, "Actually, I don't own them. They own me." Honest confession in the house of the Lord is healthy for the soul.

THE WEALTH OF THE CHURCH STAFF

The wealth of the church staff was a major asset to the congregation and community. With 20-25 capable, committed Christlike servants almost all aligned with the mission of the church, we met weekly, worshiped, prayed, played, planned, evaluated, laughed, ate and occasionally retreated together for community building and long-range planning. Evaluations helped us all stay on track or move on, if needed. Sometimes there is a painful staff infection which must be healed. It was a pleasure to lead and serve with such capable, committed, Christlike souls who loved what they did, cared for one another and who often echoed mercy and whispered love.

THE WEALTH OF CONGREGATIONAL MISSION OUTREACH

The wealth of the congregation in its mission outreach was then and still is a model of local and global Christian compassion and concern. Marvin Church is synonymous with missions in Tyler. Directed for the past 28 years by missions' champion Melissa, the downtown destination of disciples has 42 local Mission Partners it serves with in providing education, volunteers and financial resources. Recently the church sent 15 work teams to Orange, Texas over a period of six months to rebuild homes from hurricane flood damage. For many years the church has had mission partnerships in India and the former Soviet Union. Several church families have adopted children from Russian orphanages.

Since 1988 Marvin Church has conducted an annual Mission Week each June. Hundreds of saints show up for some or all the days to scrape, paint, clean, restore, construct ramps, install cooling units, mow and landscape in underserved neighborhoods. Some summers included repairing the houses of worship of underfunded congregations.

In 1996 a rookie pastor in Tyler town ascended the hot heights of the Winona Methodist Church bell tower to scrape and paint. Nothing like sweat equity to earn a new preacher acceptance in his or her new appointment. It will also earn you a turn in the popular dunking booth on the Thursday evening of Mission Week. The youth of the church loved to baptize their senior pastor by immersion every Thursday evening of the neighborhood Mission Week festival!

Retirees, teachers and students on summer break and fulltime folks taking vacation worked side by side doing God's work for a magical seven days. The meals, prayers and conversations were holy communions. Lots of love was whispered in the hammering, painting, building, eating and praying. An American musical trio with biblical names sang over 50 years ago about a hammer and justice and love. Peter, Paul and Mary were not at Mission Week, but the themes of some of their popular music echoed in the hands, heads and hearts of those serving and being served. I have never been associated with nor seen a church more mission-minded than Marvin Methodist. Love whispers in good deeds, good people and good results.

THE WEALTH OF CHURCH AND COMMUNITY JOYS

Living and serving in Tyler brought a wealth of community and congregational joys and concerns over ten years. What a privilege to welcome, pray for and present First Lady Laura Bush with a dozen Texas yellow roses on her visit to the church for a luncheon launching a literacy community initiative called "Success by Six." Pirtle Hall was packed for the program. The lifelong Methodist could not have been more kind to the church staff by personally greeting each one.

161

In 2004 the Marvin Church family studied California Pastor Rick Warren's bestseller *The Purpose Driven Life.* Over 1,500 youth and adults shared the practical Bible study over six weeks. The climax of the daily discipleship devotions and weekly services was one grand gathering of God's family at Harvey Hall at the Tyler Rose Center. We moved offsite on 4-4-04, April 4, so we could all be in one room to share our call to live our lives on purpose. Healing, hope, hallelujahs and heaven were shared in a season preceded by some bitterness and brokenness in the family of God. All shall be well, love whispers.

Being invited to speak in public but non-pulpit places is a little awkward and tempting. I once asked Sharon about such venues, "Should I try to be funny?" She laughed and answered, "No, just be yourself." While a pastor is not called to be a spiritual Jimmy Fallon, he or she must remember Psalm 2:4. What? You don't remember? "He who so sits in the heavens laughs." God has the last laugh. That is good news!

In our time in Tyler I was pleased to speak and perhaps split a few sides when addressing a variety of community occasions. One was the 2006 East Texas Oil Legends Merit Awards Luncheon remembering the truly legendary life of R.W. Fair. He was a leader in the Arp Methodist Church at age 16. One of eight children, he discovered oil on a piece of land he bought from a Methodist minister.

Walter Fair's gusher produced 23,000 barrels of oil a day. He reacted by declaring, "The Lord placed me on this site. I expect to put the income where it will help somebody besides me. You see, our family tithed before we had oil." Fair founded a foundation and gave generous grants for the evangelistic, educational and missionary endeavors of Christ's work all over the world. Mr. Fair's son and other family belonged to Marvin in my tenure and carried on the great generosity. Walter Fair believed, "To whom much is given, much is expected."

Some other formal public addresses I gave in secular settings included "Path of Memories" at the Alzheimer's Association Walk, "Hooray to the Heroes of Healthcare!" honoring the employees of the Trinity Mother Frances Healthcare System, "Religion in Tyler and Smith County, Texas" to the Tyler Pilot Club and the Rose City Kiwanis Club, "Front Windshield or Rearview Mirror?" to the All Saints Chapel and the Pirtle Real Estate Company.

My most fun public service was serving as a Celebrity Waiter for a worthy community charity. It was held at Gilbert's El Charro, a popular Mexican restaurant. We "celebrity" waiters were asked only to fill water glasses and encourage gratuities for the good cause which escapes me after 15 or so years. What I will never forget is the gentle generosity of an octogenarian Marvin member who slipped me a $500 tip for the cause. Calvin was a soft-spoken newspaper publisher whose kindness whispered love to many children of all ages. His newspaper had a Bible verse in a prominent place in each edition. It is good to have some "good news" in the daily paper.

THE WEALTH OF COMMUNICATIONS

Secular communications were a strong and vital part of the Tyler and East Texas community. Three television stations telecast local news, weather and sports. A dozen or more radio stations broadcast to all segments of the greater Tyler area. The *Tyler Morning Telegraph* newspaper has been a daily staple at many a breakfast table since 1877. The spiffy *Tyler Today* magazine launched in 1989 and has been going strong for thirty years covering the community social scene, seasonal events, the annual Rose Festival, local businesses and personalities. The magazine publishes six thick issues annually, contributing to the community through articles which offer guidance and support for persons going through transitions in their lives. I was grateful to contribute an article in 2004 on "Helping Hurting Hearts in the Holidays."

Marvin UMC and its pastors enjoyed an abundance of communications means to spread hope, encouragement and a God connection. The sermon, choir anthem and anything else we could squeeze into 28 minutes and 40 seconds from the previous Sunday was telecast to two dozen counties across East Texas. We did not solicit monetary donations from the TV congregation. Today the church still has the service on the CBS station. One can also share the service live on Facebook or YouTube. Preaching on television means several things. You can easily touch the lives of persons who cannot attend in person. Think of shut-ins, saints and sinners in hospitals and nursing homes, inmates in minimum security jails and prisons. Some folks recorded the services and shared with others. I personally know a Tyler pastor who sent video recordings of the services to his mother. Glad you liked them, Mom!

People may recognize you in public and feel they have a connection with you. "I liked (or disliked) your sermon on the prodigal daughter." Or worse, they say, "I think I know you. Do you do the weekend weather on channel 56?" It is quite enough to keep one humble. Marvin has a weekly live broadcast of a large Sunday School Class. The Friendly Class has been on the radio practically every Sunday since God was young. The live broadcast from the church began in 1931 and reaches 6,000 guests weekly. There is always a warm welcome, prayer by a class member, solo and practical Bible lesson.

I communicated with the community each Friday with a paid ad in the Tyler newspaper. It included Sunday's sermon title, text and a teaser tale from the message. Each ad also had Marvin's address, phone number, website and worship and class schedules. One day a sweet lady whispered to me in the aisle at Brookshire's Grocery Store, "I read your column even though I am Baptist." I assured her it was okay with God and me if she did so!

A prominent Baptist pastor, friend and seminary dean sent me a gracious note one day. Dr. Paul Powell wrote, "I enjoy reading your column in the Tyler newspaper. I clipped several of them and will make some good Baptist preaching." Paul was a kind, sincere ecumenical servant of Christ whose life blessed the world with abundant whispers of love. He joined the Church Eternal in 2016.

THE WEALTH OF PASTORAL CARE RESPONSIBILITIES

The decade in the city of roses delivered a plethora of pastoral care privileges and responsibilities. I was called on to baptize bunches of beautiful babies, counsel and marry 119 couples who were in love or thought they were in love, confirm hundreds of youth and commend the bodies and souls of 325 saints to God for eternity. Many Services of Death and Resurrection were held in the Marvin Sanctuary or Chapel. A fair number were in one of three local funeral homes. Some were graveside or memorial services only. One brief, tender service for a wife was conducted in the nursing home room of her husband where he was confined. The celebration of her life and faith was short, sweet and spiritual.

The most unique service was for a Jewish man. His wife was a Marvin member. It was an honor to lead the public celebration of the life and faith of this friend and respected businessman in the community. The service was comfortable to lead. Jews and followers of Rabbi Jesus of Nazareth have much in common. Holy scriptures, liturgies, prayers, rabbis and, of course, God. We are all the beloved children of God.

The dear departed over the years included children, youth, young adults, spouses, singles, parents and grandparents. One aged couple died a week apart, as if one could not live without the other. The oldest was 105 years. The youngest was DOA. I did not know the age of one lovely saint. That number

164

was between her and God. The pastor and the public were not privy to that personal information. My parents both died in our time in Tyler. I did not have a pastoral role in either service, as I needed to be a care receiver rather than a caregiver. I buried the rich and the poor. Death is the great equalizer. We are born to die. Yet our Creator whispers in love through his servant Paul, "If we live, we live for the Lord; and if we die, we die for the Lord. So, whether we live or die, we belong to the Lord."

Weddings were always happy, fun and sometimes anxious events. Some things can go awry. Someone is always late for the rehearsal. Sometimes somebody seems to smell of spirits not holy. Child ring bearers can be unbearable. Rings can be dropped, vows mumbled with uncertainty and weather unpleasant. MOTB (Mothers of the Bride) may over function in their role. Dads may shed a happy tear when giving their daughters away, causing the pastor to weep as well. Nonetheless, "Those whom God has joined together let no one put asunder." I have wondered once or twice over the years if God had anything to do with some of these couples being together.

THE WEALTH OF PASTORAL EXECUTIVE LEADERSHIP

Being the Marvin pastor brought a wealth of responsibilities and privileges. Membership in one of the country clubs provided a setting to interact with many present and prospective church members in a cordial setting. I was called to do a TV interviews on "Can Adam and Steve get married?" after a state in the Northeast approved same-gender weddings. Invitations to attend or pray or both at community gatherings were extended.

The most memorable one was in the last week of September 1998. The local social service organization called PATH (People Attempting to Help) was celebrating a special anniversary. Its executive director was a Marvin member and invited me to attend the event and a news conference. The special guest was Texas Governor George W. Bush. Like his leadership or not, he is an affable guy and baseball fan. It was nice meet and chat with him.

When there was a lull in the questions at the press conference, I raised my hand. The Lone Star State CEO nodded. I said, "Governor Bush, this Friday evening I will be in Arlington to see the Texas Rangers play the New York Yankees in the baseball playoffs. As governor of Texas, please tell us who you will be cheering to win when the Texas Rangers play the Houston Astros in the World Series?" He smiled, looked me in the eye and exclaimed, "There's a crackpot in every crowd!" Everyone in the room laughed loudly. Then the future President said, "(Astros owner) Drayton McLane is a friend of mine. I hope the Astros make it to the series. But as a managing general partner for five years, I will be pulling for the mighty Rangers!" Then Governor Bush looked at me and said kindly, "Thanks for going to the game." I trust it is a small number of pastors who have been called a "crackpot" by a powerful governor and soon-to-be most powerful person in the world. We all had a good laugh that day. Three years later the new President would be leading the nation and world in an unwanted war on terrorism.

One of the fun and serious responsibilities and privileges of Marvin's senior pastor is choosing, inviting, hosting and introducing the speakers in the two endowed lectures the church has. I stepped out of the old white American male preacher box to expand the experience and expression of the faith message. We welcomed young futurist, prolific author, seminary dean and evangelist Leonard Sweet in 1997. We invited the first woman in the series begun in 1965. Jeannette Cliff-George was a popular Christian actress, playwright, Bible Teacher and founder of a Christian theatre company in Houston.

We brought the first musician, Dr. Steven Kimbrough. We welcomed the first African American, Dr. Zan Wesley Holmes. We brought evangelicals Eddie Fox, Bill Hinson and Maxie Dunam. We flew in the first scientist, Professor David Wilkinson, an astrophysicist and pastor in the British Methodist Church. We reveled in the energy and electricity of professor, sociologist and evangelist Tony Campolo. These folks rocked the house and made me a better preacher.

Not all the ministry at Marvin was wine and roses. There were many roses and very little wine. Or whine. The toughest travail of my Tyler tenure was a gruesome murder connected to our congregation. In August 2002 I received a phone call from the Tyler Methodist District Superintendent requesting me to go ASAP to the home of one of the pastors in the district. The D.S. was recovering from surgery or would have gone himself. The church and parsonage were about 30 minutes away. Six weeks before I had seen this happy family at a Tyler hospital where they had just delivered their second child. The parents of this pastor were members of Marvin.

When I got to the home, I learned the pastor's wife had been murdered in their home several hours before. Law enforcement officers, family and church members were there. The 41-year-old pastor said he came home and found his wife dead. The scene was filled with shock, tears, anguish and anger.

How could this happen? Who would commit such a crime in the sleepy little town of Troup, Texas? After an extended visit I prayed with the mourning family, holding the hands of the pastor and his mother with others in a circle. The tears flowed freely. It was not long before an arrest was made.

The suspect was convicted and sentenced to 55 years in prison. The perpetrator was proven to be none other than the small-town Methodist minister himself. The first death in the Bible was a man murdering his brother. Sadly, sometimes shouts and acts of hate may drown out whispers of love for a time. We live with a vision of a time when human suffering and brokenness will be redeemed, and pain and tears will be no more. Until then we will need physicians, pastors, prayer warriors and pallbearers to carry us onward and upwards to our "house not made with hands, eternal in the heavens." Love wins in the end. Always has. Always will.

A generous pastoral privilege at Marvin Church was the provision for a sabbatical leave after seven years at the church. Sharon and I took two months off in the summer of 2003. The first six weeks we spent in a cabin at a Christian Retreat Center near Bozeman, Montana. After two other weeks being renewed in the glory of the Grand Teton and Yellowstone National Parks, our bodies and souls were rested and refreshed in the majesty of God's glorious creation.

We came home ready to charge into hell with a squirt gun. We had both been to Colorado several times over our lives. We both experienced the glory and grandeur of God in the Rocky Mountains. Who does not? But the thought of our ever living in the Centennial State sixteen years ago would have been as unlikely as someone saying sixteen years ago Donald Trump would one day be elected President of the United States of America.

In the spring of 2006 something strange, unexpected and almost unbelievable happened. Out of the blue came a call came from Colorado about a major Methodist church in need of a new senior pastor. Having been at Marvin Church for just over ten years and having recently made a real estate investment in the Centennial State, I listened. After prayer, discernment and discussion with the Colorado Springs Area District Superintendent and Sharon, I withdrew my name from consideration for the church.

Within weeks I received another call from a different Rocky Mountain D.S. about my possibly coming to pastor in Downtown Denver. Within a week I was asked to send a CV, sermon and answers to a multitude of questions. Soon I was invited to fly to Denver for dinner with the Denver District Superintendent Youngsook Kang and the members of the Staff-Parish Relations Committee of Trinity United Methodist Church. After dinner and an extended interview and conversation, we adjourned to the historic sanctuary seating 1,142 persons. There I preached to a dozen persons. My sermon was appropriately entitled *If I Could Only Preach One Sermon.*

One was enough. The committee asked the D.S. and Bishop Warner Brown to work with Texas Conference Bishop Janice Riggle Huie to release me to serve at Trinity. All parties agreed. The move meant a major relocation, 891 miles to a new time zone, from mild hills to mighty mountains. We elevated ten times over from 541 to 5,280 feet above sea level. We increased from 218 to 300 days a year with sunshine.

While the move from the Lone Star State to the Centennial State was unsought, unexpected and unbelievable, it opened new vistas, expanded awareness and brought new opportunities for ministry to receive, live and share the life and love of Christ. This transfer from the Texas Conference to the Rocky Mountain Conference of the United Methodist Church began our last, longest and most life-changing pastorate. Amazingly, there was much in common between with Denver and Tyler, Trinity Church and Marvin Church.

A WEALTH OF HISTORY

There is the significant wealth of history in the colorful state. Nomadic Native Americans roamed for centuries the ranges which would become the Mile-High City. Denver was founded in November 1858 as a gold mining town in the Kansas Territory. The first church in the rough and tough tiny town was organized by the Methodists. The initial services of the new Auraria and Denver City Methodist Episcopal Church were conducted August 2, 1859, seventeen years before Colorado became a state. Historians note, "The new church was an island of civilization in a wide-open frontier town." The records reflect there were no schools, hospitals, libraries or banks. The only other businesses in town were saloons, 31of them. One can safely assume there were other commercial enterprises underway in or near the saloons.

That tiny congregation hung in there, changed names, relocated and grew as the contiguous city and county of Denver did over the next 150 years. The Colorado Territory was established in 1861. In 1863 the Rocky Mountain Methodist Episcopal Conference was founded with 241 white members and 14 colored members. The conference established Colorado Seminary, the initial institution of higher education in the infant community. It evolved to become the noted University of Denver. The congregation erected its first permanent house of worship as the War Between the States was winding down. After meeting in a theatre for some time and surviving both a fire and a flood in the toddler city, the young congregation worshipped in its new home February 12, 1865. The impressive brick Lawrence Street Methodist Episcopal Church cost $22,948. It was the largest building in the young city.

Colorado Territorial Governor John Evans was a member of the congregation and a major donor. Evans was a medical doctor, philanthropist, founder of two major universities and lifelong friend of Abraham Lincoln. His connection to a massacre of Native Americans in the Colorado Territory under his watch is a blotch on his otherwise admirable life of public service. Mount Evans, a fabled Fourteener, is an easy one-hour drive west of Denver and named for Governor Evans.

Another governor connected to the church was one of its pastors who became the state's CEO. Henry Augustus Buchtel was arguably the most prominent pastor in the church's long history. Under his leadership from 1886-91, the congregation relocated a mile away, changed its name to Trinity, raised funds and built the landmark spiritual station and mission center which is still serving the community and world over 130 years later. Buchtel inspired generosity for the erection of a substantial, first-class, artistic facility "complete in every detail, even to the hitching posts on the street."

The majestic new sanctuary was erected in 1888 at perhaps the most historic intersection in the city. Across the street today is the iconic Navarre Building built in 1880 as a school for girls. Across a century it served as a hotel, gambling parlor, gentleman's club, restaurant and Denver's hottest jazz club. In the 1990s the Navarre was renovated and restored it to its Victorian roots. The Anschutz Collection of Western American Art moved in. The American Museum of Western Art is a true treasure and a treasured good neighbor to Trinity. Religion and art are intertwined telling stories, sharing beauty, building community and connecting us to many artists, art forms and the one Great Artist.

The third and youngest member of the august nineteenth-century trio of neighbors is the Brown Palace Hotel. Built in 1892, the Brown has housed every United States President in the twentieth-century, Sir Winston Churchill and the Beatles. The luxury hotel's famed Autograph Collection reflects the rich history of the angled intersection. President Bill Clinton and would-be President Hillary Clinton were our across-the-street neighbors at the Brown during the 2008 Democratic National Convention.

The new worship space at Eighteenth and Broadway seated 1,142 for worship services. Every seat was numbered with a small metal plate so assigned seats for concerts and lectures could be sold. Those plates are still in place after 13 decades, as are the metal hat holders under each balcony chair for male attendees to have a convenient place to store their hats during the services. One member, the church's Music Director, committed to give the new pipe organ. It did not hurt at all that Isaac Blake was also the founder and first President of the Continental Oil Company and the son of a Methodist minister. Each Sunday Blake directed over 100 voices in the choir. He later lost his entire fortune as a victim of the 1893 Silver Panic.

However, the stirring sounds of the mighty 4,200 pipes of the New York-built Roosevelt organ are still blessing worshipers weekly with whispers of love and the triumphs of past, present and future saints forward marching in, out and up to reign in glory. Over five-million worshipers have had their souls soothed and stirred and their hearts healed by the strains of the king of instruments and the instrument of kings. Blake's grand gift of $30,000 for his church is now worth over $2 million. The Conoco founder found you cannot take your organ with you, but you can send it on ahead.

Pastor Buchtel went on to serve as President of the University of Denver for 21 years. During that era, he also served as Governor of Colorado from 1907-1909. He chose Trinity Church's stately sanctuary as the site of his inauguration. During his service as chancellor and governor, the pastor and public servant retained his close connection to the church he built. Buchtel is still remembered daily by thousands of Denver drivers who travel on Buchtel Boulevard on the north side of the beautiful DU campus. In 2007 it was my honor to pray at the University of Denver Commencement Ceremony and to remember the Chancellor who became governor 100 years before.

The twentieth century brought changes and challenges to Denver's first church. Two world wars, a stock market crash, pastoral changes, resignations of lay leaders, financial concerns and building upkeep all took a toll at times. Yet the church helped plant a dozen new Methodist congregations across growing Denver, elected bishops from its prominent pulpit, housed the Rocky Mountain Methodist Conference offices and invested in many community and global missions and ministries. The congregation ebbed and flowed in membership and attendance across the years as pastors ebbed and flowed. In 1979 the church received only 27 new members. There was talk of closing the church, selling the property and calling it a century. Dedicated disciples dug down deeply for dollars to keep God's house open and God's people fed. Soon a savior was sent.

New pastor Jim Barnes was the right person at the right time to right the ship and return Trinity to its flagship role in Methodism and the Denver community. Noted church consultant Lyle Schaller coached Barnes and the congregation in a transformation which restored vitality in every phase of ministry. Rev. Barnes led gifted laity in an unheard-of transaction of selling future vertical development rights. In exchange, Trinity received renovation of existing space, addition of new rooms and facilities, several million dollars for the church's endowment and provision for church parking though 2084. Consultant Schaller has never seen anything it. He declared, "A miracle has happened at Eighteenth and Broadway."

Barnes guided the church to growth in every area over his seventeen years as pastor. The church launched the Second Century Foundation in celebration of its first 100 years of ministry. Since its inception the foundation has given grants totaling over $1,200,000 to local agencies providing food, shelter, childcare, clothing, personal care items, meals, job training and other support to thousands of Denver-area families and individuals. Successive senior pastors Darrell Mount, Michael Dent and Ken Brown have wisely walked in the way of the large footprints left by Rev. Jim Barnes.

In 2009 the congregation celebrated 150 years ministry of mission and ministry as the city's oldest congregation by printing a sesquicentennial calendar, offering concerts and hosting a picnic at Historic Four Mile Park.

The congregation rejoiced to receive 153 new members in its year 150. A great time was had by all. A second history book, *Trinity at 150: We're Here for Good*, was published. Penned by longtime church member and writer Don Blake, it contains scores of color pictures by church photographer Lynn Willcockson and interviews and updates from the past 22 years. Don wrote in his reflections at the close of the updated volume, "One thing is certain...Trinity has been and will continue to be an unquenchable beacon of Methodism and Christianity."

A WEALTH OF NATURAL BEAUTY

The wealth of natural beauty is a bountiful blessing to anyone approaching Denver. Look west and inhale the mighty Rocky Mountain range and be blessed with towering, often snow-capped peaks. From various vantage points you will view Pike's Peak to the south and Long's Peak to the north. The Cherry Creek and the Platte River are life-giving running waters which have brought rich plant, animal and human life to the region for millennia. The confluence of these streams was the site of Denver's first church. Today it is another community focal point of spiritual devotion, an REI flagship store where one can learn to kayak or climb a fourteener. There are four National Parks in Colorado, including nearby Rocky Mountain National Park.

A WEALTH OF THE MEDICAL COMMUNITY

The wealth of the medical community is an awesome asset to the Front Range. My pastoral care ministry took me to over 30 different hospitals in the Denver area. Several large healthcare centers were faith-based, including Rose, National Jewish Health, Presbyterian, St. Anthony, Adventist and St. Joseph's. Other major medical centers were Sky Ridge, Swedish, Denver Heath, Children's and the UC Health and Anschutz Medical Campus. The Craig Hospital is a world-renowned rehabilitation hospital which specializes exclusively in neurorehabilitation and research. Both Sharon and I were the recipients of top-quality medical care in our dozen Denver years. One of our Trinity members, a urologist, served as president of the Colorado Medical Society and led the battle against the opioid epidemic in the state and nation.

A WEALTH OF THE ECONOMY

The economic wealth of the community is evident in many ways. While Tyler seemed to have a church on every corner, Denver has a bank or two at each intersection. The U.S. Mint makes tons of money literally each year just a few blocks from Trinity Church. The mint produces billions of coins each year for the American public. While we preferred "silent offerings" (cash, checks and credit cards), coins from the mint were always welcomed, too, in Sunday's offerings, especially from children! The sooner young disciples learn the simple truth that God owns it all, the better off they will be.

Country clubs, gourmet restaurants, high-end automobile dealerships, gated high-rise residences and palatial estates dotted the Denver landscape. The generosity of the well-to-do was evident in the many charitable foundations, endowments, charity events and gifts which blessed the community, congregations and those in need. Denver and Tyler both excelled in great giving.

A WEALTH OF EDUCATION

The wealth of education is evidenced in in the many learning opportunities and options available in the community. There are seven universities and a professional school in the immediate area. The University of Denver, University of Colorado at Denver, Regis University, Metropolitan State University, Colorado Christian University, Aspen University, American Sentinel University and the Art Institute of Colorado offer post-high school learning opportunities. As in Tyler, there are many elite private academies for pre-kindergarten through college prep schools. There are also medical, dental, nursing and other professional healthcare education opportunities.

Quality public schools abound in and around the city and its suburbs. The headquarters of Denver Public Schools relocated a block away from Trinity Church in 2013 and opened a new Downtown Expeditionary campus, a K-5 DPS public charter school and vocational training center. I occasionally took folks to lunch there to share the fare of aspiring student chefs. The future is bright for those who receive education and training for a culinary career. Former DPS Superintendent Michael Bennet was elected to the U.S. Senate in 2009 and is still in office. He is an effective public servant and was one of a score of candidates for the Democratic presidential nomination ten years later. Who says education does not pay?

A WEALTH OF SPIRITUALITY

The abundance of spirituality is evident in in Denver's many congregations. Churches, synagogues, temples, mosques and other holy watering holes to fill the souls of saints and sinners are all available. Some have massive facilities, staff and property.

There are three major seminaries in the area. The Iliff School of Theology, adjacent to the University of Denver, was founded in 1892 and is connected to the United Methodist Church. I was pleased to serve on its board for nine years. President Tom Wolfe is a strong leader, good friend and trusted pilot of planes, people and pressures. It was a pleasure to serve as his and Marilyn's pastor.

Denver Seminary in Littleton was begun by the Conservative Baptist Association of Colorado in May 1950. St. John Vianney Theological Seminary is a Roman Catholic institution committed to preparing persons for spiritual leadership in parishes. Denver is also home to the Rocky Mountain Bible College and Seminary, educating saints to serve in ultraconservative congregations.

The annual Easter Community Sunrise Service at the lovely Red Rocks Amphitheatre in nearby Morrison is a popular place to proclaim the Resurrection. Over 10,000 folks fill the iconic outdoor venue for the service sponsored by the Colorado Council of Churches. Several years ago, a nasty snowstorm blew through and the red rocks became white rocks. The service was cancelled but the resurrection was not. Christ kicked butt anyway and delivered us from sin and death. Whispers of love fell with fresh snow and new beginnings were on the way as spring would soon spring forth in full bloom and new life.

A WEALTH OF GUESTS

The wealth of guests who came to Denver to speak, entertain, inspire or play was staggering. We were privileged to encounter up close and personal some very interesting individuals. They included Academy Award Winner Diane Keaton (learned she was raised Methodist), Saturday Night Live Host, U.S. Senator and Presidential nominee George McGovern (son of a Methodist minister), U.S. Senator Rick Santorum, cellist Yo-Yo Ma, Heisman Trophy Winner Tim Tebow, Episcopal Bishop Michael Curry who preached at Trinity UMC in 2015 - best known for marrying Prince Harry and Meghan Markle in 2018 - country singer Randy Travis - best known for *Forever and Ever, Amen* and Charles Haley, a Dallas Cowboy Hall of Fame National Football Player who battled and beat a difficult bipolar diagnosis and illness.

At Red Rocks we were entertained again by our Texas Methodist friend Willie Nelson, James Taylor, Celtic Woman, Bob Dylan and the Fab Four. The guys in the tribute band looked, talked played and sang like John, Paul, George and Ringo in paying homage to the Beatles. However, they were from California. Sharon and I still danced through the night, held each other tight when we saw them standing there. The Fab Four were fabulous!

Yet our favorite Denver concert was Jennifer Nettles of Sugarland fame doing a solo concert at the Paramount Theatre two blocks from the church. We scored seats on the eighth row. The women outnumbered the men in the audience by two to one. This was the night I learned that desperate women will brazenly enter the men's restroom to find relief from over hydrating in the first half of a concert. When you have to go, you have to go. They had to go.

Trinity Church was delighted to connect with the Tattered Cover, a popular independent bookstore chain in Denver launched in 1971. The four locations host 600 author events annually. The TC also has book nooks in each DIA terminal. Late in my Denver tenure we were invited by the bookstore to partner with them in hosting well-known authors from across the nation who came to the church to speak, be interviewed, take questions and sign books. How much fun was that to have a thousand folks, many them secular souls who had never been in our historic building, show up an hour early to sit and soak in the beauty of the sacred space.

Our popular guests included U.S. Senator Al Franken interviewed by Colorado Governor John Hickenlooper, Astronaut Scott Kelly, Secretary of State Madalyn Albright, Journalist Dan Rather and YouTube actor, author, producer and singer Joey Graceffa. All of them packed the house. It was my pastoral privilege to welcome our guests and share a brief word on Trinity's history and ministry in the community, as well as gently plugging the annual magical Christmas Eve services at Denver's first church. Perhaps the more important information I was compelled to share was the location of the restrooms, water fountains and emergency exits for the 1,000+ guests, many of whom had never been in the 1888 edifice. What fun to chat with these popular and prominent folks in the green room before each program. I especially enjoyed visiting with Dan Rather whose brother Don had been an active member of one of my early congregations in Texas. Funnyman Franken resigned from the Senate a week after his visit to Trinity. His monkey business was not funny business.

In 2008 when the Democratic National Convention met in Denver, I wrote a letter to lifelong United Methodist Church member and Presidential candidate Hillary Rodham Clinton. On behalf of the Trinity United Methodist

Church family, I invited her and her family to worship at Denver's first church on the Sunday before the convention began the next evening. Her office replied with thanks and interest. When it became obvious before the convention that Senator Barrack Obama would be the nominee, I heard nothing more from her staff.

Interestingly, Secretary Clinton and daughter Chelsea are scheduled to speak and be interviewed on their new book at Trinity Church in downtown Denver in late November 2019. The Tattered Cover event sold out 1,000 tickets as soon as they became available. If becoming president does not work out, writing a book is not a bad fallback.

A WEALTH OF THE QUALITY OF LIFE

The wealth of the quality of life makes Denver a destination for many folks. The city's Park and Recreation provisions are without rival in the region. The first park was created in 1868. Just over 150 years later there are now nearly 20,000 acres of urban parks and mountain parkland. Facilities for picnics, golf, swimming, disc golf and boats are available. City Park with the Zoo and Museum of Nature and Science give all a premier place to park and play for a day or two. On one visit we saw the Titanic Ship Exhibit. The experience was almost too up close and personal.

The Denver Zoo opened in 1896 and is home to 4,000 animals on 80 acres. The 650 species are cared for by 350 employees and 600 volunteers. Wide jogging, walking and bike paths abound throughout the city and surrounding satellite communities. One can traverse unimpeded for a dozen miles via various under and occasional overpasses. The city has 29 recreation centers in which to swim, exercise, play basketball, do yoga and many other individual and team physical activities. Many of the programs are provided at no or low cost to Denver residents. Turning 62 in the Mile-High City has its advantages!

A WEALTH OF COMMUNITY SERVICE

The abundance of community service opportunities was a blessing. I delighted to belong to the Downtown Denver Rotary Club, one of the oldest clubs in the country. Rotary's motto is "Service Above Self." Club 31 had 300 members and met weekly for lunch at the nearby Denver Athletic Club. Rotary International is perhaps best-known for its work to eliminate polio in the world. Our club was diverse with female, African American, gay, young and progressive voices in leadership.

The programs were always timely and informative. One of the best was former Wyoming Senator Alan Simpson who spoke recently at President George H.W. Bush's funeral in the National Cathedral. Because of my proximity to the Colorado State Capitol, I was regularly invited to pray at the opening of either the Colorado Senate or House when they were in session. In 2012 the President of the Colorado Senate, a Democrat, published at his own expense a book containing the prayers offered in the Senate that year by many and various Colorado pastors, priests, rabbis, senators and the Roman Catholic Archbishop. I was humbled and grateful to have four prayers published in the book.

I was most honored to represent the Christian community in praying at the "Colorado Remembers 9-11" observance on the tenth anniversary of the terrorist attack on America. On a beautiful sunny Sunday afternoon 35,000 Coloradans filled Civic Center Park between the State Capitol's and the City and County of Denver's impressive edifices. Two large hook and ladder fire trucks suspended a huge American flag for all 35,000 citizens present to salute and pledge allegiance.

Colorado's governor, two U.S. senators, seven U.S. congressional representatives were all on the stage with the spiritual leaders from the four major world religions. Each of us clergy had a designated point in the program to pray. I was praying first. The complete invocation will be in *Spirituality 2020: Public Service, Prayers and Proclamations.* Spoiler alert: Since the Beach Boys were to give a concert in the park when the remembrance was complete, I did pray for "Good Vibrations" in my invocation for the gathering which had a very strong military and law enforcement presence. The Beach Boys knew where they were. To the delight of the throng, they altered one of their biggest hits that day in Denver to whisper, "I wish they all could be *Colorado* Girls."

This invitation to share in this sacred memorial was a most high and holy honor. One cannot forget the renowned Colorado Children's Chorale singing a spiritual offering to God, after which a military unit immediately fired off their rifles. The hot bullet casings were suddenly rolling around on the compact stage. All I could think of was an old-World War ditty called "Praise the Lord and Pass the Ammunition."

All of us born before the final decade of the twentieth century will never forget where we were on September 11, 2001. May God bless those 3,000 souls suddenly lost to us, yet never to the Holy One. Echoes of mercy and whispers of love bring hope and healing to those scarred by deep loss.

A WEALTH OF GENEROSITY

The wealth of Trinity United Methodist Church perhaps surpasses its rich history with all its ebb and flow. The congregation is wealthy in generosity. In the past 40 years its members have shared tens of millions of dollars to preserve, protect and upgrade God's holy house. Generous giving to the annual Mission and Ministry of Christ, Second Century Foundation and other mission appeals has refocused the direction of the congregation to serving others.

The generosity is in time and talent, as well as treasure. Some members teach children or work with youth or rock babies. Some set tables. Some cook or wash dishes. Some usher or greet at the door or in the parking lot. Some provide physical security and some spiritual security. Some sing, some ring. Some sit, some stand. Some pray, some visit. Some call, some clean. Some lead, some follow. All are generous in some way. All give freely. All receive graciously. Generosity abounds in Trinity hearts. Generous whispers of love echo and abound all around. What a blessing to serve a dozen years in such a family of great generosity.

A WEALTH OF MISSION AND OUTREACH

The wealth of mission and outreach was and is essential to Trinity's being. This is a church which cares for others. The church has had many local mission partners in the downtown area including Metro-CareRing where a room is named for the church, Warren Village, St. Frances Center, Capitol Hill Community Services, Olin Hotel, Turnabout and Redemption Fellowship. The church serves hot meals in a sit-down Fellowship Hall setting three days a week in conjunction with CHCS. Multiple recovery groups meet in the church five days a week. I loved sitting in the AA meetings from time to time to welcome and bless our daily guests. We rejoiced to have hundreds of committed, caring, honest children of God to come to a safe place for help, hope and healing.

The church organized, trained and deployed an Early Response Team to assist with provisions, clean-up and recovery following fires, floods and other losses. Youth teams travel to Guatemala every other summer to build homes and relationships with students for whom we provide annual scholarships. In the sesquicentennial year 2009 the congregation gave $500,000 for construction of the John Wesley School in Guatemala, birthing kits in Liberia and establishing the Redemption Fellowship congregation in downtown Denver for those touched by incarceration, addiction and any other affliction.

A WEALTH OF WORSHIP, MUSIC AND THE ARTS

An abundance of music, worship and the arts is in Trinity's DNA. The modern gothic sanctuary, stunning commissioned resurrection window and 4,275 powerful organ pipes ranging from less than one inch to 32 feet, encourage, edify and elevate all who enter the sacred space for Sunday worship, weddings, funerals and memorial services, concerts, baptisms, graduations, lectures and other gatherings. The sanctuary was overflowing with worshippers at a noon service on Friday, September 14, 2001, three days after America was attacked. The Mormon Church Choir twice presented a sacred musical in the Methodist Church a few years ago. Tuesday organ recitals are a staple for the four Tuesdays of Advent .

The Stiles Chapel provides a more intimate space for weddings, funerals, prayer, counseling and baptisms. The location, architecture, traditional worship and hospitality attract many guests to Trinity's sanctuary. In my twelve years as pastor, we welcomed major league baseball umpires, actors and crew from Broadway shows coming through town, foreign ambassadors, bishops, tons of Texans on vacation, convention attendees, annual National Western Stock Show guests in their cowboy best and God knows who else.

Trinity Church majored in traditional worship for contemporary people. Creeds, prayers, hymns, silence, a children's message, and sermon were standard fare. And yes, there was always an offering. We also received annual offerings for special missions. The church was at its best when there was a critical need – a typhoon in Japan or a year-end shortfall in the church's annual mission and ministry for Christ.

When people passed away, fell away or moved away, it was okay as others stepped up. Easter Sunday at Trinity was my favorite day of the year. It is springtime. There is a breakfast. The Brass Choir plays. There are lilies on the altar honoring loved ones. The choir sings Handel's *Hallelujah Chorus.* Anyone is welcome to sing with them. Jesus is up. We are ready to charge into hell with a squirt gun. Most everyone is a happy camper. Sharon prepared a special lunch of ham, potato salad, baked beans and cobbler. While Jesus rose on Easter Sunday, with pastors everywhere I took a nap and Monday off.

THANK GOD FOR CHRISTMAS EVE

The biggest day of worship each year is not Easter. It is most often not a Sunday. It is December 24. Though most Bible scholars believe Jesus was born in the springtime of 4-6 BCE, no one really knows. Maybe Macy's marked 12-

180

24 for making the most money in a magical month. More people come to worship on Christmas Eve than any other day of the year. At Trinity we welcomed between 3,000 and 4,000 children of all ages depending on the weather. It can be bitter, biting cold or just cold.

December 24 is magical, mysterious and majestic at Trinity. Five candlelight services are conducted for the convenience of our many guests. We do our best to provide radical hospitality to all. Snow-blown parking lots, gregarious greeters, hot chocolate and coffee and, most importantly, a candle for every worshipper, glowsticks for young children and an offering plate for every usher.

There is nothing to compare with 1,000 voices singing "Silent Night" while holding lighted candles. One Christmas Eve a couple of years ago there was suddenly a putrid, pungent smell coming from the center balcony. During the quiet, dignified lighting of the candles, a woman momentarily caught her hair on fire! It was immediately extinguished, but the smell was atrocious. The head usher believes the lady was already likely a little lit before arriving at the 9:00 p.m. service.

I did not preach at every service, but you can bet your bottom dollar I gave the annual Christmas Offering appeal. Associate Pastor Linda called me "fearless." I just told it like it was. On December 24, 2017, my last Christmas in Denver, I said, "We need $250,000 to complete all of our mission and ministry commitments for the year. We have five services tonight. Your share is $50,000." Those present laughed at every service and then gave at every service.

One couple wrote a special note to me on their Christmas Offering envelope. It read, "Merry Christmas, you longwinded bastard." Inside was $4 cash. You cannot win them all. Give them to God's grace. By the end of December, the members and friends of the church had given over $270,000 for the appeal. We began 2018 with money in the bank. God and God's people are good. Love whispers in generosity.

A WEALTH OF MUSIC AND ARTS

The Trinity Music and Arts Ministry began around 2000 under the guidance and skilled direction of Judith Mitchell. For a score of years, she has brought energy, vitality and creativity to the ministry. TMAM attracts folks who want to develop their sacred gifts. Various ages learn to sing, ring, chime, dance, act, draw, paint and create to the glory and in the way and spirit of the Master

Artist. Judith has welcomed and found a place for hundreds of souls searching to serve with their nascent gifts. Many folks are attracted to Trinity not because they themselves are musical or are artistic, but because they are blessed by others who are. Director Judith is able and willing welcome all. The TMAM program is generously supported by the prayers and gifts of many in and beyond the ministry. Love whispers through music and arts.

A WEALTH OF MARRYING AND BURYING

The attractive, historic church and its central location made it a destination site for sending off loved ones at life's end or uniting couples in holy marriage for life. Our pastors shared the marrying and burying. Pastor Linda was kind to let me assist in one of her weddings a decade ago. Knowing me to be a sports fan, she kindly asked if I would assist her. It was an elevating experience. The groom was six-eleven, his bride six-one and his best man seven feet tall. Linda and I felt we were in the valley of the giants. Groom Nene is gentle, kind and the most vertically gifted Brazilian I have ever met. He just completed his eighteenth season in the National Basketball Association.

All our pastors buried as well as married God's precious children. One funeral and burial service I conducted was for a Trinity member named Joe. He was a World War II German Concentration Camp survivor and recipient of two Purple Hearts. Joe came home, recovered from his wounds and earned two college degrees. He married Peggy in 1955. They had three daughters, all of whom were competitive figure skaters and performed professionally with the Ice Capades. The family joined Trinity Church. Joe opened Joe's Skate Services where he sharpened ice skates for 39 years in Colorado. He sharpened over 75,000 pairs of blades over the years. Several were worn by Olympic champions Dorothy Hamill and Scott Hamilton who dubbed Joe the "Blade Doctor."

Joe lived by the saying engraved near his workbench at the South Suburban Ice Arena, "No Extra Charge for the Magic." He thought that if the kids believed he was putting magic in their skates, they would skate better. Scott Hamilton, a cancer survivor, came to Joe's service at the church to serve as a pallbearer and deliver a eulogy for Joe from the Trinity pulpit. I deeply admire anyone who fights to overcome cancer, then does a backflip on ice skates at age 50 to celebrate! There was magic in Joe's blading, Scott's skating and Jesus' saving.

A Wealth of Communication

The wealth of communication was essential to Trinity Church's birth, growth and rebirths over 160 years. Whether it was telegraph or telephone, snail mail or email, website or Facebook, the church has stayed connected to its community. Attractive signage, seasonal billboards, targeted mailings, and new resident letters have all been used across the decades to draw guests. The old days of knocking on doors are long gone. The best way to grow a church is by personal invitation.

Some attention came our way from the media through press releases, radio spots and news organizations wanting a trusted voice from the Denver faith community. Several times I was interviewed by local television outlets on a variety of timely topics. One was on church folks bringing guns to church. That came after the 2017 Texas church shooting in which 26 persons were killed and 20 more wounded by a gunman on Easter Sunday. The reporter wanted to know pointblank if Trinity members bring weapons to worship. I had never had a show of hands on arms! I shared we have armed, uniformed police officers onsite at all services and other levels of security in place. Following the interview, I learned some of our members are locked and loaded for far more than praising the Lord. Gee, I trust they do not get too wound up on the next sermon on tithing.

The most compelling television conversation I was a part of was "Preaching to a Purple Congregation" extended interview. Popular local NBC news anchor Kyle Clark of the Next program quizzed Presbyterian Pastor Mark Meeks and me for twenty minutes in the Trinity sanctuary on the provocative theme. I am confident we both offended some viewers and comforted others. Kind of like Jesus did.

The two local newspapers were near the church and kindly connected with us through our sesquicentennial in 2009. One year the Denver *Post* did a story on electronic donations via church kiosks for debit and credit cards. The article was cleverly entitled, "Giving God Credit." A majority of Trinity's giving came via bank drafts and credit or debit cards. Your gifts can be there even when you cannot be. No longer is it necessary to be present and park your posterior in the pew so you can plop your pledge in the plate!

A Wealth of Professional Sports

The wealth of pro sports at 5,280 feet made Denver a desirable destination for any athlete, would-be athlete or sports fan. Sharon and I attended 10-12

Colorado Rockies games every year at cozy, cool Coors Field, an easy walk from the church. We often went with or met friends. The team made the playoffs four seasons in our dozen-year Denver duration. My son and I were present at Coors for the first-round clinching game win over the Phillies in 2007. Unfortunately, the Red Sox swept the Rox in four games in the World Series. A joy of every home fan is singing *America the Beautiful* during the seventh inning stretch. When it the comes to the line *For purple mountains majesty,* the fans shout it out without a doubt that Providence prefers purple!

We saw the popular Denver Nuggets advance to the NBA play-offs seven times in our Colorado time. Sitting with my son under the basket, front row for the Nuggets-Cavaliers game, it does not get any better than that. I could have reached out and touched LeBron James several times during the game. I would have done it only once for I would have been taken away and banned from the Pepsi Center for life. Childhood wisdom: Look, but don't touch!

The Crown Jewel of Colorado sports has always been the Denver Broncos. Even God seems partial. Ever seen a Broncos blue and orange sunset? That settles it. That and fifteen Division Titles, eight Super Bowl games and three Super Bowl victories. The last was in 2016. When I arrived in Denver in 2006, I was given an official NFL Broncos jersey by the Board of Trustees with my name and the number 3 on it. Why a 3? For Trinity, of course! I went to a game or two almost every year. The team went to the playoffs four times, made two trips to the annual ultimate game and won Super Bowl L (50) on February 7, 2016.

There was no rioting, cars burned, or arrests made in Denver. Unheard of! Two days later a Victory Parade passed through downtown Denver a block from the church. Our staff went out and took it all in. One million happy camper Coloradoans showed up to celebrate and dance in the streets. The weather was ordered by the Chamber of Commerce. Peyton Manning could have been elected mayor, governor or perhaps president. That is an interesting thought looking back. The best game I ever saw in person was the 2013 Monday Night Football season home opener. My son flew up from Dallas and we saw the Broncs demolish the Ravens 49-37. Peyton Manning threw a record seven touchdowns. He was one of the best, if not the best quarterback ever.

A WEALTH OF SPECIAL EXPERIENCES

The plethora of special experiences was a bountiful blessing. Sharing in the annual Marade was a cool, even chilling experience. What is a Marade? It combines a march and a parade honoring the life and legacy of Dr. Martin Luther King, Jr. in Denver. As it was on the third Monday of January, the temperature was almost always in the mid-twenties. Do not leave home without your mittens, earmuffs and mug of hot something. The Marade stretched from the MLK statue in City Park to Civic Center Park, annually attracting thousands of God's children of all colors.

The Trinity Church Choir was pleased to sing the National Anthem at a Colorado Rockies game every other season. Pastors were welcomed to sing if they came to two rehearsals. Take me out to the ball game! One season the Rocky Mountain Conference met in Denver. After the Sunday morning ordination service at the Tech center was concluded, 600 delegates and friends descended on downtown for the Father's Day game on Methodist Day at Coors Field. Bishop Elaine Stanovsky threw out the ceremonial first pitch. Baseball legend Tommy Lasorda was on the field to make a pitch for prostate cancer prevention. He was a hoot-and-a-half. I do not know how much Coors beverage the Methodists may have consumed that Father's Day, nor do I remember who won the game. Nonetheless, it was a day of Holy Communion and a good time was had by all on a sunny day honoring our fathers and our Heavenly Father.

Regarding honors, I was surprised and humbled to receive in 2015 the Paul and Paula Murphy Human Sexuality Award from the Center for the Church and Global AIDS organization. As my close colleague Kent Ingram remarked, it is not often a pastor receives a sex award. The recognition came for a sermon on homosexuality I had preached at Trinity several years before. The message drew more letters, cards and calls than any other sermon preached in 35 years. The lengthy *Bringing the L Word Home* will be in my upcoming book of proclamations and prayers. With the nice etched glass plaque came a check for $500. That was a generous gift, but it was my pleasure to hand it back over to the nonprofit organization whose mission is to support and advocate for persons infected and affected by HIV and AIDS throughout the world.

Another special experience came when we moved to Colorado. We had never lived in our own home. We lived in dorms, apartments or parsonages for over thirty years. They did not belong to us. Trinity Church provided a housing allowance for its pastors. We could choose to live anywhere we wanted and could afford. Sharon and I rented a modest older Denver home for six months to learn the lay of the land. We then bought our first residence in the thriving suburb of Centennial. It was a great place to bike around the Cherry Creek and Quincy Reservoirs. We were seventeen miles from Trinity. After four years of commuting by light rail, bus and car, I had a midlife crisis. It was time to move. Not just move but move downtown. Not just move downtown but move into a high-rise.

We downsized from four bedrooms to two in a condo two blocks east of the church. We went from seventeen miles away to 1,700 feet away from the church. Sometimes I went for a week or more without getting my car out of the underground garage. We were on the twelfth floor. That was good and bad. We had lovely views on two sides of our rental, but lots of light and noise invaded our home every night. Sirens and streetcleaners were always about. Snowplows began many winter mornings at 3:30. The Mile-High City never sleeps.

When our black poodle Gabby needed to go outside, it meant an elevator ride. The sirens sometimes seemed to stir her systems. I could not train Gabby to operate the elevator, so when she had to go, I had to go with her. The Portofino Tower had some nice amenities – a lap pool, workout center and locked storage - but walking dogs in the snow was not one. The most fun convenience was a garbage chute. All we had to do to get rid of refuse was to walk 15 feet from our door, open the chute by the elevator door and drop our bags down to the basement dumpster. Twelve seconds was my door-to-door record to dash to the trash and be back in a flash!

The greatest adventure from the tower time was the windy spring day our large patio umbrella blew loose from its moorings and suddenly set sail over the lunchtime passersby below on Eighteenth Street. Sharon and I watched aghast as the potentially lethal object began its leisurely descent. My life passed before me. I immediately imagined the bold headline in the *Denver Post,* "Pastor impales passerby with giant umbrella!" I was helpless for several seconds as the umbrella descended in this direction and that. Not soon enough it grounded itself without damage to people or property. I exhaled with a heartfelt confession of faith, "Thank you, Jesus!"

Soon we moved to a quiet neighborhood full of Jewish and Christian people, gay and straight people, left and right-handed people, Democratic and Republican people. We all got along and liked each other. Why? I believe it was because we lived next to a cemetery where 300,000 human beings are at rest. We were reminded daily of our mortality. We are here not for long. Let us love our neighbors as we love ourselves. Let us be kind to others, as we would like them to be kind to us. I believe it was a Jewish rabbi who advocated affection for all of God's precious children. We all need that sacred reminder from time to time. I need it every day.

A most extraordinary opportunity to extend hospitality to strangers came when the Democratic National Convention came to Denver in 2008. I was no stranger to political conventions, having been in hot, humid Houston when President George H.W. Bush was nominated for a second term in the cavernous Astrodome on August 20, 1992. My gratis seat on Level Seven was so high up that I was above the balloons being dropped at the end of the evening. Most political speeches are like a Texas longhorn steer – a point here, and a point there and a lot of bull in between – maybe like some sermons I have heard and have preached.

Trinity Church did its best to welcome the many guests to town. We got the names and addresses of all the over 100 Methodist delegates and invited them to Sunday worship at Trinity if they arrived in town early. Fifteen showed up, were greeted and prayed for. Delegates and other guests to town were invited through signs on the church and newspaper ads to come to Denver's first church during the week for worship, rest, concerts, tours, prayer and bottled water. Some went to other venues for liquid refreshment and entertainment.

We would have extended the same hospitality if the Republicans came our way. Being from the Lone Star State, I was invited to offer the blessing at the Texas Delegation Breakfast on the first morning of the DNC. The prayer gave thanks for recently departed Texas giants Governor Ann Richards and U.S. Senator Lloyd Bentsen. Richards is remembered for remarking at the 1988 Democratic National Convention that Vice President George Bush was "born with a silver foot in his mouth." She was a hoot and-a-half. Google her hilarious observations of life. My wife's favorite Ann Richards' quote is, "I don't want my tombstone to read, 'I kept a really clean house.'"

A WEALTH OF SNOW SKIING

The wealth of snow skiing venues and vistas was an asset to the Centennial State. Thanks to all the Texans and others who come to Colorado to ski, the economy is strong. What fun to ski with family, friends, staff, church members and sometimes alone.

Snow skiing is a spiritual experience – quiet, outdoors, cool, clean and close to God. Loveland was my favorite ski area as it was an hour from downtown Denver and had inexpensive lift tickets, bunches of beautiful blue runs, ample parking, nice vistas and cheap eats. On top of all that, it had the best name. Loveland! I skied at a dozen different downhill destinations across the state. My last and best skiing came in March 2018 at Breckenridge with my six-year old grandson. The $165.00 senior ticket was worth every penny. With my MCI it is time to retire to safer, saner and slower sports. Anybody for bowling? Oh my!

Travel Adventures

Being a pastor means more than being able to marry, bury and save Uncle Harry. While serving in six fulltime post-seminary parishes over 39 years, I was able to follow in Methodism's main man's ministry who declared, "The world is my parish." The church's global mission and ministry eventually afforded me and sometimes Sharon the opportunity to travel and experience some unusual, historical and spiritual sites and settings. While there is no place like home, travel broadens one's appreciation of diversity, democracy and diets.

DIGGING TO SAVE LIVES

What do you call a dozen Methodist pastors from Texas taking off a week to travel to Haiti? A day at the beach? Hardly. Our God guys got down and dirty digging fishponds to stock and grow tilapia to combat hunger and malnutrition in the northern rural mountains of the Caribbean nation. The Volunteers in Mission team in April 1985 was the first of several church groups to dig ponds 40x40x4 feet in size to help provide protein in the diets of the children in the poorest country in the Western Hemisphere.

The aquaculture project was designed to serve as a teaching model for other communities in Haiti to duplicate. Most of us left a lot of our clothes with our new friends. What wonderful worship to share in a two-hour service with our brothers and sisters in Christ! Their joy and gratitude to God was contagious. By the grace of God, perhaps the work begun that week preserved the precious people in and around Cap Haitien.

HOLY LANDS AND UNHOLY TERRORISTS

Two months after returning from Haiti, it was up, up and away again. Along with three other pastor couples, we led dozens of members of our Texas congregations to the lands called holy for millennia. Our tour took us to Egypt, Israel, Cyprus, Rhodes, Greece, Switzerland and Italy. In Egypt my wife's camel at the Pyramids threw her off and cracked her tailbone. Ouch! This happened on the second day of a two-week trip. Ouch! Ouch! We did not take out the tailbone insurance rider. Ouch! Ouch! Ouch! Sharon was a true trooper the rest of trip. In Israel we ran where Jesus walked. So much to see, so little time. The money changers and money takers were not just in the Temple, but everywhere in the Holy Land

Jesus was not in his tomb. He got up already and went before us. Lots of people got dunked or sprinkled at the River Jordan. Some Methodists drank wine. Nobody walked on water. We all went down in the grotto where Jesus was believed to have been birthed and burped. There were some dirty diapers which looked as if they came from the first tour, not the first century. Everyone sang *Silent Night* in her or his native language. Way cool!

We boarded the Italian cruise ship *Achille Lauro* at Ashdod, Israel. It took us around the Mediterranean Sea to various ports of call. We pastors learned about the topless deck on the ship. Our wives wanted nothing to do with it for themselves or their husbands. We learned how tiny windowless cabins on a rocking sea can deepen one's prayer life.

Something we learned four months after the cruise was that PLF terrorists may well have been on our ship. The *Achille Lauro* was hijacked in October by members of the Palestine Liberation Front. The hijackers killed a Jewish American passenger by tossing him and his wheelchair into the sea. Authorities expect several PLF folks were onboard months before doing reconnaissance. The invaders also terrorized the 600 passengers and crew members. Two movies were made about the ship-jacking. No true holy people threaten and terrorize the lives of fellow passengers on the journey of life. The Holy One does not go for unholy business.

ANCIENT-MODERN MEGACITY

In 1994 I was invited with some Bellaire Church members to go on a United Methodist Church South Central Jurisdiction Mission Tour to Seoul, South Korea. Though I was born during the Korean War, most of what I knew about Korea was from watching MASH. There were six of us from Bellaire UMC, including a couple and their young adult daughter whom they had adopted as a child from Korea. Reverend Won Kie Kim of Los Angeles led this culture and waistline expanding experience. We worshipped at the Kwang Lim Methodist Church which had 60,000 members. We saw the Yoido Full Gospel Church with 800,000 members and weekly attendance of 200,000. It has 500 pastors. That must be one long staff meeting!

Seoul was a bustling big city 25 years go. The community began in 2323 BCE. Today there are 10 million souls in Seoul. In our visit we drove past the 1988 Summer Olympics Games venue. We visited the DMZ, looking over into North Korea. Supreme Leader Kim Jong-un was 10 years old at the time. A most memorable moment on our trip was a personal visit with U.S. Ambassador to South Korea, Dr. James Laney. A Methodist minister, he served as the president of Emory University from 1977 to 1993. Laney was appointed Ambassador to South Korea by United States President Bill Clinton in October, 1993. He was involved in defusing the 1994 nuclear crisis during his tenure. I had a couple of crises in my ministry, but none was of a nuclear magnitude.

The day we had our appointment with Ambassador Laney happened to be a day with someone being upset about something somebody else said or did. There was some shouting, shoving and sign waving. Armed guards were present, but there was tension as we were hustled into the American Embassy. We were all a little anxious when we were asked to turn over our passports and cameras as we passed through the next level of security. Finally, we reached top floor and spent a delightful hour with Ambassador Laney.

He served as U.S. ambassador to South Korea from 1993 to 1997. In 2009, Emory's graduate school was named the James T. Laney School for Graduate Studies. Maybe at age 91 he will come out of retirement and lend some timely wisdom on the present tension on the Korean Peninsula.

DON'T BLAME IT ON RIO

In 1996 the World Methodist Council was to meet in Rio de Janeiro, Brazil. Texas Conference Bishop J. Woodrow Hearn graciously nominated me to serve as a delegate, no expenses paid. With a child beginning college at a private school that fall, a trip of that magnitude was not financially feasible. Some generous lay leaders in the congregation learned of this nomination and stepped up and funded the travel so I could attend the august assembly in August in America South.

Rio is a beautiful place to visit. Home to five million, the huge seaside city is world known for its Copacabana and Ipanema beaches, Sugarloaf Mountain and Christ the Redeemer, the colossal statue of Jesus Christ with outstretched arms at the summit of Mount Corcovado. It was completed in 1931 and stands 98 feet tall. The statue is the largest Art Deco-style sculpture in the world and is one of Rio de Janeiro's most recognizable landmarks. The city is also known for its sprawling favelas, or shanty towns. Taking a tour of the city shared not only its magnificent beauty, but also the great poverty of many peasants who live in squalor.

My time in Rio will always be marked by two things which happened to two family members back in Texas, and the grace of a fellow pastor at the airport. Within a couple of days my aunt who lived next door to my mother died unexpectedly. Then word came that my sister was brutally terrorized and assaulted in a home invasion while visiting a sorority sister in Los Angeles. I needed to come home to Texas immediately. It is not easy to leave a foreign land suddenly, even with a family crisis. The hotel concierge was helpful but could do only so much. American Airlines did its best to get me from Rio to Tyler, Texas. With grace and grit they arranged an itinerary which include seven airports in 24 hours. Hello Rio, Brasilia, Miami, JFK, LaGuardia, DFW and Tyler. Do not try this at home or anywhere else, unless absolutely necessary.

When I arrived at the Rio Airport, I discovered that I had to pay a special early departure surcharge. It was $70 and had to be paid in cash. How much cash did I have? Seventy dollars. Crisis averted. In the airport I ran into Dr. Hal Brady, pastor of First UMC in Dallas. He graciously gave me a $20 bill to help out. When I landed in Tyler the next night, I still had my $20 backup bill. I later mailed it to Hal with a note thanking him for his kindness. With a kind heart like that it is no wonder he is still preaching in his eighties on the internet from Decatur, Georgia.

WELCOME TO WESLEY WORLD

In 1998 Sharon and I took a group of chronologically gifted members of Marvin Church to England and Scotland on a Wesleyan Heritage Tour. We experienced the beauty St. Paul's Cathedral, Westminster Abby, London Bridge, Oxford, Buckingham Palace, the Tower of London and Epworth. Helping some of our seniors "Mind the gap" almost made me lose my mind. We toured Stonehenge and a ton of historic cathedrals. One tourist to Great Britain wrote in his diary daily "ADC." When asked what that meant, he replied, "Another damn cathedral!"

Church of England priest John Wesley (1703-1791) began a methodical movement to reform, renew and reignite the Anglican Church. Though he never left the Church of England, he was a passionate proclaimer of God's grace for all. His brother Charles Wesley wrote 6,000 hymns which are still sung around the world over 250 years later. John offered sound advice, "Beware you be not swallowed up in books! An ounce of love is worth a pound of knowledge." He confessed, "I set myself on fire and people come to watch me burn." A favorite is, "Though I am always in haste, I am never in a hurry."

Though an Oxford don, John was a practical theologian bringing good news to all. On his deathbed at 88, Brother John confessed, "The best of all, God is with us." All parents love to quote JW, "Cleanliness is indeed next to godliness." Of course, everyone on the planet earth embraces two-thirds of Brother John's economic strategy, "Make all you can, save all you can, give all you can."

In 2002 Wesley was listed at number 50 on the BBC's list of the 100 Greatest Britons, drawn from a poll of the British public. Wesley's house and chapel, which he built in 1778 on City Road in London, are still intact today. The chapel has a thriving congregation with regular services as well as the Museum of Methodism in the crypt. Numerous schools, colleges, hospitals and other institutions are named after Wesley. In 1831, Wesleyan University in Middletown, Connecticut, was the first institution of higher education in the United States to be named after Wesley. The now secular institution was founded as an all-male Methodist college. About 20 unrelated colleges and universities in the United States were subsequently named after him. Today 80 million persons are connected to Methodist and Wesleyan branches of the Christian tree.

RETURN TO WESLEY WORLD

Sharon and I came across the pond again three years later to vacation and attend the 2001 World Methodist Conference in Brighton, England. While our first trip to England was all about buses, this time we rented a car for a week, as well as rode trains. Funny how those drivers went in circles on roundabouts and drove on the left side of the road! We got the hang of it pretty quickly. However, the narrow lanes with high hedges on the remote roads led to some scars and scratches, dings and dents in the Dent's car, say 400 pounds for the pounding we gave our rental. Little harm, little foul.

Our carless days in London led us to lean on the London Underground. Also called the Tube, the public transportation system got us everywhere we needed to go, even to a chapel on Aldersgate Street where John Wesley felt his heart "strangely warmed" 250 years ago and where he "believed in Christ and Christ alone for his salvation." While Wesley rode 250,000 miles on horseback to proclaim the good news for 50 years after his spiritual heartburn, we rode 50 miles from London to Brighton on a modern train to attend the meeting of Methodists in the seaside resort dominated by a pier, a pavilion and playground for adults of all ages.

Our hearts were familiarly warmed with powerful Methodist singing and praying, preaching and teaching and communing with bread, wine and holy conversation. As with Rio's World Methodist gathering, this one was a celebration of diversity in ages, attire, accents, color, gender and education. Our lengthy and many services reminded the thousands present we are all one in Christ. We were most moved to hear David Wilkinson, an astrophysicist from England, speak. Soon we welcomed him to Tyler to deliver the Pirtle Lectures in the Marvin sanctuary. Wesley World would soon come to Texas!

IMAGINING NO MALARIA

In 2006 Denverite Rick Reilly wrote column about malaria in *Sports Illustrated*, challenging his readers to donate at least $10 for the purchase of anti-malaria bed net. Rick's popularity brought the issue to national attention. Tens of thousands of Americans across the country donated, leading to the creation of the Nothing But Nets campaign. What's better than saving a life with a ten spot? Led by Bishop Thomas Bickerton, the United Methodist Church got in on the ground floor in imagining no malaria.

Imagine No Malaria was a comprehensive anti-malaria campaign run by The United Methodist Church. This extraordinary effort to put faith into action to end preventable deaths in Africa, especially the deaths of children, has raised many millions to empower the people of Africa to overcome malaria's burden. Imagine No Malaria has worked in partnership with the United Nations Foundation and the Global Fund to reduce the number of deaths of children caused by malaria in African countries.

As Co-Chair with Rocky Mountain United Methodist Women President Robin Ball, I had the opportunity to travel to Angola in October 2012 with Bishop Warner Brown, Bishop Elaine Stanovsky, Robin, Lay Leader Kunle Taiwo and retired pastor and former missionary to Angola Burl Kreps. We pastors preached in Angolan Methodist congregations the Sunday we were there. The challenges of preaching through an interpreter are three. The sermon is twice as long. The interpreter may mistranslate a word or phrase. A Texas accent can throw off the best translator! We distributed bed nets from house to house, did radio interviews, ate dinner with the Angolan Host Bishop and toured Methodist work in the area.

Our trip inspired us to come home and raise $1 million in our conference for Imagine No Malaria. It took a year, but we did it. Our denominational goal was to raise $75 million. We exceeded $68 million, just over 90% of the goal. Thanks be to God for those who dream and work for a world without preventable diseases. Who would think that love could whisper through a bed net?

194

Letters to the Editor

With the mass expansion of the internet in the last two decades, readership of daily newspapers has declined significantly. Nonetheless, letters in the paper have long reached a segment of the community quickly at no expense with a spiritual value or observation. Unless noted, these letters all appeared in the *Denver Post*. Letters from around the world today can be read daily via the internet. Facebook and other electronic forums sometime bring more heat than light.

DEATH OF ANOTHER YOUNG BRONCOS PLAYER   FEB. 28, 2007

Re: *stunned Broncos ponder the randomness of death," Feb 26 sports story*

For the second time in as many months, our community mourns the death of a 24-year-old member of the Denver Broncos football team. Again, we read team players and coaches responding to these unexpected losses by saying, "This just makes you realize we don't know how much time we have. That's up to our maker," and "This was not our call. This was God's decision."

If the divine must be invoked to explain these sad deaths, let it be said that God created the world finite and free. Physical evil such heart failure is the natural implication of a finite world. Moral evil such as drive-by shootings is the tragic implication of a free world. May we also take comfort in the belief that the Almighty knows our pain in such losses.

Michael D. Dent, Senior Pastor, Trinity United Methodist Church, Denver

MISSING THE CONVENTION   MAY 18, 2008
ROCKY MOUNTAIN NEWS

Thank you for your interesting ten lists of 100 things about the Democratic National Convention just 100 days away. On your list of former presidential and vice presidential nominees likely to be at the convention is Lloyd Bentsen. As a U.S. Senator and Secretary of the Treasury, Mr. Bentsen was a highly respected gentleman. If he shows up in Denver this August, please note his appearance with a bold headline. He left the political world permanently May 23, 2006, two years ago this week. May this beloved statesman from my home state continue to rest in peace,

Michael D. Dent, Senior Pastor, Trinity United Methodist Church, Denver

DENVER'S OLDEST CHURCH NOVEMBER 22, 2008

Thank you for your special section on "Denver: 150 and Counting" (Nov. 21). The pictures and articles were informative and captivating. While there were four mentions of saloons, liquor laws, and a prominent brewery establishment in 1873, nowhere was made note of Denver's first church. Founded August 2, 1859, when there were 31 saloons, but no schools, hospitals, or libraries, what is now Trinity United Methodist Church was home to many early city and territorial leaders, including Governors Evans, Elbert and Pitkin. One of its pastors. Henry Augustus Buchtel, was elected governor in 2006.

Church members were instrumental in founding both the Iliff School of Theology and what is now the University of Denver. The congregation's present home, built in 1888, is a downtown landmark, with its signature stone spire and gothic sanctuary.

Trinity remains a vital congregation with almost 2,000 members and will celebrate its sesquicentennial throughout 2009 with the theme, "We're Here for Good."

Rev. Michael D. Dent, Denver
The writer is Senior Pastor of Trinity United Methodist Church

COACH'S LIFE LESSONS APRIL 3, 2010

Re: *"Karl's still coaching, but just not hoop,"*

Dave Krieger's column was both personal and powerful. Particularly poignant was the observation of the coach's young daughter: "It seems like there's a lot of death in the world."

Five-year-old Kaci Grace Karl is correct. There is a lot of death in this world. Dreams, hopes, marriages, and souls also die. How timely that a child's awareness of human mortality is shared in the week that Jews and Christians are observing Passover and Easter, traditions which celebrate holy deliverance and triumph in the face of suffering and death.

May the hopes and prayers of many of all faiths surround and strengthen Coach Karl and his family in his bout with cancer.

Michael D. Dent, Senior Pastor, Trinity United Methodist Church, Denver

NUGGET OF IRONY
FEBRUARY 16, 2011

Thanks for the chuckle from the Feb. 14 sports section. Just above the Nuggets Briefs article headlined, "With Melo or without, Karl sees success," was a blurb headlined, "Eye exam wouldn't hurt." The inescapable irony, intentional or not, was a sweet Valentine's Day gift.

Michael D. Dent, *Denver*

JOSH DAVIES FOR CITY COUNCIL AT-LARGE POST
APRIL 20, 2011

For five years I have had the privilege of knowing Josh Davies as his friend and pastor at Denver's first church. During that time, I have seen him invest his time, talent and treasure in the Denver community. In addition, he was the first-elected lay delegate in the Rocky Mountain Methodist Conference to the denomination's most recent international meeting. As a delegate, Josh advocated on behalf of the marginalized in the faith community in the face of strong opposition. He has proved himself as a passionate, courageous and respected leader.

Genuine public service takes persons of vitality, approachability and responsibility. Josh is such a leader. I am honored to endorse him for Denver City Council at-large member. Josh Davies is a wise choice for the common good of the Mile High City.

Michael D. Dent, Denver
The writer is Senior Pastor of Trinity United Methodist Church

REACTIONS TO COLORADO'S 9/11 EVENTS SEPTEMBER 13, 2011

Kudos to the sponsors of Sunday's "Colorado Remembers 9/11" and to Gov. Hickenlooper and Mayor Hancock for hosting this event and including a multifaith component in the program. The brief blessings from Buddhist, Christian, Islamic, and Jewish spiritual leaders were warmly welcomed by the 35,000 sun-drenched citizens.

The close juxtaposition on the stage of clergy members and soldiers firing a salute may have been a disconnect for some. Yet it called to mind the title of a song from another war-era, "Praise the Lord and Pass the Ammunition." At one point, the four diverse spiritual leaders stood and held hands in a circle, sharing genuine gratitude, and offering mutual encouragement. That spontaneous expression of unity is a sign and symbol of hope for our diverse nation and world.

Michael D. Dent, Denver
The writer is Senior Pastor of Trinity United Methodist Church

GUNS, MENTAL ILLNESS, AND THE CONNECTICUT SCHOOL SHOOTING DECEMBER 18, 2012

Friday's tragedy in Newtown echoes the tale of young children murdered in and around Bethlehem after the birth of Jesus. This "slaughter of the innocents" by a paranoid person with power is sadly repeated with increasing frequency. There is a lot we don't know about this latest massacre.

As Jews and Christians light candles in this season, most all people of faith acknowledge these realities:

1. Life is fragile, unpredictable and therefore precious.
2. Moral evil is the tragic implication of a free world.
3. Community is good and vital to our well-being.
4. The Creator compassionately cares for the children who suffer.

Whatever our faith orientation, may we work to overcome evil with good.

Michael D. Dent
The writer is Senior Pastor at Trinity United Methodist Church

JOYS TO CELEBRATE

FEBRUARY 2010
TYLER MORNING TELEGRAPH

Last month my wife and I were privileged to be in Tyler to participate in the grand-opening ceremonies of the Meadow Lake Senior Living Community.

What a joy to celebrate on a sunny, 65-degree January day the launch of the city's first faith-based, nonprofit continuing care retirement community.

The first phase includes 54 executive homes, 80 garden apartments, 34 memory care assisted living apartments, 20 traditional living apartments, 30 skilled nursing residences, a gorgeous community center, and a lakeside lodge. The campus will eventually be home to 250-300 residents and will employ 129 full-time staff members.

Meadow Lake began with a dream more than 20 years ago when Tyler community leaders James Fair, Bob Irwin, and Quintan Chamness donated a lovely 92-acre plot of land to their church for development as a retirement community.

Congratulations to Marvin United Methodist Church and the Sears Methodist Retirement System for partnering to make this dream a reality. Tyler, Smith County, and East Texas will long benefit from this gift to the common good. Folks from as far away as Colorado are already making plans to make Meadow Lake their retirement home.

Michael D. Dent
Senior Pastor
Trinity United Methodist Church
Denver, Colo.

(Former Pastor, Marvin United Methodist Church)

NOTE: This final letter to the editor was found in a folder from my first pastorate 45 years ago. It was published in the weekly Bolivar Peninsula newspaper and includes the folksy reply of the editor in the coastal Texas community

NEIGHBORLY NEWS

DECEMBER 11, 1974

Dear Friend:

Thank you for the opportunity to have our community activities printed free in your fine paper. Would you please print the following news in your issue of week of December 11?

"The Meaning of Christmas" will be presented on Wednesday, December 18, at 7:00 p.m. at St. Matthew's United Methodist Church in High Island. The musical drama is being put on by the combined efforts of Baptist, Presbyterian, and Methodist Churches of High Island. A candlelight service will follow the drama with refreshments and fellowship period afterwards. The public is invited to attend. We appreciate your being of public service by printing such news. Thank you again.

Sincerely,
Michael D. Dent

Editor's Note: Thank you, Rev. Dent, for your letter.

Everyone needs some encouraging news along the way of life. Reminds me of an angel's whispering love long ago, "Behold, I bring you good news... great joy... for all the people...a Savior is born..." No better news than that!

Lobbying the Legislature

When one is called to pastoral ministry, the tasks which come to mind are to preach, teach and do outreach. A pastor has the responsibility to marry, bury and save Uncle Harry. One country cleric cast his tasks as "Win 'em, wash 'em and work 'em." Our call is to collect the cash. Our vocation is to visit the sick, the shut-ins, saints and sinners. Our privilege is to pray with parishioners in sad, glad and bad times. Our call is to save souls. One preacher asked his congregation one day who wanted to go to heaven. Everyone, save one, raised a hand. The pastor asked the single negative soul, "Brother Smith, don't you want to go to heaven?" Brother Smith replied immediately, "Of course I want to go heaven. I just thought you were getting up a group to go tonight!"

Pastors also have a biblical responsibility to do justice, to care for the sick and to watch over the young. Three times in my ministry I had the call to travel to state and national legislative assemblies and visit representatives regarding the health of thousands of at-risk children and youth or those on death row. I traveled a few blocks, a few hundred miles and across the nation to voice concern over the need to do what is just, fair and compassionate.

ALCOHOL ADS IN AUSTIN

Having spent a year of preparing, conducting and analyzing an alcohol project for my doctoral project, I was ready, willing and able to testify at a state legislative committee in the spring of 1998 in the State Capitol in Austin, Texas. Marvin UMC Lay Leader David Eikner and I drove from Tyler to Austin to invest a day to convey our concerns. The issue was the prominent presence of alcohol advertising in a State of Texas publication which was directed at older children and teenagers. It seemed incongruous to allow such commercial advertisements in a state-produced publication for all ages. Underage alcohol consumption did not need an assist from the Lone Star State.

The members of the Texas committee we met with were grateful and respectful of our concerns. We shared copies of the offensive Budweiser ads. David and I both had teenage children. We knew the pressures, problems and pervasive presence of adult beverage advertisements in the lives of our sons and daughters. Legislators do listen. The legislative committee we spoke to was responsive to the issues we raised. Eventually the ads were removed. The omnipresent tee-shirt declares "Keep Austin Weird." I am grateful when folks in Travis County "Keep Austin Wise."

LEAVE THE KILLING TO GOD

Growing up in Texas in the middle of the twentieth century instilled a culture of capital punishment in many communities. If you were convicted of a violent crime and did not have significant financial resources, you might have a date with fate and with Old Sparky in Huntsville. Texas, which is the second most populous state of the Union, has executed 567 offenders from the U.S. capital punishment list since the resumption in 1976, more than a third of the national total. One of those came from my home church. RIP, George.

Too many innocent people have been executed. Execution eliminates the chance for rehabilitation. Killing people who kill people to show that killing is wrong is not logical. Execution is an act of vengeance. Innocent persons have been executed. State sanctioned murder is contrary to the Love Ethic of Jesus, the Prince of Peace. The Jewish and Christian scriptures proclaim, "Do not take revenge, my dear friends, but leave room for God's wrath, for it is written: 'It is mine to avenge; I will repay,' says the Lord."

I can personally testify to the pain of losing an immediate loved one in a manslaughter conviction. My brother was only 33, a son, brother, husband, new father and practicing medical doctor. Killing his killer would not take away our family's painful loss. That is why I chose to go to the Colorado State Capitol three blocks from my church in downtown Denver to testify against capital punishment in the spring of 2008. Only one person has been executed since 1977 by the state of Colorado since the reintroduction of capital punishment. That was in 1997. Let's leave it at that, for God's sake.

PARTNERING TO SAVING LIVES

In October 2012 I spent a week in and around Luanda, Angola in Africa as a part of the Imagine No Malaria Campaign of the United Methodist Church. Within a week of returning to Denver, I was invited to travel with a handful of folks from across the USA to Washington, D.C. to spend a couple of December days lobbying. Our task was not difficult. We fanned out to visit with the state's two U.S. Senators and seven congressional representatives to request their continued support for the HIV/AIDS/Malaria programs initiated under President George W. Bush. Such lifesaving programs cannot be taken for granted.

Unfortunately, not a single Colorado elected official was in or available. I visited each of their seven offices, left business cards, notes and materials on the HIV/AIDS/Malaria initiatives. With a little extra time on my hands, I went to the office of my former congressional representative from Texas. Louie Gohmert was in, kindly greeted me and then asked me to wait for him in one of the rooms in his office suite. I went in and there was someone already waiting to see Louie. The guy looked familiar. He introduced himself, "My name is Steve Forbes." Yes, that Steve Forbes, former USA presidential candidate and scion of the Forbes fortune. We visited a bit before the congressman came in and invited us to be his guests for his Tuesday night tour of the Capitol. Having plans already for dinner with my fellow Methodist lobbyists, I declined.

When I got back to Denver, I sent Mr. Forbes a letter to his office in New York City inviting him to invest $1,000,000 in the Imagine No Malaria Campaign. A week later a letter from the Big Apple arrived. I quickly opened the envelope and found inside the nicest rejection letter I have ever received. The Bible says, "You have not because you ask not." Steve was flattered to be asked but was already committed to many other quality charitable causes at the time. While he did not give at that time, others did. Many Methodists made monetary gifts to mash malaria. The Imagine No Malaria campaign received $68,000,000. Love whispers when gifts large and small are given to save the lives of children. Lobbying to save lives is always in season.

THE LITTLE ROCK NINE

On May 17, 1954 the U.S. Supreme Court issued its historic *Brown v. Board of Education*. The court declared all laws establishing segregated schools to be unconstitutional. The court called for the desegregation of all schools throughout the nation. Resistance to desegregate was strong. All-white schools in cities throughout the South continued. In Little Rock, Arkansas, the school board agreed to comply with the high court's ruling. After a year of stalling, the Superintendent of Schools submitted a plan of gradual integration in May 1955. The school board unanimously approved the plan to be implemented in the fall of the 1957. Nine black students were chosen to attend the previously all-white Little Rock Central High, based on the criteria of excellent grades and attendance.

On September 4, 1957, the approved students made an unsuccessful attempt to enter Central High School, which had been previously segregated. The Arkansas National Guard, under orders from the governor, and an angry mob of about 400 converged on the school and prevented the nine from going in. Two weeks later a mob of about 1,000 people surrounded the school again as the students attempted to enter. The following day, President Dwight D. Eisenhower took control of the Arkansas National Guard from the governor and sent soldiers to accompany the students to school for protection. Soldiers were deployed at the school for the entirety of the school year, although they were unable to prevent incidents of violence against the group inside the school. Members of the nine were spat on, yelled at and had acid thrown in their faces.

Fifty years later in Denver the Little Rock Nine members were honored by the Iliff School of Theology in a Community Luncheon celebrating their courage, faith and endurance. The spacious place was packed. The emotional event was a highlight in my nine years of service on the Iliff Board of Trustees. I was in a Hall of Heroes that day.

Five years later one of the nine came to speak to a full house at Trinity Church. Denverite and United Methodist Carlotta Walls LaNier graduated from the University of Northern Colorado and began working at the YWCA as a program administrator for teens. She later founded LaNier and Company, a real estate brokerage company. Connecting closely with Carlotta was a brush with a sad and painful part of American history. Little Rock Central High

School still functions as part of the Little Rock School District. It is now a National Historic Site which houses a Civil Rights Museum, administered in partnership with the National Park Service, to commemorate the painful events of 1957.

JFK ASSASSINATION

I was eleven years old when my president was killed in my home state. With the whole nation, my family watched and wept for four unbelievable days. Shock and sorrow swept our nation. The world cried with us. My parents ordered a copy of *The torch is passed*, a pictorial and prose recording in 100 pages of four painful, almost unbelievable days for our nation. The large, hardbound, marron-colored book cost $3 and was produced by the Associated Press. Its subtitle was *The Associated Press Story of the Death of a President*. I read that volume many times, never expecting I would one day make a connection with a prominent player in that day's tragic drama.

For nine years I served as the chair of the Ethics Committee at Trinity Mother Frances Hospital in Tyler. Dr. Bill Turner, a young cardiovascular surgeon in Marvin Church, was kind to invite me to speak at the April 2002 Texas Surgical Society semi-annual meeting in the Rose City. Seated next to me at the breakfast event was a delightful doctor who was the President-elect of the American College of Surgeons, no small honor. Dr. C. James Carrico was a medical school classmate of our near and dear neighbor, Dr. John Hudnall.

Decades ago one late fall Friday around noon bullets were fired in downtown Dallas. Confusion reigned as a motorcade suddenly sped off to Parkland Hospital. A 28-year-old, first-year surgical resident named Jim Carrico was the first physician to care for President John F. Kennedy. The young doctor inserted a tube into the barely breathing leader of the free world and stayed with him for 25 minutes until gun violence took another soul home. It was not the only murder in Dallas which made world headlines that sorrowful weekend. Dr. Carrico believed the Warren Commission's conclusion that Lee Harvey Oswald was the lone assassin in Dallas November 22, 1963.

Dr. Carrico did not get to serve his term as the ACOS president. He died of colon cancer in July 2002. The Presbyterian physician received many honors and trained a plethora of physicians across his medical career. His legacy of leadership and service is testimony to the Great Physician. Dr. Carrico whispered love, mercy and grace across two-thirds of a century. I am deeply humbled to have crossed his path. May his tribe increase.

TEXAS A & M BONFIRE COLLAPSE

The phone at the Marvin Church parsonage rang at an ungodly hour on November 18, 1999. It was just a few minutes past three a.m. No one calls at that hour with good news. Our daughter was calling from College Station where she was a freshman at Texas A&M University. She said, "Dad, the bonfire collapsed!" Half-asleep, I muttered, "I'm sorry, but do you know what time it is? Thanks for letting us know, but it is time to go back to sleep." Martha screamed into phone. "No, you don't understand. People have died!" She could see the tragedy from her eighth-floor apartment window.

In a decades' long tradition, A&M students spend weeks carefully crafting a 59-feet tall stack of about 5,000 logs for a gargantuan bonfire to be ignited a night before their annual football game with their bitter rival University of Texas Longhorns. Martha was sadly right. Of the 58 present and former students working on the stack when it collapsed at about 2:45 a.m., twelve were killed and 27 were injured. Delicate rescue operations took over 24 hours as rescue and recovery workers sought to avoid other collapses. Within a few hours, fifty news satellite trucks were on the campus broadcasting the devastating tragedy around the world.

Our family had four direct connections to this sad event. Not only had our daughter experienced the frightening fallout firsthand, we knew one of the twelve students who was killed. Nathan Scott West was a member of Bellaire United Methodist. I was his family's pastor from 1992-1996. Third, many Texas A&M graduates and students were from Tyler or lived there.

Marvin Church quickly decided to offer to the community a Memorial Service for anyone who wanted to attend. The above the cut headline in the . *Tyler Morning Telegraph* read "500 ETexans Pay Homage To Dozen Who Died At A&M." The November 23 article was accompanied by a color picture of my proclaiming the promise that "nothing can separate us from the love of Christ." The president of the Tyler A&M Club read the names of the twelve students who had died four days before. The local television stations reported on the service. Great was our grief at this tragic loss. Greater still was our faith.

Fourth, our family already had tickets and plans to attend the Aggies-Longhorns game in College Station. On November 25, 1999, the date that the bonfire would have burned, the university held a vigil and remembrance ceremony. Over 40,000 people lit candles and observed up to two hours of silence at the site of the collapse, before walking to Kyle Field for yell practice. At the stadium, fans relit their candles as the Parsons Mounted Cavalry fired the Aggie cannon twelve times, once for each victim. Former U.S. President George H. W. Bush, whose Presidential Library was built on the A&M campus in 1997, his wife Barbara, Texas Governor George W. Bush and his wife Laura, all attended the remembrance ceremony.

The following day the Aggies upset the highly ranked Texas Longhorns, 20–16 in the annual rivalry game. The kickoff was preceded by a flyover of F-16 jets, all piloted by former A&M students, in the Missing Man formation. At half-time, the Texas Longhorn Band dedicated their performance to the students lost and injured in the collapse and ended by playing "Amazing Grace" and "Taps." Then removing their white hats in a show of respect, they walked off the field. There was not a dry eye in the house between the over 80,000 fans of both teams.

The Fightin' Texas Aggie Band also played a tribute to the victims and, contrary to the strong tradition, marched off the field in a silent cadence. Aggie students, who normally sit only when the opposing band plays, stood throughout both performances and gave both bands extended standing ovations. I believe God whispered love to all that emotional day. I also believe God may have worn maroon that therapeutic afternoon.

OBAMA NOMINATION

In 1992 I attended the nomination of President George H.W. Bush for another term. Sixteen years later came another invitation to the nomination of another candidate seeking to succeed President George W. Bush. Most everyone in Denver was excited that the city was chosen to host a national political convention in 2008. The main color of the four days was not blue, but green. Such major gatherings bring significant national and international attention to a city. Those four days were filled with hustle and bustle. Press, protestors, police, partygoers and past and present public servants all filled the streets, hotels, bars, restaurants and taxicabs. All contributed to the City and County of Denver's coffers.

All the events of the week centered around the Pepsi Center, home of Denver's pro basketball and hockey teams. As the week wore on, there was pressure on the powers which be to expand the opportunity of the public participation in the historic event of the first African American to be

210

nominated for President by a major political party. Late on Wednesday, August 27, I received word I could have up to ten tickets for the nomination for President of the United States. The historic event was moving from the Pepsi Center to Invesco Field, home of the Denver Broncos. The ten tix went in flash. Pastoral colleagues and my son and his attorney friends were all excited to share history .

Rocking out with Stevie Wonder and Sheryl Crow, listening to former Vice President Al Gore and Vice President nominee Joe Biden and then being a part of history in witnessing the first African American to accept nomination by a major party was a night to remember. The junior senator from Illinois, born in Hawaii, educated at Columbia University and Harvard Law School, a community organizer, Barack Obama accepted the official nomination of his party. Two months later he was elected President of the United States while in his forties and served the maximum two terms. Change happens.

SAND CREEK MASSACRE

Have you heard of the Sand Creek Massacre? I had not before arriving in Denver in 2006. But soon I was educated in a sad, sordid and savage chapter of U.S. and Colorado Territory history. The Trail of Tears is the name of the forced relocation of Native American nations in the United States in the nineteenth century. The trail became a flood of tears on November 28,1864 when almost 700 U.S. troops began a daylong siege on a peaceful village of Arapahoe and Cheyenne Native Americans. The sad facts of the attack intensify the deep pain and grief of the tribes attacked:

1. The camp had been granted sanctuary by government officials.
2. The camp was flying American and white truce flags.
3. The camp consisted primarily of women, children and elderly men.
4. At the end of the day, U.S. army soldiers killed and mutilated the bodies of nearly 200 women, children and aged men. Unborn babies were cut from their mothers' wombs. Body parts of Indian men and women were taken to Denver and displayed as trophies in the theatres of the young town. The perpetrators were hailed as heroes.

Who led this Colorado Volunteer Calvary of the United States in this savage massacre? An ordained Methodist Minister who said, "Damn any man who is in sympathy with the Indians."

When Pastor John Chivington's funeral was held in 1894 the sanctuary of what is today called Trinity United Methodist Church, 600 persons attended.

211

They heard the pastor declare, "When Colorado lifts aloft the scroll of honor, the name of Colonel John Chivington will be emblazoned near the top." To his dying day, Chivington declared, "I stand by what I did at Sand Creek."

The most earnest effort to bring healing came in the Sand Creek Sesquicentennial observance at the 2014 Rocky Mountain Annual Conference meeting in Pueblo, Colorado. A score of buses transported 600 delegates to the Sand Creek Massacre National Historic Site 23 miles from the tiny town of Eads in rural Southeast Colorado. The daylong pilgrimage was largely filled with quiet reflection and sober tears as we walked through the silent, expansive massacre site and imagined the savagery of that atrocity 150 years before. Not an uplifting day, to say the least. A Community Dinner that evening included long overdue recognition of and presentations of gifts to descendants of massacre survivors. Some healing and hope emerged as testimonies of the day were shared.

As you can surmise, Trinity Church has never been a place where any Native American would want to go near. Yet, a miracle occurred in November 2014 on the sesquicentennial of the slaughter of nearly ten score innocent human beings. Dr. Henrietta Mann, whose great-grandmothers were in the Native American camps at Sand Creek when they were attacked by Pastor Chivington, came to town. Miraculously, both of her antecedents survived the massacre and imprisonment. In a long shot that she would accept, Trinity Church Associate Pastor Miriam Slejko invited Dr. Mann, a college professor in Oklahoma, to attend a small dinner at Trinity on the 150th anniversary of the Sand Creek slaughter. She was understandably reluctant, but eventually chose to attend. The event was awkward as there was the lingering pain of the past. Nonetheless, there were genuine whispers of healing and hope for the future.

For five years in Denver I lived across the street from Fairmont Cemetery where Colonel Chivington is buried. There is no mention on his massive marker of the Sand Creek Massacre or his being a Methodist minister. Sometimes I was tempted to spit on his grave. Truth be told, I may have. Nonetheless, may he rest in peace with all the victims of this hideous, heinous, horrific happening in human history.

FIRST INCLUSIVE EPISCOPAL ELECTION

In June 2015 I was honored by my colleagues in the Rocky Mountain Annual Conference when they elected me to serve as a delegate to the 2016 Western

Jurisdictional Conference meeting in Scottsdale, Arizona. Have you ever been to the desert in July? The temperature reached 112 degrees. It was still in the triple digits at 10 p.m. It was also hot in the conference sessions as the 100 delegates worked on their main task over four days. What can be controversial about electing a person to serve in a prominent position of power? That would surely never happen in the United Methodist Church or the United States of America, would it? Try twice in five months in 2016.

Every four the years five Methodist Jurisdictional Conferences meet simultaneously across the nation to elect episcopal leaders. These spiritual leaders are elected for life, though there is a mandatory retirement age. In 2004 as a delegate from the Texas Conference, I was part of the South Central Jurisdictional Conference in Corpus Christi which elected five bishops. Our task in Arizona was simple, electing just one bishop. Prayers, interviews, conversations and printed materials help discern and decide on candidates fit for the office. There were nine pastors called to offer themselves as a bishop in the church of Jesus Christ.

The delegates took nine ballots between business sessions, meals, prayers and worship services over three days. Candidates withdrew along the way. Three candidates remained competitive through 16 ballots. On ballot 17, one candidate received 88 ballots. There were twelve abstentions. Dr. Karen P. Oliveto. Ph.D., was duly elected to the episcopacy. Former seminary professor and dean, she had served the past eight years as senior pastor of Glide Memorial United Methodist Church, a diverse 12,000-member congregation in the Tenderloin neighborhood of San Francisco.

Her election made history and headlines around the world as the first openly gay bishop in the United Methodist Church. The groundbreaking election challenged some sections of the Methodist and other Christian bodies, while bringing comfort and celebration to others. Dr. Oliveto was consecrated as a bishop in the church on July 16, 2016 at Paradise Valley United Methodist Church. The theme of the conference chosen months before, *Crossing Thresholds*, came to pass. One definition of a threshold is "any place or point of entering or beginning." The church was entering a new age of welcoming and valuing diversity in God's family. Despite protest and challenge by some folks in the church, ecclesial authorities determined the election was in order.

The Western Jurisdiction College of Bishops assigned Bishop Oliveto to serve the Denver Area. She has brought passionate, powerful gospel preaching, sharing the good news of God to all of God's children since taking office. She has received numerous death threats during her tenure. Bishop Karen is grounded deeply in a genuine spirituality, compassion for those on the margins and courage and patience to work in transforming the hearts and minds not yet open to inclusivity. She brings a humble heart of obedience to the twin command of Jesus, who when asked what the greatest commandment of all is, answered, "Love God and love neighbor."

Growing up in Texas meant high levels of exposure to sports of all kinds. I loved watching sports, playing sports and reading the sports page. Baseball, basketball and football stars were idolized. Professional athletes made much money, were on television and only worked part-time. Just like today, some of them misbehaved. They got in in trouble with booze, betting or broads. Some were arrested, convicted and did time behind bars. There are a few bad apples in every bunch, athletes and pastors alike. It was my good fortune to come across and connect with some folks who were not only the best ever in athletic competition, but who were also genuinely nice people.

THE WORLD'S GREATEST WOMAN ATHLETE
Babe was the best. I did not ever meet her personally, though my dad worked with her brother at the Mobil Oil refinery in Beaumont. Mildred "Babe" Didrikson Zaharias was born in 1911 in Port Arthur, Texas, raised in my nearby hometown and came to worldwide fame in 1932 when she won two gold medals and one silver medal at the 1932 Olympic Games in Los Angeles.

She excelled in golf, basketball, baseball and track and field. After the Olympics, she turned to professional golf and winning. Babe won ten Ladies Professional Golf Championships and 48 total professional tournaments. She is widely regarded as one of the greatest athletes of all time. She was named the tenth Greatest North American Athlete of the twentieth century by ESPN. The Associates Press AP chose her as the "Female Athlete of the Year" six times. In 1950, AP overwhelmingly voted for her as the "Greatest Female Athlete of the First Half of the Century." Zaharias was inducted into the LPGA Hall of Fame in 1951

She fought a two-year battle with colon cancer. She used her fame to raise funds for cancer treatment. Babe also served as a spokesperson for the American Cancer Society. Her work in this area was honored by U.S. President Dwight Eisenhower on a visit to the White House. Babe's battle ended on September 27, 1956. In 1957 she posthumously received the Bob Jones Award, the highest honor given by the United States Golf Association in recognition of distinguished sportsmanship in golf. It was accepted by her husband George four months after her death. Several golf courses are named after her. The Babe Didrikson Zaharias Museum is on I-10 in the heart of Beaumont.

My affection and appreciation for Babe came from riding my bicycle many times to the Forest Lawn Cemetery near the Neches River in the north end of Beaumont to visit her grave. I was not inspired by the lists of her athletic awards, achievements and accomplishments. There was no mention of them. The only athletic reference on her tombstone was a quote from famed sportswriter Grantland Rice, "It's not whether you win or lose, but how you play the game." That wisdom has whispered confidence, compassion and conviction in my call and career as a pastor. Thanks, Babe, for playing the game of life with grit, gusto and grace. You were the best.

THE WORLD'S STRIKEOUT KING

Major League Baseball has produced hundreds of great pitchers over its 150-year history. Perhaps the best ever came from the Lone Star State. Many would agree. Nolan Ryan played in 27 seasons, more than anyone else in MLB since 1900. Ryan ranks first all-time in strikeouts, fewest hits allowed per nine innings, no-hitters, one-hitters, two-hitters and three-hitters. He played during the administrations of seven U.S. Presidents, from Lyndon Johnson to Bill Clinton. These records are likely never to be broken. Ryan was elected to the Baseball Hall of Fame in 1999, in his first year of eligibility, with 98.79% of the vote. He was the first Hall of Famer inducted as a Ranger. That year, he ranked 41st on *The Sporting News* list of the 100 Greatest Baseball Players and was elected to the Major League Baseball All-Century Team.

I was blessed to cross paths with the Strikeout King In addition to seeing him pitch several times over his career, I met him at a book signing in downtown Houston in the 1980s. When my fellow Texas Methodist came to Colorado in 2008 to serve as Grand Marshall of the National Western Stock Show Parade in downtown, we met in our best cowboy hats, shirts and jeans. He and Ruth, his wife of now over 50 years, were the perfect pair to participate in the prominent parade and pose for pictures.

How long did the Ryan Express ride the rails as a pounding pitcher? He once said, "When I came into the game, the minimum salary was seven thousand dollars, and I'd have to go home in the wintertime and get a job." Today Ryan's estimated net worth is over $100 million. Mamas, don't let your babies grow up to be cowboys. Let them be doctors and lawyers and fastball pitchers and such. Baseball was good for Nolan Ryan. The Strikeout King was good for baseball.

BEATING THE BABE'S RECORD

When Babe Ruth retired from Major League Baseball in 1935, he had set a career record of 714 home runs. The record seemed untouchable. For almost 40 years it was until a team player from Mobile, Alabama showed up and showed out year in and year out. Henry Aaron let his bat do his talking. He came be to be called "Hammerin' Hank," playing for the Braves in Milwaukee and then in Atlanta. He consistently hit 35-45 homers each season. Seemingly suddenly, the Sultan of Swat, as Ruth was known, was having his seemingly unbreakable record threatened. Records are made to be broken, but having a black man break a mark set by a mythic white hero was almost too much for some.

As Aaron closed in on the 714 career home runs record, he received thousands of letters every week during the summer of 1973, including hate mail. The Braves had to hire a secretary to help him sort through the avalanche of supporters and detractors. The stress and strain took a toll. He was the recipient of death threats during the 1973–1974 offseason from people who did not want to see him break Ruth's nearly sacrosanct home run record. The threats extended to those providing positive press coverage of Aaron. Lewis Grizzard, sports editor of the *Atlanta Journal*, received many phone messages calling journalists racist names for covering Aaron's pursuit of the home run record. While preparing the massive coverage of the home run record, he quietly had an obituary written, afraid that Aaron might be murdered.

As it turned out, Aaron finished the 1973 season one home run short of the Babe. Ruth's widow denounced the racism and declared that her husband would have enthusiastically cheered Aaron's attempt at the record. Aaron tied Babe Ruth's record, April 4, 1974, in his very first at bat—on his first swing of the season in Cincinnati. The Braves returned to Atlanta, and on April 8, 1974, a crowd of 53,775 people showed up for the game. It was a Braves attendance record. The game was also broadcast nationally on NBC. I remember being glued to the TV. In the fourth inning Aaron hit home run number 715, breaking Ruth's record. While cannons were fired in celebration, two college students sprinted onto the field and jogged alongside Aaron for part of his trot around the bases, temporarily startling him. Don't try that stunt today! The announcers declared, "There's a new home run champion of all time, and it's Henry Aaron!"

Aaron hit his 755th and final home run on July 20, 1976. After the 1976 season, Aaron rejoined the Braves as an executive. On August 1, 1982, he was inducted into the Baseball Hall of Fame, having received votes on 97.8 percent of the ballots, second only to Ty Cobb, who had received votes on 98.2% of the ballot in the inaugural 1936 Hall of Fame election.

Hank Aaron's MLB record for home runs was broken in 2007 by Barry Bonds. Bonds was a record-setting Major League Baseball player whose accomplishments were tainted by allegations of performance-enhancing drugs. I cherish the opportunity I had to meet and visit with Hank Aaron in 1998 in Downtown Tyler, two blocks from my church. He was present with his wife for a fundraiser for Texas College, the historically black college affiliated with the Christian Methodist Episcopal Church. Byllie Aaron graduated from Texas College in Tyler. What a special evening to hang out with Hammerin' Hank, who broke Babe Ruth's HR record! Mr. Aaron could not have been more gracious and kind to visit with. Hank and Byllie Aaron, now in their mid-80s, are philanthropists invested in making the planet a better place for all.

THE GREATEST COWBOY OF THEM ALL

America's Team, they have been called. The Dallas Cowboys, winners of five Super Bowls and participants in three more, have made the National Football League play-offs 33 seasons. The Cowboys are the most valuable sports franchise in the world, valued at $5 billion in 2019. They are the only team in the NFL to have had 20 consecutive winning seasons.

The Texas team has had many stars across its sixty years. They include Don Meredith and Don Perkins, Cornell Green and Randy White, Dak Prescott and Dez Bryant, Tony Hill and Tony Dorsett, Emmitt Smith and Kevin Smith and a hundred more. Who was the greatest Cowboy? Some might choose Captain America, popular Quarterback and U.S. Navy veteran Roger Staubach, or offensive, defensive and special teams player Deion Sanders. I would cast my vote for a player who was born in Texas, reared in Texas, played college football at Texas Christian University where he was an All-American star and then played fourteen seasons of professional football in Texas.

Bob Lilly is considered one of the greatest defensive linemen in National Football League history. As the anchor of the Cowboys' "Doomsday Defense," he helped the team win its first Super Bowl title in 1972. He was named an All-Pro seven times, and was selected to play in 11 Pro Bowl games. Lilly's agility and quickness helped him score four defensive touchdowns in his career. Affectionately known as "Mr. Cowboy," his name was the first inscribed in the Dallas Cowboys Ring of Honor, above Texas Stadium and the current AT&T Stadium.

Lilly was inducted into the Pro Football Hall of Fame in 1980, his first year of eligibility, and was the first player who spent his entire career with the Cowboys to be elected to the Pro Football Hall of Fame. The *Sporting News* named him a member of the All-Century NFL Team and "the greatest defensive tackle in NFL history." In 1999, he was ranked number 10 on The Sporting News' list of the 100 Greatest Football Players, the highest-ranking defensive lineman and the highest-ranking Cowboy.

After his retirement from pro football, Lilly moved to Waco, Texas, where he successfully operated a beer distribution business until 1982, when he witnessed the impact of a traffic crash caused by drunken driving. That tragedy truly transformed his life. He divested his alcohol investment and launched his landscape photography career.

I met Bob Lilly in Tyler one October in in the late 1990s when he was the speaker and I was the invocator at the at the annual Rose Festival Men's Luncheon at the Sheraton Hotel in Tyler. We talked over lunch about football, of course, but also about faith, family and life. The now great-grandfather is a wise man. He knew how to play the game, how to respect your opponent and when to move on in life. Now 80, Bob Lilly still lives in Texas, respects his opponents, lives out his faith and is regarded by many as the greatest Cowboy of them all. He has my vote.

Holy Ground

Everyone needs some sacred space. We seek special places where the veil between this world and the eternal world is thin. We sing of "We Are Standing on Holy Ground," where the presence of the Divine is palpable. The Holy One commanded Moses to remove his shoes, for the place he was standing was holy.

Saints and sinners alike make spiritual journeys to Jerusalem, Mecca, Normandy, Washington, D.C., Gettysburg and other consecrated sites and shrines. Some sacred spaces may be quite simple with only a candle, quiet space and devotional materials. Sacred space may be alone in the car, on a walk or run, or in a special place in one's home. I have heard God's name beseeched on a beautiful golf course.

Where is your Holy Ground? How do you experience a thin place on your spiritual journey? When and where do you come into presence of the Creator and Redeemer of heaven and earth? I have worshipped and preached in several churches which were thin places. Yet there are three spaces which have special significance because the transforming spiritual presence in each.

LAKEVIEW METHODIST CONFERENCE CENTER

Lakeview is aptly named. There are three lakes on the 1,000+ acre woodsy property twelve miles from Palestine in deep East Texas. It is more of a retreat center than anything else. Annual retreats for pastors, pastors' spouses, retirees, United Methodist Men and Women groups, Sunday School classes, college groups and other entities utilize the facilities. They include the beautiful Peace Chapel, Sparling Dining Room, Great Hall, Tabernacle, Copeland Center, classrooms, tennis courts, canteen, playground, boats, hiking trails, athletic fields, infirmary and five cabin clusters. Lakeview can welcome groups as large as 1,000.

In 1962 the assembly was given an attractive motto, "Our stock in trade is spiritual experience." That proved prophetic for me as that was around the first time I went to Lakeview. It was a father-son retreat. I was impressed by all the men in our cabin reading their Bibles and praying together before lights out. Over the next 42 years I spent at least six months of my life directing summer camps, attending annual pastor retreats, leading staff retreats, speaking to the Conference Methodist Men and even attending a called meeting of the Texas Annual Conference.

Lakeview is a sacred space where people are present and open to the Spirit and one another. Literally living, eating, praying, playing and praising God together builds bonds with Christ and each other. Many love whispers were spoken and heard there. A week at church a camp was as good or better than a year of Sunday School. None present at youth summer camp can ever forget the spiritual lyrics of vespers with the guitars playing and sopranos leading the singing the camp favorite song gently with tweaked local line:

> Have you seen Jesus my Lord? He's here in plain view.
> Take a look, open your eyes He'll show it to you.
> Have you ever stood in the family
> With the Lord there in your midst?
> Seen the face of Christ on your brother?
> Then I say you've seen, Jesus, my Lord
> Have you seen Jesus my Lord? He's here in Lakeview.
> Take a look, open your eyes He'll show it to you.

Lakeview was, is and always will be Holy Ground. Many commitments and recommitments to Christ have been made there. Calls to ministry were extended and answered. Oral Roberts once preached there. A beaucoup of bishops brought the Word alive to fatigued preachers. The Lord alone knows how many dominoes and '42' games have been played there. One of my close clergy friends had his ashes scattered at Lakeview. That makes for truly Holy Ground.

LAITY LODGE RETREAT CENTER

Located on the banks of the Frio River in the lovely canyon in the Texas Hill Country twelve miles from any town, Laity Lodge is sacred space. Founded in 1961 by grocer magnate and lay evangelist Howard Butt, Jr., Laity Lodge has been welcoming guests to its retreats for almost 60 years. Dr. D. Elton Trueblood, a noted 20th-century American Quaker author and theologian, was the first speaker. Individuals, families, classes and friends come for a week or a weekend to receive rest, renewal and refocus. Some families are in their fourth generation of coming to the canyon.

There is an intentional effort of lodge staff to provide an ecumenical, comfortable, spiritual setting and space. Guests are awakened to a sense of the sacred. God's goodness and nearness are experienced and expressed in the Holy Ground's beauty, hospitality, individual and community worship and

222

spiritual exercises.

Frederick Buechner, popular American preacher, theologian, ordained Presbyterian minister and the author of more than thirty published books, spoke at Laity Lodge several times. Now 93, Fred said, "On my first visit to Laity Lodge, I knew it was a holy place. The high hills spoke of it. The river spoke of it. ... I don't believe I have ever known a place as full of human kindness and openness and grace as I have found in virtually everyone I met there."

Sharon and I echo that high praise for the hospitality, humanity, humility, holiness, spiritual warmth and graciousness of the staff, as well as the high-quality speakers and musicians who brought us all to spiritually sacred spaces. We were moved to remove our shoes as we received the Word through the words of Howard Butt, Jr., Don Murdock, David Redding, Howard Hovde, Eugene Peterson, Buckner Fanning, Jeannette Clift-George, Christopher de Vinci and Dave Williamson. The music each summer in Creativity Week was provided by the best. Stephen Clapp, Dean of the Juilliard School from 1994 to 2007, and Charles Webb, Dean of the Indiana University School of Music for 24 years, were musicians every summer we attended. It does not get any better than that.

Laity Lodge was designed and built to be attractive, comfortable and inviting. The Great Hall main meeting space was created to be the "the most comfortable living room in the Hill Country." The founders were intentional in their radical hospitality. They worked on conveying the message, "You are a guest in our home ... a place we love deeply and have prepared just for you." We always felt warmly welcomed, highly valued and spiritually comfortable. Sharon and I were reawakened to a sense of the sacred in the many thin places at Laity Lodge.

In addition to the Great Hall, there were several hospitable havens available. The large library in the lodge led many souls to a thin place to read, relax and rest their eyes. The bookstore contained books written by LL authors, devotional classics, various Bible translations and, of course, some lodge swag. Sharon still has an attractive green sweatshirt with the Laity Lodge logo on it from fifteen years ago, as well LL mugs and a ring. The Quiet House is a secluded, contemplative retreat built in 1978. Located a short hike from the Lodge, this small, comfortable house provides an opportunity for silence, stillness, meditation and prayer for an individual or a married couple.

The Lodge was completely rebuilt in 2017. The primary lodging accommodation has 16 guest rooms for 1-3 guests. Each features a king bed and an extra-long twin bed, essentially dividing the room into two zones. All rooms include built-in desks and private bathrooms with large windows opening to the meadow and the river bluff. Served in the Great Hall, the meals are healthy, nutritious, delicious and abundant. The retreat center property is dotted with hammocks, benches, trails and non-motorized watercraft to explore up and down the Frio River. The Blue Hole swimming spot is the favorite place for all ages to cool off in the summer heat after a hike, tennis match or Bible Study.

For six-plus years Sharon and I were blessed by a benefactor to attend the annual Creativity Week sessions where, guess what? We created! I built a porch swing, made a pinch pot, threw a pot, took a creative writing class, designed and sculpted a bonsai tree and added creative shots to my tennis game. Sharon took silversmithing, watercolor, block printing, pottery, jewelry making and birdhouse building. It was like an adult Vacation Bible School on steroids! One year we shared a relaxing year-end spiritual retreat with teaching, reflection and experiencing Laity Lodge with much cooler and shorter days. Not a bad place to welcome a new year with prayer, music, reflection and the presence and power of God's grace and goodness. Lots of love is whispered at Laity Lodge. Look online to learn more of this hallowed space. We hope to return there soon.

YMCA OF THE ROCKIES AT ESTES PARK

There is much Holy Ground in the Rocky Mountains of Colorado. One is amazed by the snowy towering peaks, clear cool streams, bright fields of flowers and vast array of animals large and small which have peacefully coexisted for millennia. The scenery is truly breathtaking. Every morning for almost 13 years we would wake up in the morning in the Rockies, pinch ourselves and declare with glee, "We live here!"

Did you know Colorado has two state songs? The first is old and largely unknown. The second is known worldwide. We lived in Denver when the state adopted an additional official song. You likely know it. In 2007 the Colorado State Senate, by joint resolution, determined that "Rocky Mountain High" should be accepted as a second song. The song tells the tale of a young man coming into a state of grace and self-awareness through the natural beauty he encounters in the mountains of Colorado. Transplant John Denver - he of the nice adopted Colorado name - wrote the autobiographical song in 1971. He lived the last twenty years of his life in Aspen. The Colorado Rocky Mountains were sacred space to John Denver. They are today to all who view them as far as 50 miles away.

The YMCA of the Rockies at Estes Park is Holy Ground. Opened in 1907 near the village of Estes Park, the Y provides a spiritual environment where families, friends, individuals and groups are inspired by its scenic beauty, peaks and wildlife. The camp is surrounded on three sides by Rocky Mountain ridges and ranges. Groups of five to 5,000 come for retreats, reunions, conferences and vacations. The accommodations are comfortable, convenient and cost-effective. One of the two YMCAs of the Rockies two facilities, the Estes Park Center offers a variety of affordable accommodations, including family and family reunion cabins, and comfortable lodge rooms located close to the Center's core recreational, dining and meeting facilities.

My connections to the EP-Y have included the United Methodist Rocky Mountain Annual Conference meeting, a Trinity UMC Youth Retreat, my wife's Trinity Women Annual Retreat and a score years of attendance at the annual Rocky Mountain Preaching Seminar. A group Texas Methodist pastors retreat to comfortable, cool Colorado in the fall to plan, prepare and project sermon titles, texts, themes and series for the next twelve months. We bring computers, Bibles and notes. The six to twelve pastors work independently for the most part, share illustrations, enjoy daily hikes and share evening meals, fellowship and worship. We encourage one another and solve all of the problems in our congregations. Well, some of them. Those evening meals are holy communion.

There are 58 verses in the Bible which refer to mountains. One commands "Go out and stand on the mountain before the LORD, for the LORD is about to pass by." There you go! Go to the mountains to get close to the Most High God. I grew up singing, "Lord, plant my feet on higher ground." We named our Colorado mountain home "Higher Ground," not only because it was at an elevation of 8,600 feet, but we felt extremely close to the Divine in the alpine outdoor cathedral of the Sangre de Cristo ("Blood of Christ") Mountains of the Rockies in Southern Colorado.

Run, do not walk, to the Rocky Mountain nearest you. Visit the vast vista of the Rocky Mountain National Park, adjacent to the YMCA of the Rockies at Estes Park. Depending on the season, you can drive two miles above sea level and encounter a herd of elk, as well as black bears, moose and eagles. This is our Father's world. A day in the park is worth a thousand elsewhere to our souls. The air is thin, as are plentiful places and spaces to meet your Maker on earth. Where is your Holy Ground?

The Preacher and the FBI

Most every older boy, teenage guy and adult male wanted to see the "The Untouchables," an American TV crime drama which ran weekly from 1959 to 1963. The show fictionalized Eliot Ness's experiences as a Prohibition agent fighting crime in Chicago in the 1930s with the help of a special team of agents handpicked for their courage, moral character, and incorruptibility, hence nicknamed the Untouchables. I became an admirer of the show and of the Federal Bureau of Investigation. As with all boys of that era, we wanted to join the FBI because we joked it meant "female body inspector." Funny then, but not today. A member of my Beaumont home church, Frank Rooks, was an agent of the Federal Bureau of Investigation. Texas's Jefferson County Sheriff Dick Culbertson, my mother's boss for 25 years, attended training at the Quantico FBI Marine Corps Base in Virginia.

From 1965-74 the ABC TV network churned out 240 one-hour episodes of "The F.B.I." The popular drama starred Efrem Zimbalist Jr. as Inspector Lewis Erskine. It was "must see TV" for many. Sponsored by Ford Motor Company, you can guess what type of cars the agents drove! With the endorsement of then Bureau Director J. Edgar Hoover, the show was like an ode to the F.B.I. Hoover even allowed some scenes to be filmed at F.B.I. headquarters in Washington, D.C. Inspector Erskine was all business. He didn't laugh, love or play. But he usually got his man! Zimbalist was supposedly approved by Hoover personally. At the end of many shows, the actor would appear to ask viewers for their help in finding real life fugitives and assorted bad guys.

TYLER FBI CONNECTIONS

During my ten-year pastorate in Tyler two young FBI Special agents and their families joined Marvin Church. One was from my hometown of Beaumont. David and Peter were bright and brave, as well as wise and witty. When David received an assignment, he would pack his bag, kiss his wife goodbye and tell her two things, "I'll be back be back between two days and two weeks. Don't watch the news." One such assignment was in Afghanistan. And I thought the ministry had rough days. Both of these dedicated agents were sent to my parents' hometown of Hemphill in deep East Texas to assist in a most challenging assignment.

I remember the day and moment the disaster struck. As I was backing out of my parsonage driveway in Tyler on the first Saturday of February 2003, I heard and felt a terrible explosion, yet had no idea what had just happened. Soon the nation learned the tragic news. The Space Shuttle Columbia disintegrated during atmospheric entry, killing all seven crew members. During the launch of its 28th mission, a piece of foam insulation broke off from the Space Shuttle external tank and struck the left wing of the orbiter. When Columbia re-entered the atmosphere of Earth, the damage allowed hot atmospheric gases to penetrate the heat shield and destroy the internal wing structure, which caused the spacecraft to become unstable and break apart.

President George W. Bush shared with the nation, "My fellow Americans, this day has brought terrible news and great sadness to our country. At nine o'clock this morning mission control in Houston lost contact with our space shuttle Columbia. A short time later debris was seen falling from the sky above Texas. The Columbia is lost. There are no survivors...." He then shared the names and ranks of the seven astronauts. Our nation was stunned and saddened.

Almost immediately, FBI agents David and Peter were summoned from Tyler with other FBI agents to lead in the recovery of the space shuttle and its crew members. They were assisted by NASA, local law authorities and the U.S. Forest Service. It was grim work. Peter and several others assisting in the effort were hospitalized briefly from exhaustion. Neither Tyler agent was released from duty until the task was completed. All the astronauts and space shuttle pieces were recovered from across deep East Texas and Western Louisiana. The primary debris field was in and around Hemphill, Texas, where I had spent many summers playing at my grandparents' homes and dreaming of being an astronaut someday. Since the astronaut call never came but the preaching gig did, I never made it to the Federal Bureau of Investigation until I was 59. It was worth the wait.

ATTENDING THE FBI ACADEMY

In early 2011 a regular worshiper at Trinity Church and Denver civic leader invited me to apply for acceptance to the FBI Citizens' Academy. Academy class members are community leaders and are nominated by a Bureau employee or a previous academy graduate. To be eligible, one must be at least 21 years old, with no felony convictions and must live and work in the local office area. Because of the classified investigative techniques discussed, nominees must also undergo a background check and get an interim security

228

clearance. It would have been a severe embarrassment for the pastor of Denver's oldest church to fail the background exam!

Two dozen men and women were accepted in the 2011 Class. The Academy offers members of the community an up-close and personal look at how the Bureau operates. The program brings civic, business and religious leaders together to experience firsthand how the FBI investigates crimes and threats to national security and learn about the various tools and techniques the FBI employs to carry out its mission.

Our class met weekly in the evenings for three hours for eight weeks. Most sessions were taught by agents and experts from the Bureau Laboratory and Training divisions. Our meetings were usually at the FBI Denver Division Headquarters in northeast section of the city. Believe me, it is a secure setting. The staff and agents at the division bureau were all professional, courteous, helpful and patient with us.

Because the FBI Academy is where new agents are trained, the Citizens' Academy curriculum mirrors new-agent training. That means class members received plenty of hands-on instruction, from shooting firearms and learning how to fingerprint and handcuff suspects, to collecting evidence from a crime scene and operating vehicles under emergency situations. We shared in simulation exercises of drawing and retuning fire. Our class had several field trips. We spent an eye-opening evening at Denver International Airport touring the expansive space and its extensive facilities. There is far more security there than meets the eye. We rode a special RTD (Regional Transportation District) Bus in the city, visited Invesco Field (home of the Denver Broncos) and a pair of undisclosed locations which provided the FBI support, resources and intelligence.

Two of our classes were led by FBI Special Agents who distinguished themselves on a large stage in their service to their country. What an honor to get to know these men. Both were named Jim. The first Jim was portrayed in a 2001 American war film produced and directed by Ridley Scott. West Point graduate Jim Yacone served eight years in the U.S. Army and is a decorated combat veteran. He joined the FBI in 1995 as a special agent. His hazardous military service was shared in *Black Hawk Down*, a book and then a movie by the same name. In 1993, U.S. forces were part of a United Nations mission to end the civil war and humanitarian crisis in Somalia. The helicopter Jim was piloting was shot down and crashed. The ensuing firefight became known as the Battle of Mogadishu.

In March 2008 Jim Davis was named Special Agent in Charge of the Denver Division of the FBI. He had previously served as Legal Attaché in the U.S. Embassy in Baghdad, Iraq. This Jim entered the duty with the FBI in 1985, investigating white collar crime. In 1989, he was transferred to the Chicago Division and was assigned to an undercover operation involving fraud in the commodities markets. He then served on the Public Corruption Squad, where he was the case agent on a three-year undercover operation which resulted in over two dozen convictions, including six City of Chicago Aldermen. He was promoted to supervisor of that squad in 1996.

Jim #2 was transferred to FBI Headquarters in August 1998, where he was responsible for supervising FBI agents assigned to the independent counsel investigation of Secretary of the Interior Bruce Babbitt. In September 1999, Jim was promoted to Unit Chief of the National Press Office. Jim's face came to the world as part of Operation Red Dawn, an American military operation conducted on December 13, 2003 near Tikrit, which led to the capture of Iraqi dictator Saddam Hussein. Jim's picture accompanying the fallen dictator made front pages around the globe.

THE MACHINE GUN PREACHER

Most every FBI Citizen Class participant looks forward with the greatest anticipation to Range Day. It is the final class and the agents cooked lunch for the soon-to-be academy graduates on a beautiful July Saturday. Best of all, we shared fun, fellowship and firearms. Under close supervision of the agents, we got to shoot a variety of weapons in a secluded, safe, secure range south of Denver used by area enforcement entities for practice. We discharged rifles and pistols. Those who wished were permitted to shoot a rapid-fire gun, again with an agent at your side and in control

A machine gun is a fully automatic mounted or portable firearm designed to fire rifle cartridges in rapid succession from an ammunition belt or magazine. Did the pastor pop off a belt of bullets in the blink of an eye? What do you think? Though not a registered gun owner, I had shot guns in the Boy Scouts. I had not discharged a gun in 45 years. It was time to do it again!

Our Range Day concluded with a group picture of the class members and the seven to eight agents who taught us the in the months together. Thirty of us were standing, kneeling or sitting on the large armored Denver Division FBI Vehicle brought out and used only in PR poses, riots or championships won by the Avalanche, Broncos, Nuggets or Rockies. IOW, not too often.

230

Two weeks after Range Day, each class member received in the mail from Washington, D.C. a happy surprise. We each were blessed by the U.S. Department of Justice Federal Bureau of Investigation with a lovely letter and framed certificate on August 17, 2011, recognizing our successful completion of the FBI Citizens' Academy. Both were signed by the Director of the FBI, Robert S. Mueller, III. The Vietnam Veteran, Purple Heart Winner, Bronze Star Recipient, University of Virginia Law School Graduate and wise Public Servant has been hailed throughout his life and career as being objective, apolitical and nonpartisan. "Bobby Three Sticks" is still in the news at age 75 in 2019.

Going through and graduating from the FBI Citizens' Academy was the most fun, interesting, exciting and expanding community experience in my long ministry. It was a privilege to learn from, hang out and partner with these dedicated public servants who risk their lives to protect ours. Agents in the Denver FBI Division arrested an admitted terrorist in adjacent Aurora during the period our Academy was meeting. Those feds were still pumped up the next time we met!

Strange But True

There are many happy celebrations in a pastor's calling. What is more delightful than joining a joyful couple in Holy Marriage, or baptizing a beautiful baby or welcoming a Confirmation Class into membership in the Body of Christ? Those are holy, happy and healthy happenings! Over 44 years it was my pastoral privilege to be a participant in many mountaintop moments and memories. Unfortunately, some strange, unexpected events occurred, not always with happy endings. As Forrest Gump taught us in the 1994 film, "Mama always said life was like a box of chocolates. You never know what you're gonna get." Sometimes strange things happen on a pastor's watch. Five of these seven weird events involved weddings. Anybody surprised?

THE WALKAWAY GROOM

In 1999 Julia Roberts starred in and as a *Runaway Bride*. Four times she left grooms at the altar. The zany film grossed $309 million. I have had a pregnant bride or two, but never a runaway bride. However, I once had a groom walk away. Fortunately, it was not at the wedding. That would have been a disaster. Like most pastors, I required meeting with any couple who wanted to get married. This is usually done months before the wedding. This premarital conference includes confirming the date, time and location, going over the order of the service, choosing scriptures for the service, discussing their future and praying with and for the family in the making.

The longest and most important part of the premarital conference is their independent written completion of a four-page questionnaire on their families of origin, education, vocation, spiritual journey and other appropriate information. That is when the wedding train went off the track and crashed. The groom got up, walked out and never said a word. I was shocked and speechless. This was very early in my ministry. Was it something I said or did?

The bride-to-be apologized and explained why the groom walked away from the premarital meeting. What do you think? Was he nervous about entering this lifetime commitment? Had he had a bad day at work? The gentleman bolted because he could not read. He was embarrassed by his illiteracy. I never saw the couple again. That was over 40 years ago. I wonder what happened to the walkaway groom. I pray they got married and all is well for them today. They surely raised my awareness that not all major challenges in life are visible to others.

OPEN WEDDING

The couple was in their fifties. They had each been married before. They were professionals, established in the community, but new members of the church. They asked if I would marry them. Of course, I would. Could the wedding be in the sanctuary? Sure. Could it be on a Sunday? I guess so. Could we have it right after the 11:00 a.m. service? If you give me time to greet our guests after the service. Could we invite the entire church family to stay for the nuptials? That would be unusual, as many Marvin Methodists move on quite quickly to meals at one of the country clubs, cafeterias, cafes or home cooking.

We had the Sunday noon wedding open to all. Not all came. The bride and groom, pastor and musicians did their thing with rings on Sunday soon after noon. There were some guests. There is a first time for everything. Most importantly, Jesus showed up and showed out in the prayers, music, scripture, vows, rings and commitments made. I had not officiated at a Sunday wedding nor an open service before. Nor have I since.

WHAT IS SHE WORTH?

The doorbell rang at the Edom parsonage one weekday afternoon in the fall of 1978. An older couple at least in their fifties was at the door. I was not usually at home in the daytime but happened to be that particular day. They wanted to get married. They had a proper license to wed. The preacher who was supposed to tie the knot was a nearby no-show, so I was drafted into pastoral service. I was glad to officiate.

We had the brief wedding in our living room. Sharon was our witness. When the prayers, vows, rings and pronouncements were completed, everyone was smiling and rejoicing in the creation of a new family. As the officiant, I signed the wedding license. It is tradition for the groom to give the pastor a monetary gift for services rendered. The groom bluntly asked, "How much do I owe you?" We had a new baby and I was still in school. Money was tight. I did not want to insult the man nor stifle his generosity, so I smiled and said to him looking at his new bride, "What is she worth?" He reached into pants pocket, pulled out his wallet and from a wad of cash he placed a $5 bill in my hand. While I was frankly hoping for more, I was grateful to be able to take Sharon to dinner that week with the wedding honorarium. We were most hopeful the bride was worth a stash of cash.

FUNERAL HOME BAPTISM

David and Joanne had it all. They shared a thriving medical practice, a magnificent, multi-story home on the lake and two beautiful young daughters. Then came the boy, Bradley. He was so loved by his beloved parents, sisters and Grandma Joanne, all a part of the Atascocita United Methodist Church family. Then one night tragedy struck in their home. Bradley somehow got tangled up in the sheets of his crib and smothered to death. Unbelievable. Shock, sadness and sorrow swept across the community.

As a caring community, folks in the church and across Northeast Harris County brought food, prayed prayers, sent flowers, gave memorials and held their children a little tighter. It was my pastoral privilege to meet with David and Joanne to plan the Service and Death and Resurrection for their son, their only son.

As we gathered to do so at their home, we realized Bradley had not been baptized. Call it benign neglect, third-child syndrome or whatever, his parents asked me to baptize him. Doing so at the funeral was not a viable option. We decided to administer the Sacrament of Holy Baptism in the Rosewood Funeral Home in Humble, Texas after the last guests departed the visitation. It was quiet at 9:00 p.m. David and Joanne, Bradley's sisters and grandmother and I gathered for this sacred task in the Chapel.

> *Brothers and sisters in Christ:*
> *Through the Sacrament of Baptism*
> *We are initiated into Christ's holy church.*
> *We are incorporated into God's mighty acts of salvation*
> *And given new birth through water and the Spirit.*
> *All of this is God's gift, offered to us without price.*
> *Bradley Briscoe, I baptize you in the name of the Father,*
> *And of the Son, And of the Holy Spirit. Amen.*
> *Dying, Christ destroyed our death.*
> *Rising, Christ restored our life.*
> *Christ will come again in glory.*
> *As in baptism Bradley put on Christ,*
> *So in Christ may he now be clothed in glory.*

The next day over 500 folks came to Atascocita United Methodist Church to express their grief, celebrate their faith and give God thanks and praise for the life and eternal life of Bradley Briscoe. His parents generously donated funds to the church to construct a playground in loving memory of their beloved, baptized baby boy.

SLAPPED BY A STRANGER

Serving in a diverse setting such as Downtown Denver has its drawbacks. Other than Sundays, parking is limited and expensive. Various Sunday annual community festivals, parades, runs, bicycle races and marathons all limit normal access to downtown worship venues. Worship guests may come from the shelters, streets and settings where boundaries are not respected, nor mental health assistance is readily available.

Every Sunday morning at Trinity a pastor serves the Sacrament of Holy Communion. immediately after each service. The invitation is extended to all. Anywhere from 20-40 souls may step forward to kneel or stand and receive the bread and cup. Some saints stay and pray. Some eat and run. Four pastors or ministerial interns rotated in serving the good gifts of God.

On my final Sunday to serve the Sacrament in April 2018, something strange occurred. A man walked down the center aisle not in his Sunday best nor on his Sunday manners. He was on a mission. His mission? To slap the senior pastor hard on his face. I was stunned.

Several people saw and heard the facial strike happen. The Head Usher who had been at the church for over three decades had never seen anything like it. Dave was shocked, but wisely chose not to confront the individual. No one seemed to recognize the guest. He did not return on my last two Sundays, nor ever again to my knowledge. Jesus was slapped around at the end of ministry. He forgave his foes. Not a bad lesson for all to learn.

THE BULLDOG WORE A TUXEDO

One of the great joys of serving as a pastor is the privilege of uniting couples in holy marriage. I have officiated at hundreds of weddings in a variety of venues. The most memorable was in September 2007 on a mountain summit at the Keystone Resort an hour west of Denver. We had to take two gondolas to get to the peak where the vows and rings were to be exchanged. Ascending to the top took our breath away. Fortunately, there was a dirt back road which allowed access for the caterer, florist, band and aging guests to be transported into the clouds.

The wedding couple were a winsome pair of young attorneys. She was from Texas and practiced aviation law. He was a Colorado native working in transactions. A hundred or more family members and friends made it to the mountain top that Saturday night to witness an elaborate elegant exchange of rings and vows sealed with a promise and a kiss. The attendants were dressed to the nines.

The bride was beautiful. The groom was handsome. The weather was perfect. It was well planned as most weddings are. However, this wedding had a most special attendant. The couple's pet bulldog named Patch was present and participated in the ceremony. Yes, Patch the bulldog wore a gray tuxedo as the groomdog. He matched the other male attendants. It was the most unique family celebration of the marriage covenant I have ever been a part of. Patch was far better behaved than some guests I have seen in various weddings. After all, all dogs go to heaven. We know God cares for the animals of the planet. (Psalm 147:9)

THE SUMMER SNOWY WEDDING

We lived in Colorado for twelve years. The Colorful State is a lovely landscape lending itself to many outdoor events, including weddings. I performed at least a half-dozen outside weddings on a high Keystone mountain, beside a Frisco stream, in a Golden city park and two on the grounds of the world-renowned Broadmoor Hotel in Colorado Springs. A herd of deer showed up at that misty outdoor marriage ceremony, as if on command. The most recent outdoor Colorado wedding I performed was on June 22, 2019, the first day of summer in the beautiful town of Breckenridge. I had been the groom's family pastor in Tyler for ten years and seen groom Chris grow up from ages 10-20. It was a joy to be invited to officiate at his wedding.

Bride Megan grew up in Amarillo, so lots of Texans attended the summer wedding. Summer heat in the Lone Star State often begins in early May. No one anticipated the possibility of snow in the summer. Especially a bride with a strapless dress. The weather was fine for the Friday rehearsal, dinner and welcome party. Everything was ready to rock and roll for a lovely outdoor wedding on the initial day of summer. As is said in both Texas and Colorado, "If you do not like the weather, wait five minutes and it will change."

Well, can you guess what happened in Breck? The weather changed! The temperature dropped. Sleet fell. The sun disappeared. The outdoor wedding was threatened. Plan B to shift the wedding inside was in place. When you have planned thirty years for that perfect day, what is a little snow among friends? Come snow or high water, the calendar says the first day of summer.

The 150 guests waited anxiously for the bride's decision. Inside or out? Seventy-two or 32 degrees? Cover or strapless bridal gown?

The decision belonged to the bride. She requested that I shorten the service, if possible. I did. Megan chose well. The snow stopped minutes before we were to begin the service at 5:00 p.m. The temperature rose to a balmy 35 degrees. The service was a breeze, so to speak. No one was distracted by the weather. In twenty minutes, a covenant was created, a family formed and two became one in the eyes of their Creator. Very soon a license was signed, pictures taken, drinks served, dinner set, cake cut, and toasts lifted. How many couples can claim it snowed on their wedding day on the first day of summer?

Spiritual Wit and Wisdom

Pastors have the privilege and responsibility to proclaim good news. We serve a Creator who "sits in the heavens and laughs." (Psalm 2:4). Over the years I have received much witty and wise insight into the human condition. These tidbits from personal, scriptural, long lost or anonymous sources contribute to our spiritual, financial, social, physical and mental wellbeing.

Money is like manure. Pile it up and it stinks. Spread it around and it does a lot of good.

You can't take it with you, but you can send it on ahead.

Some days you are the windshield, and some days you are the bug.

The cemetery is filled with indispensable people.

Undertakers are great people. They are the last ones to let you down.

The seven last words of the Church: "We never did it that way before."

There is a first time for everything.

The tomb was empty, but it does not mean my mind has to be.

To walk fast, walk alone. To walk far, walk together.

We all drink from wells we did not dig. (Deuteronomy 6:11)

Sometimes it is better to ask for forgiveness than permission.

There is nothing that can separate us from the love of God. (Romans 8:38-39)

God is the Savior of all, especially of those who believe. (I Timothy 4:10)

Jesus in four words: " Love God, love neighbor."

"I just want to go home and sleep in my own bed." (Personal confession of my former parishioner Alex Atherton, age 12, after his Bellaire team lost to Venezuela in the final game of the of the Little League World Series in Williamsport, PA in 2000.)

"If I hate, that means Hitler won." (Alice Cahana, Auschwitz Concentration Camp Survivor and our next-door neighbor in Houston. She died in 2017 at age 88.)

For we brought nothing into this world, and it is certain we can carry nothing out. (I Timothy 6:7)

Tradition is the living faith of the dead. Traditionalism is the dead faith of the living.

The Church is like Noah's Ark. You cannot stand the smell on the inside, except for the storms on the outside.

Every saint has a past. Every sinner has a future.

God is in the details.

No one is so bad he or she is not welcome at the Lord's table.

No one is so good he or she does not need the Lord's table.

He who sits in the heavens laughs. (Psalm 2:4)

Heartbreaks Redeemed

If you live for very long, you will experience pain, loss and suffering. No one is exempt. You may lose a parent, spouse, sibling, job, home, self-esteem, limb, faith or hope. Any significant loss or change in our lives brings grief. The classic stages of grief are denial (not me), anger (why me), bargaining (maybe not me), depression (perhaps me) and acceptance (why not me). It may take many months and often years to come to a modicum of peace and acceptance. The hardest task of a pastor is caring for parents whose child has died. Such a death is out of order. Children are to bury their parents far into the future. But far too often, the roles are reversed.

BROKEN HEARTS

Two young teenage boys in the neighborhood I grew up in died of brain tumors within a year. Their parents were sad and sorrowful. I did not know anything about cancer. I felt very bad for these families. I wondered if I would die if I got a brain tumor. Across the years I have been called on to care for far too many families whose son or daughter departed this life far too soon by any measure.

Some of the deaths came after prolonged, painful illnesses. Death has come as a friend, bringing release when physical healing was not possible. It has come with little or no warning. One bright, beautiful daughter in our Marvin Church family had just earned her master's degree when her body was suddenly invaded by an insidious infection. She died within a week despite the best medical care available in the Texas Medical Center's St. Luke's Hospital. Valerie was 24, preparing to do great things in life. Great grief. Good grief. Necessary grief. Loving loss. God weeps. The Father saw his Son die. He weeps with us and for us. God gives us the good gifts of tears, time, talk, trust, touch and thanksgiving to heal.

While it is impossible to compare losses, some families were most deeply wounded in the sudden, violent losses of their offspring. Klein Church member Rob was playing a round of miniature golf with his friends on a Friday night in a Houston suburb when suddenly a drunk driver crashed into the course, ran over the 12-year-old, dragged and mangled the boy's body. It was not possible to have an open casket.

Another 12-year-old, Trent, was a member of the church's Confirmation Class. The night before he was to profess publicly his faith and become a full member of Marvin Church, he took a gun and took his life. Maybe it was a suicide. Maybe it was an accident. We all wept that very Holy Week. Trent's grandmother and my mother were first cousins. Hearts are broken. Tears are spilled. Anger is expressed. Trust is deepened. God shares our grief.

HEALED HEARTS

What do you do when an earthly life comes to its end? You give God thanks for the life. What do you do when hearts are broken? You put them back together by God's grace. That is what Valerie's parents and close friends did. John and Marilyn wept, of course. Tears are truly therapeutic. This couple stayed connected to their faith friends in worship and their Seekers Sunday School Class at Marvin Church. They showed up when it was hard to sing and to pray. They wrote how blessed they were to have their beloved daughter for 24 years. They shared, "The best way to counteract grief is through thanksgiving." They were deeply grateful in their deep grief. They were humbled by two families who named daughters after Valerie. Scholarships were created and funded in her name to assist others. Flowers are given annually on her birthday by several families in honor of her life.

What do you do when an earthly life comes to its end? You give God thanks for the life. What do you do when hearts are broken? You put them back together by God's grace. That is what a young Trinity Church family did when tragedy struck on a hot summer day in 2009. Two-year old Colin was suddenly swept from his family in an instant by the rushing water of a cool Colorado stream. Despite the best efforts of his family and others along the banks of the stream, the child could not survive. Shock, sorrow and sadness spread through the family, church family and community.

Such events require legal investigation and closure. Six days later on a holiday weekend, Colin's family, friends and church family gathered 800 strong in the 1888 sanctuary for a Service of Death and Resurrection celebrating his short life and his family's faith. After the Word of Grace and Greeting, the congregation lifted its collective voice in *The Hymn of Promise.* All present prayed together *The Prayer of St. Francis* and *The Lord's Prayer.* Readings from the well-named Book of Lamentations and the Gospel of Matthew connected comfort with pain. The closing Hymn of Hope was *Let There Be Peace on Earth.*

Colin's parents redeemed their grief by working with others to organize a lacrosse tournament which raised $25,000 for scholarships in memory of their son and given to Colorado students. They also expressed gratitude in writing to the public and all others who helped on the day of their tragedy. They thanked the dozens of "regular" people who rushed to help strangers in a time of crisis. These pained parents publicly praised police officers, firefighters, EMTs, doctors and nurses who acted with skill and urgency attempting to save their son.

Chris and Sara wrote, "We especially recognize the man who was at work on a construction site when he risked his own life and safety to jump into Gore Creek to pull Colin from the water, and the people who performed CPR immediately after. These selfless, brave and heroic people – and others like them – have set a new higher standard of honor for us." This extraordinary couple directed memorial gifts to be made to Trinity Church, the local volunteer fire department, Colorado's Alzheimer's Association, Children's Hospital, Denver Rescue Mission, Meals on Wheels and St. Frances Center.

What a magnificent way to transform grief to grace. Give to others. A week after burying their son, Chris and Sara received a most special gift. They learned they were going to have another child. The God of love and the love of God whispered in their hearts, "Earth has no hurt which Heaven cannot heal."

Most folks look forward to retiring at some point. Because pastoral ministry is my calling, I thoroughly enjoyed preaching and teaching, visiting in hospitals and homes, baptizing and confirming, marrying and burying, serving local and global communities. I was disappointed to enter formal retirement a little earlier than anticipated. Nonetheless, Sharon and I are grateful beyond measure to have served eight pastoral assignments over 44 years. We were called to lead and share in nine capital campaigns for new constructions, renovations and mission investments. Four of those were at Marvin and Trinity, my final two pastorates.

TIME TO TURN OUT THE LIGHTS

Our final assignment was our longest. Serving the Divine in Downtown Denver for a dozen years was a delight. Retiring was not a delight. Dis-ease is not the way to go. The church's and my health demanded a decision to depart sooner rather than later. It was all for the best and the best for all. I could claim with St. Paul, "The time of my departure has come..." Several dozen family and friends from Georgia and Texas showed up for my final service, including four couples from our first full-time appointment in Spring, Texas in 1979. As the contemporary Christian chorus correctly claims, "Friends are friends forever if the Lord's the Lord of them."

Over a thousand saints were in worship Sunday, April 22, 2018 to send us into the next chapter of life called retirement. We worshipped, sang, celebrated, laughed, cried, exchanged gifts and hugs. It was a gracious send-off to the next chapter of life. With the help of longtime good friends, Sharon and I literally moved the next day to our retirement home at 8,600 feet elevation in the southern Colorado Rocky Mountains, arriving physically exhausted and emotionally exhilarated. We spent the next two months getting settled as fulltime residents in the Paradise Acres development, home to over three dozen attractive homes high in the Sangre de Cristo ("Blood of Christ") range of the Rockies. We were ready to relax, rest, renew, recover and roll into retirement!

In June we flew to Salt Lake City for the Rocky Mountain Annual Conference meeting in Ogden, Utah. Two significant things happened in LDS Land. The Methodists and the Mormons meshed in a day of community service projects. Wearing gratis UMC.org tee-shirts with the word "love" in dozens of languages, the garments declared, "GOD SPEAKS ALL LANGUAGES." In smaller letters was the tag line, "Open Hearts. Open Doors. Open Minds. The People of The United Methodist Church."

On a more personal note, the Conference officially approved my retirement from active ministry after four and a half decades of service. We twelve 2018 retirees had served a total of 289 years in pastoral ministry. The Conference gave each of us a special gift, a small desk clock with the conference logo and a commendation from the Bible, "Well Done Good & Faithful Servant." I set my new retirement clock to 5:00 and took out the battery. It is always 5:00 somewhere, and always at my home now!

Just after we got the telephone land line and satellite TV service installed in our retirement home, we joined the Two Peaks Fitness Inc. in little La Veta, twenty miles and thirty minutes from our new full-time home. We united with the United Methodist Church in La Veta and became "Friends of the La Veta Library." We wrote all our retirement thank you gift notes and planned a retirement celebration trip and Canadian cruise for October, courtesy of the generous Trinity Church family. It was now time to relax, read, rest and receive a retirement pension. All is well. Everything is fine. Life could not be better.

Not so fast. The year not from heaven was about to begin.

IT ONLY TAKES A SPARK

Smokey Bear has been sharing timely wisdom for 75 years. A campaign began in 1944 featuring Smokey and the slogan "Smokey Says – Care Will Prevent 9 out of 10 Forest Fires." His slogan changed in 1947 to "Remember... Only YOU Can Prevent Forest Fires" and has been associated with Smokey Bear ever since. Completely extinguishing a campfire was drilled into my mind by the Boy Scouts of America. In church Youth Choir we sang:

> It only takes a spark to get a fire going,
> And soon all those around, can warm up in glowing.

Sadly, a spark set off of a fiery blaze on June 27, 2018 about nine miles northeast of Fort Garland, Colorado, twenty miles from our home. The fire was unpredictable. We could smell the smoke. Evacuation where we lived was optional at that time. We watched the TV coverage on the Colorado Springs stations through the evening. I was worn out from the day's drama and went to bed at 9:30 p.m. and was soon fast asleep. Sharon then learned on the 10:00 p.m. newscast that the winds had changed, and the flames had jumped U.S. Hwy 160 to the north, suddenly making our home three miles away in Paradise

Acres at risk from the fire. She woke me with urgent commands, "Get up! Get dressed! Get packed! We have to get gone!"

I was sleepy and resistant to the urgency of the moment. My bride quickly explained, "You don't understand. The winds have shifted. The fire is headed this way!" That news got my attention. Suddenly the old values clarification exercises of fifty years ago came to mind. In church youth group we were told, "Imagine your house has caught fire. You have time to grab only three things. What would you take? Family picture album? Baseball card collection? Your pet? Beatles or Beach Boys' albums?

Well, Sharon and I picked and packed our two SUVs quickly with our computers, a few family pictures, jewelry, valuables, three changes of clothes, toiletries, a pair of shoes, checkbooks, Bibles and a box of files with notes for this book. And yes, the white six-pound Maltese dog Sugar Magnolia (AKA "Maggie") made it into Sharon's SUV. Kiss goodbye all of furniture, lamps, beds, dishes, tools, food, rugs and the like. We really thought we would be returning soon. The sober reminder of Holy Writ hit home, "For we bring nothing into this world, and we take nothing out of this world."

FLEEING THE FIRE

We hit the dirt Pass Creek Road headed north around 11:00 p.m. There were few stars and scant light on the Huerfano County Road that night. We drove in separate vehicles at least 45 minutes before reaching a paved road. We gave thanks, jumped on State Highway 69 toward Walsenburg. It was well past midnight when we arrived. There are at least six chain hotels in Walsenburg at Interstate 25. "No Vacancy" signs shone in every hospitality establishment. Hundreds of folks were fleeing the fire by now. We stayed in our vehicles and headed north on I-25.

No vacancies in Colorado City, the next town. Finally, at 3:00 a.m. we got the last room at a Pueblo chain motel. Dogs were not accepted. Maggie had to stay in our car in the parking lot. We paid $160 to sleep restlessly for four hours. We then drove to Denver where a kind couple from Trinity Church put Maggie and us up for four nights. Donald and Beth were a soft place to land. They abundantly blessed us, fed us and de-stressed us. Jesus said, "I was a stranger, and you welcomed me." We were rested, renewed, revitalized and refreshed in their care. We wondered if we still had a house. The fire raged on. We chose to retreat to Texas. Nothing like some grandkid hugs to lift the spirit!

The fire in adjacent Huerfano and Costilla Counties had continued to spread. The Spanish Peaks Music Festival at the La Veta Airport for the Fourth of July weekend was canceled. Before evacuating south for two weeks, Sharon and I went to La Veta to register as official evacuees of the Huerfano Spring Fire. We were issued bright green Evac TAGs with a barcode, priority color and ID Number. After the fire was eventually put out, this would allow us to return to our property. This process helped minimize the gawkers and looters who show up when such tragedies occur. Fire and other disasters bring out the best and the worst of humankind.

It took us two days to get home and assure in person our Texas family we were alive and pretty well. While at our son's home, we watched a live internet feed of the Spring Fire being battled in the mountainous forests very near our Colorado home. It was eerie seeing the specially equipped airplanes and helicopters flying over and dropping red fire retardant over familiar terrain.

While in the Lone Star State I had the joyful privilege of baptizing my new grandson. As soon as the short sacrament was sealed with a song and a kiss, my son and I departed for Colorado. We were quite anxious to learn if Sharon and I still had a home to live in or not. The authorities will not give such news except in person. Nineteen days passed before we would learn if our home called Higher Ground, we had bought in 2006, was still above ground. As a Volunteer Fire Department Chaplain, I had seen homes reduced to nothing but ashes. I anticipated most everything we owned had gone up in smoke.

RECOVERING FROM THE FIRE

Here are the Spring Fire Facts. The blaze burned 108,045 acres of private and public property. It was not declared 100% contained until September 10, 2018. More than 140 homes and structures were lost to the fire. At least 120 others were damaged. The fire was human caused and the suspect was charged with 141 counts of first-degree arson — one count for each home destroyed by the fire. Jesper Jorgenson, 52, a citizen of Denmark and reported by immigration authorities as being in the United States illegally, was arrested and charged with arson for allegedly starting the fire. It was the third-largest wildfire in Colorado history.

When my son and I arrived in La Veta on July 15, a rumor was confirmed. Our home was still standing. That was the good news. That was also the bad news. Of the 37 homes in our Paradise Acres community, 21 had burned to the ground. We grieved for our friends. We felt pain and some strange pangs of guilt that our home survived. All some of our neighbors had left were foundations, chimneys and ashes. Mostly ashes. The burn smell lingered for months. Most of the hundreds of trees nearest our homes were now just black sticks. The hummingbirds and other flying friends, turkeys, deer, rabbits, squirrels and occasional bear and elk had all abandoned the land.

Like a good neighbor, an insurance adjustor was on scene soon to cut checks. Money cannot restore the beautiful gifts of neighbors, trees, abundant animals and human community. We literally tasted ashes for a time. The smoky smell settled here and there and everywhere in Paradise Acres. It was Paradise Lost.

The impact of the fire was far-reaching and is still being felt. These headlines from the weekly local *Huerfano Journal* newspaper in the months following the fire reflect the devastation experienced in our new retirement setting: "Property losses in Huerfano County top $8.2 million in Spring Fire," "Fire and flood have economic impact," "If locusts come, I'm leaving" and "La Veta plans for worst case scenario flooding." Floods, burn scars and landslides often follow fires in the mountains.

It can take a decade or more for the land to heal. And as much or more for the mind and soul to heal. When the fire was under control, we did not suffer flood and landslides. But all hail broke lose in mid-July. The one-inch frozen ice pellets relentlessly pounded our pair of vehicles for 30 minutes in La Veta. Sharon's SUV was totaled. Mine sustained $12,000 in dents. The hail hitting the metal roof sounded like maniacal machine gunfire, drowning out all conversation. Again, like a good neighbor, an insurance adjuster was soon there to cut checks.

While our home survived the fire, it was uninhabitable for eight months. Higher Ground sustained significant scorching and a dozen cracked windows from the heat of the fire. We were hit with $90,000 in interior smoke damage and cleaning costs. Giant deodorizing fans ran 24-hours a day for a week throughout the home. All of our coats, clothes, linens and curtains were shipped to Denver to be cleaned and deodorized. It was nice to have clean home and clean clothes, but we could not live there. The water system was compromised by the fire. We were unable to wash dishes, clothes and ourselves. The toilets would not flush. Adios, Paradise.

Like a good neighbor, our insurance company put us up in a hotel for a week in Trinidad, and then a B & B, paid for some our meals and eventually installed a cistern. Paying to have water delivered on icy roads in the Colorado winter was a dicey, pricey proposition we did not relish to survive.

Soon after living with family in Texas for the two weeks, we landed back in La Veta, population 800, twenty miles from Higher Ground. For four months we resided in Harding's Corner B & B. Sara Harding was an angel, another soft place to land. She served much more than breakfast. She was a port in our storm. Though against house rules, Sara fell in love with Maggie and allowed the puppy to reside in our room. We lived in the B & B for four months. It often became a B & L and B & D. Sara and Sharon bonded as best buds. Sara, Pastor Janine and all the saints in the little La Veta United Methodist Church family embraced us and others in our time of need with care, prayer and gentle kindness. Our recovery from the fire was hastened by our church family. The small congregation helped many folks big time during and after the fire. The Body of Christ is often at its best in a time of crisis.

BROADCASTING THE FIRE

Bad news attracts viewers, hence the maxim, "If it bleeds, it leads." Along with a Huerfano County Commissioner and the Paradise Acres HOA President, Sharon and I were interviewed by Colorado Public Radio early in August 2018. Nathanial Minor, the young radio reporter, met us at Higher Ground, took pictures for the CPR website and quizzed us for a special news program broadcast statewide several times. We learned two things about CPR. First, they do quality, in-depth reporting. Second, many folks listen to the broadcasts. As soon as the report went on the air, we began getting calls and emails from church members who had heard it on the radio or read it online. The interview is still on the CPR website as of November 2019. Google "In The Spring Creek Fire's Wake, Heartbreak Before A Long Recovery."

Nathaniel's radio piece was accurately entitled. "He noted, "The name 'Paradise' seems almost cruel now. Paradise Acres is a subdivision in Southern Colorado where more than 20 homes in the subdivision were destroyed by the Spring Fire in July. It was one of the areas hardest hit by the massive Spring Fire." The fire was, indeed, depressing, destructive and defeating, but no one perished in the Colorado flames. Lest we forget, four months later near Paradise, California, 55 persons lost their lives in fires. Many died in their cars, trapped by a wildfire in a campground blaze. Our fire in Paradise Acres paled in comparison.

The CPR reporter shared how we had moved in full-time two months before the conflagration spread. He also included pictures of the acres of burned trees next to our gently charred retirement residence. The final words

250

of his broadcast were, "Michael Dent said he's gone through many of the phases of grief. He's stuck in depression now. So, he turned to the Bible, a book he has used thousands of times before to counsel others. Two passages have stood out. 'I'll never leave you, nor forsake you,' and 'The creator says, 'And when you walk through the fire you shall not be burned.' As he recited these lines from the Bible, Sharon listened intently. She then rested head against her home, and quietly wept." Tears, time, talk, trust, touch and thanksgiving are divine gifts to get us not over, but through the tough times of life. My guess is the Bible is not often quoted on public radio.

MOVING ON FROM THE FIRE

Wonderful as it was, we could not live in the lovely La Beta B&B forever. In our third month of staying with sweet Sara, we decided to scan the land with a plan for more space for us and Maggie. We drove to Texas in September and looked at homes for rent near our children. The daily heavy traffic in the Dallas area where our son and his family live was not a good match for my MCI. We surveyed some nice rental properties in north Texas where our daughter and her family. However, those neighborhoods emptied out during the day, leaving a lonely ghost town setting. That social isolation was the last thing we needed.

Next, we decided to check out Tyler where we lived and served for just over ten years before the higher calling took us to Colorado. Sharon noticed that the closer we got to the Rose City, the more relaxed and animated I became. I seemed to feel my blood pressure coming down and my spirit lifting. We were pleased to be coming home to a place that was right for us.

Somehow a couple in our previous congregation heard we were looking for a place to live. Don and Jane had a charming, cozy brick home erected in 1952, the same year I was built. They let us set the rent for the 2BR, 1B home. We signed a six-month lease and paid fair rental value. We moved in on All Saints Day 2018. I had the personal pleasure of raking and bagging at least one million leaves on the half-acre lot the next four months!

Only three families were able to stay and live in Paradise Acres during the cold season. Though our Good Neighbor eventually provided a cistern for our Colorado property, Sharon and I were not physically nor emotionally able to endure the winter weather, unreliable water delivery, possible road washouts, landslides and loss of electrical power.

Returning to Tyler was the right move, putting us two hours or less to our children and grandchildren. We returned to Marvin UMC and to Sharon's wonderful Seeker's Sunday Class. She rejoined the church on the second Sunday we were back. The preacher that day was longtime clergy colleague Scott Jones, now Bishop of the Texas Annual Conference. I voted for Scott when he was elected to the episcopal office in 2004 in Corpus Christi.

Tyler's beauty, Marvin's hospitality, the city's healthcare resources and our many friends in and beyond the church made Tyler the place of peace we needed at this time of recovery. We had experienced PTSD from the significant trauma and drama we shared over the past four months of fire, forced relocations and loss of friends and community.

The congregation's music ministry, dynamic and missions and outreach are superb. Over 1,100 saints share in four traditional or casual services each Sunday. The annual Mission and Ministry of Christ through Marvin Church is $4.5 million. It has been my pastoral honor to be invited occasionally to assist in the liturgy, serve communion, perform weddings and speak at the Meadow Lake Retirement Community. Tyler is the first Certified Retirement City in Texas, a recognition based on its low taxes and high level of healthcare.

In March 2019 Sharon and I bought a one-level home in Tyler. The city is truly home now. We belong in the Rose City. It is a community filled with love whispers and whisperers of love. It is close to most all of our living family members. In July 2019 we sold Higher Ground, our mountain getaway for over twelve years and our retirement home for two months. Though the home's value was reduced by 25 percent in value by the Spring Fire, we were delighted to sell it to a couple who lost their Paradise Acres home of 30 years in the fire. It was a win-win transaction between two Methodist couples. We were glad to leave the surviving furnishings, linens, appliances, dishes and pots and pans for Mike and Jeanne.

Sharon and I are happy that the home has a bright future under new ownership. We cannot choose what happens to us in life. We can choose how we respond to the trials which eventually come the way of us all. Whatever and wherever the home we live in on earth, Jesus whispers in love, "Those who love me will keep my word, and my Father will love them, and we will come to them and make our home with them." Thank you, Lord, for your promise and presence in our homes and hearts.

Final Whispers of Love

One of the best words in the world is thanks. Lives grounded in gratitude are normally happy, healthy and whole lives. Cicero said, "A thankful heart is not only the greatest virtue, but the parent of all other virtues." Apostle Paul called followers of Jesus to "Give thanks in all circumstances." Jesus himself did so the night he was betrayed by a brother. That was a genuine whisper of love. As I reach two-thirds of a century of life, my heart beats with thanksgiving for grandparents, parents, siblings, public and Sunday School teachers, coaches and scout leaders who were subtly infusing every fiber of my being with an eagerness for studying, serving others, sharing gifts, doing my best, being trustworthy and, most of all, loving God and neighbor.

I am thankful for God's call and claim on my life, and the affirmation of the church when I shared that calling to preach. Saintly souls said, "I am praying for you." Those prayers were whispers of love. Pastors opened their pulpits to a young, inexperienced student so I could share and sometimes shout God's grace and whisper God's love. Words are insufficient to express my everlasting gratitude for the education, experience and encouragement given to me and others to serve as whisperers of divine mercy. Many pastors, colleagues and friends have been role models, prayer partners, encouragers and steadfast sources of strength. Thanks Charles, Dick, Bill, Wayne and others for years of prayer and sermon preparation retreats in Estes Park.

Praise God for all the saints at High Island, Edom, Klein DeKalb, Atascocita, Bellaire, Marvin and Trinity United Methodist Churches with whom we were privileged to serve. May your tribe increase! I look forward to reconnecting somehow, some way, some day.

PLANNING FOR THE END

Sooner or later we all check out. We are all terminal. The death rate is 100%. Ready or not, here comes the great equalizer. No one gets out alive. We live and we die. Are you ready to depart? In a Sunday night service, the pastor asked everyone present, "Do you want to go heaven?" All but Jim raised a hand. The preacher noticed the lone dissenter and asked him in front of the congregation, "Jim, don't you want to go to heaven?" "Sure, I want to go to heaven." The exasperated pastor exclaimed, "Well, why didn't you say so when I asked?" Jim answered innocently, "Well, I thought you were getting up a group to go tonight." Jim was ready to go, yet not ready to leave. Are you ready to step on the Heavenly Train? There is room for all. The tickets are paid for and available to all, saints and sinners alike.

My plans are made. Cremation is the way for me. Ashes to ashes, dust to dust. No casket, vault or makeup. Ditto for Sharon. My Service of Death and Resurrection is completely planned, except for the date. No time soon, I hope! The hymns, musicians, scriptures, memorials, worship leaders and location are chosen. Let the Marvin Organ cut loose to the glory of God! The potato salad flavor is still up for grabs.

GIVING FOREVER

Sharon and I have tithed for all our married life. Giving ten percent is biblical, blesses others and is easy to calculate. We have aligned our earthly estate to continue to do heavenly good long after we have left the building. Someone said, "You cannot take it with you, but you can send it on ahead."

Three cheers for congregations which have foundations, endowments, scholarships, missions and other means of providing for God's good work to continue long after the saints go marching in. Abel is commended by God for giving in such a way that his faith is still speaking. Such giving whispers love from generation to generation.

TOO GOOD NOT BE TRUE

Over 500 times in my pastoral ministry I have had the sacred task of journeying with a family to the cemetery to speak the final words of commendation and thanksgiving for their loved one. Several of those committals were for members of my family. The most emotional and painful committal service was for three members of one family, ages 27, 22 and five years. Along with the young pilot, they perished in a fiery private plane crash on Easter Sunday 1980 near Tomball, Texas.

I was connected to the family from having officiated at the wedding of a third daughter just months before. The mother and child were buried in the same casket. The Klein Funeral Home was filled to overflowing with flowers, friends and firefighters. The father of the two young women incinerated in the crash was, ironically, a captain in the Houston Fire Department.

Such sudden losses remind us how fragile, unpredictable and precious life is. We tend to deny our mortality. The Service of Death and Resurrection and graveside Committal Service both offer comfort, hope and assurance in times of grief and loss. The proclamations, prayers and promises affirm God's truth which is too good not to be true:

> "Jesus said, I am the resurrection and the life.
> Those who believe in me, even though they die, yet shall they live,
> And whoever lives and believes in me shall never die.
> I go to prepare a place for you.
> I am the Alpha and the Omega, the beginning and the end, the
> first and the last.
> I died, and behold I am alive forevermore,
> And I hold the keys of hell and death.
> Blessed are the dead who die in the Lord.
> They will rest from their labors for their labors will follow them.
> Because I live, you also shall live.
> I will dwell in the house of the Lord forever.
> Thanks be to God who gives us the victory through our Lord
> Jesus Christ."

THE WHISPER TEST

Those powerful love whispers from the Bible have the last word. For years a love whisper called "The Whisper Test" story has been circulating on the internet. Whether fact or fiction, I do not know. What I do know is that it conveys valuable truth. Mary Ann Bird was born with multiple birth defects. She suffered not only from her physical impairments but also with the emotional trauma of being different from others. Mary Ann shares her story in her own words:

> *I grew up knowing I was different, and I hated it. I was born with a cleft palate, and when I started school, my classmates made it clear to me how I looked to others: a little girl with a misshapen lip, crooked nose, lopsided teeth, and garbled speech. When schoolmates asked, "What happened to your lip?" I'd tell them I'd fallen and cut it on a piece of glass. Somehow it seemed more acceptable to have suffered an accident than to have been born different. I was convinced that no one outside my family could love me.*
>
> *There was, however, a teacher in the second grade whom we all adored -- Mrs. Leonard by name. She was short, round, happy --a sparkling lady. Annually we had a hearing test. Mrs. Leonard gave*

the test to everyone in the class, and finally it was my turn. I knew from past years that as we stood against the door and covered one ear, the teacher sitting at her desk would whisper something, and we would have to repeat it back -- things like "The sky is blue," or "Do you have new shoes?" I waited there for those words that God must have put into her mouth, those seven words that changed my life. Mrs. Leonard said, in her whisper, "I wish you were MY little girl."

EPILOGUE

Thanks for sharing the journey of whispering love in the graces, places and faces of family, friends, flocks and faith folks across the first 67 years of life. I know not what tomorrow may bring, but the day for whispering love, echoing mercy and sharing stories of grace is ever present. Love is therapeutic and blesses. Grace abounds. Mercy echoes. Love whispers and weeps, gives and forgives, strengthens and soothes, saves and seals, searches and finds, welcomes and blesses. Love never ends. May its whispers and the Whisperer bless you on the journey ahead. There is no place love cannot whisper.

UPCOMING PUBLICATION

Look online in early 2020 for *Spirituality 2020: Public Service, Prayers and Proclamations*. This election year offering will focus on timely and timeless truths for a nation divided by immigration, healthcare, war, marriage equality, racism, fear and mistrust.

Made in the USA
Columbia, SC
10 December 2019